Little Rock on Trial

LANDMARK LAW CASES

&

AMERICAN SOCIETY

Peter Charles Hoffer

N. E. H. Hull

Series Editors

RECENT TITLES IN THE SERIES

Murder in Mississippi, Howard Ball

The Vietnam War on Trial, Michal R. Belknap

Sexual Harassment and the Law, Augustus B. Cochran III

The DeShaney Case, Lynne Curry

Brown v. Board of Education, Robert M. Cottrol, Raymond T. Diamond, and Leland B. Ware

The Battle over School Prayer, Bruce J. Dierenfield

Nazi Saboteurs on Trial, Louis Fisher

The Great New York Conspiracy of 1741, Peter Charles Hoffer

Griswold v. Connecticut, John W. Johnson

M'Culloch v. Maryland: *Securing a Nation*, Mark R. Killenbeck

The Slaughterhouse Cases, Abridged Edition, Ronald M. Labbé and Jonathan Lurie

Mapp v. Ohio, Carolyn N. Long

Dred Scott *and the Politics of Slavery*, Earl M. Maltz

The Snail Darter Case, Kenneth M. Murchison

Animal Sacrifice and Religious Freedom, David M. O'Brien

The Yoder *Case*, Shawn Francis Peters

The Insular Cases *and the Emergence of American Empire*, Bartholomew H. Sparrow

San Antonio v. Rodriguez *and the Pursuit of Equal Education*, Paul Sracic

Slave Law in the American South, Mark V. Tushnet

The Confederacy on Trial, Mark A. Weitz

The Times and Trials of Anne Hutchinson, Michael P. Winship

Race and Redistricting, Tinsley E. Yarbrough

The Battle for the Black Ballot, Charles L. Zelden

For a complete list of titles in the series go to www.kansaspress.ku.edu

TONY A. FREYER

Little Rock on Trial

Cooper v. Aaron and School Desegregation

UNIVERSITY PRESS OF KANSAS

Published by the University Press of Kansas (Lawrence, Kansas 66045), which was
organized by the Kansas Board of Regents and is operated and funded by Emporia
State University, Fort Hays State University, Kansas State University, Pittsburg State
University, the University of Kansas, and Wichita State University

Library of Congress Cataloging-in-Publication Data

Freyer, Tony Allan.
Little Rock on trial : Cooper v. Aaron and school desegregation /
Tony A. Freyer.
p.   cm. — (Landmark law cases and American Society)
Includes bibliographical references and index.
ISBN 978-0-7006-1535-3 (cloth : alk. paper) — ISBN 978-0-7006-1536-0
(pbk. : alk. paper)   1. Cooper, William G. — Trials, litigation, etc.
2. Aaron, John — Trials, litigation, etc.   3. Segregation in education —
Law and legislation—United States. [1. African Americans—Civil rights.]
1. Title.
KF228.C6545F74   2007
344.73'0798 — dc22
2007016899

British Library Cataloguing-in-Publication Data is available.

Printed in the United States of America

10 9 8 7 6 5 4 3 2 1

The paper used in this publication meets the minimum requirements of the
American National Standard for Permanence of Paper for Printed Library Materials
z39.48-1992.

CONTENTS

Editors' Preface *vii*

Acknowledgments *xi*

Introduction *1*

1. The Little Rock NAACP Decision to Sue, 1954–1956 *13*

2. *Aaron v. Cooper:* Rights at Bay, 1956–1957 *47*

3. The Crisis Erupts, 1957 *89*

4. *Cooper v. Aaron:* Delay Won and Appealed, 1957–1958 *135*

5. The *Cooper v. Aaron* Opinions: Unanimity and Division, 1958 *169*

6. Protean Precedent since 1958 *202*

Epilogue *232*

Chronology *239*

Bibliographic Essay *245*

Index *255*

Landmark law cases leave their mark on many people, reveal basic legal and political issues, and change the world. This may seem an extreme claim, but no case better captures that definition than *Cooper v. Aaron*. Before the confrontation between the federal government and Governor Orval E. Faubus of Arkansas was over, the entire world had seen the heroism of the black young men and women who walked the long hard walk into Little Rock's all-white schools. The "well-morticed high wall" of segregation, as one civil rights lawyer had called the southern system of Jim Crow, had forever cracked.

As high political drama captured on the new medium of television, nothing matched the Little Rock school crisis. A reluctant president, a resolute High Court, a cunning state governor, the people — black and white — of Little Rock, the Arkansas National Guard, U.S. paratroopers, and a world torn by the cold war all participated. The state and the city, divided along class and racial lines, mirrored a nation of states coming to grips with the broken economic promises of liberalism. The back stories of initial good faith and subsequent backsliding in the city school board, the fate of teachers caught in the middle and parents who had to make painful personal decisions, and the political ambitions of Faubus and others preening themselves in the spotlight of "massive resistance" by white southern "citizens' councils" makes this account both rich and rewarding.

Faubus won a third term in a landslide victory, campaigning as a segregationist. To some observers, it seemed a reprise of the tragedy of the "redemption" of the South after Reconstruction. Then, the high hopes for racial justice embedded in the Reconstruction and Court decisions like the *Slaughter House Cases* (1873) crashed to the ground with the imposition of Jim Crow and the retreat of the Court in the *Civil Rights Cases* (1883). But Faubus and the segregationists ultimately lost, and segregation lost, because people of good faith, white and black, gained control of the school board, and this time, public opinion in the North and the Court in the nation's capital did not surrender to racialist partisanship. The road to desegregation was still long and hard, but if Little Rock was not the end for the segregationists, it was surely the end of the first round of massive resistance.

As constitutional law, the case established once and for all the supremacy of the federal judiciary and the High Court. Although the Court had asserted its hegemony as interpreter of the U.S. Constitution as far back as *Marbury v. Madison* (1803), and announced that state law was subject to its authority in *M'Culloch v. Maryland* (1819), it had never faced an opponent as entrenched as southern segregation. Indeed, the Court had done much to dig those trenches itself in *Plessy v. Ferguson* (1896). But the world had changed, and so had the Court, as it proclaimed in *Brown v. Board of Education* (1954).

Would that landmark decision be drained of substance by deliberate and persistent subterfuge and trickery? Would the law of the land be mocked by those responsible for the education of all the citizens of the country? Would a claim that public disorder would result from desegregation — disorder fomented by the die-hard segregationists (the "heckler's veto") — undo what decades of civil rights litigation had accomplished? *Cooper v. Aaron* provided an answer. But here too there was a back story. In bringing the case, the NAACP Legal Defense Fund (LDF), led by Thurgood Marshall and seconded by Wiley Branton of Arkansas, abandoned gradualism and its facade of accommodation and instead opted for direct confrontation with southern segregation. In doing this, the legal side of the civil rights movement aligned itself firmly with the direct action wing led by Martin Luther King, Jr., and other activists.

The Court had allowed, if not encouraged, accommodation and gradualism in *Brown v. Board of Education* II (1955). Thus, the Court did not come to the decision in the Little Rock case without internal debate. Although the opinion was unanimous and signed by all nine justices (unique in the Court's history), in fact it was largely written by the Court's most liberal member, newly appointed Justice William J. Brennan. The changes he made to accommodate the other justices were not unusual, but the high drama of the Supreme Court convening a special term and the stakes of the opinion lent to each word a heightened impact. Justice Felix Frankfurter, denied the prize of rendering the opinion and increasingly upset with Chief Justice Earl Warren for not following his advice, signed on but wrote a concurrence, causing much contention among his brethren.

No one is better placed, more knowledgeable, or more sympathetic in the best sense of the word, to write this story than Tony Freyer. For more than two decades he has researched and written about aspects of the Little Rock crisis. With access to almost all of the participants, care and candor in his judgments, and an intimacy of detail, he has crafted an account that is both highly readable and an original scholarly event. If *Cooper v. Aaron* is a landmark case, Freyer's account is a landmark accomplishment.

ACKNOWLEDGMENTS

I am grateful to the following individuals and institutions for facilitating the completion of this book. Longer ago than I wish to remember, Peter Hoffer proposed I write a study of *Cooper v. Aaron*. I join a growing list of authors in expressing heartfelt pleasure at working with Editor in Chief Michael J. Briggs and the staff of the University Press of Kansas. University of Alabama School of Law dean Kenneth C. Randall, the Edward Brett Randolph Fund, and the Alabama Law School Foundation, as well as the Office of Academic Affairs, which endowed me with the university research professorship, provided essential financial support. David Warrington, head of Harvard Law School Manuscripts, provided access to the Felix Frankfurter papers and the Fred N. Fishman papers. The staff of the Seeley G. Mudd Manuscript Library at Princeton University made possible my use of the John Marshall Harlan papers. I continue to benefit from the Library of Congress Manuscripts Division's expert staff for research on the papers of the NAACP and NAACP Legal Defense Fund along with the papers of the justices of the U.S. Supreme Court — especially for this project, the papers of Justice William J. Brennan. Particularly helpful was Daun van Ee. The University of Alabama Library staff, including Paul M. Pruitt, Penny Gibson, Creighton Miller, and Diana May have always rendered expert and friendly assistance. I am also indebted to my secretary, Caroline Barge.

In the bibliographic essay at the end of this book, I thank the various publishers for their permission to cite or otherwise draw upon pieces I have written. I wish to thank as a group, too, the clerks who served the members of the Supreme Court deciding *Cooper v. Aaron*.

Since I began my academic career in Little Rock in 1976, my gratitude to Zu has grown, as dedications in other books have shown. For reasons all four of us appreciate, this book is dedicated to Allan and Rachel.

Introduction

As time passed, images originating from the *Cooper v. Aaron* litigation persisted. The Supreme Court's decision in 1958 reflected an equivocal outcome of the Little Rock school desegregation crisis, which had erupted the preceding September when the city school board attempted to comply with the historic decision of *Brown v. Board of Education* (1954). Two media photographs transmitted around the world in September 1957 gave the protracted litigation ongoing power. The first picture focused on a young black woman walking with dignity among leering white adults and national guardsmen, amidst whom stands a young white woman, her face contorted in hateful rage. In the second photograph the words *Little Rock Central High School* identify a castle-like edifice; ascending its stairway are nine black young people protected by helmeted, rifle-bearing U.S. Army troops. These enduring images suggest that the Little Rock crisis and the Court's *Cooper* decision marked a significant turning point in the U.S. civil rights struggle. Still, the seemingly more clear-cut achievements associated with Martin Luther King, Jr., and the civil rights movement eventually overshadowed the more ambiguous results the Supreme Court implemented through litigation in *Brown* and *Cooper*. This book argues that the images and events of the Little Rock confrontation and *Cooper v. Aaron* paved the way for later civil rights victories, and in so doing reaffirmed the U.S. constitutional democracy based on judicial supremacy.

The strategy of nonviolent resistance aligned African Americans with the nation's dominant cold war liberal consensus. More particularly, former civil rights lawyer Derrick Bell contended, King and his fellow leaders established a convergence of interests between the African American civil rights struggle and the majority of northern white Americans who favored democracy and constitutionally sanctioned minority rights, whereas they feared communism and the cold war. In addition, this convergence of interests gradually achieved in Washington, D.C., the perception that segregationists were aiding the communists' anti-American propaganda, especially given southerners' often violent defiance of civil rights, which politically isolated the South. A similar pattern of convergence emerged in the national and global reaction to the civil rights issues the Eisenhower administration confronted during the unfolding conflict in Little Rock. Initiated from 1955 to 1956, the *Cooper* litigation eventually mobilized the Little Rock black community as never before. On September 3, 1957, Governor Orval E. Faubus, claiming that civil disorder was imminent, defied a federal court order by commanding the Arkansas National Guard to block desegregation of Central High School. For the next three weeks of intractable confrontation, and then during the succeeding two years, Faubus, Eisenhower, the school board, the Little Rock black community, the NAACP, prosegregationist whites, and the federal judiciary shaped the nation's and the world's perceptions of U.S. democracy.

The Little Rock confrontation sharply defined the African American struggle for civil rights and the contending constitutional claims of federal and southern public officials. On September 20, 1957, the federal court found Faubus's assertions of impending disorder unsubstantiated, whereupon the governor complied with the court order and withdrew the National Guard. On September 23, however, nine black young people entered Central, but were forced to leave when outside the school rabble rousers galvanized the crowd into a threatening mob. Shortly thereafter, President Eisenhower enforced the court order by federalizing the National Guard and dispatching paratroopers of the 101st Airborne to Little Rock. Troops remained at Central until the academic year ended, but segregationist-supported youths harassed the nine black students relentlessly. Tension again mounted during the summer of 1958. Faubus campaigned for a third-term gubernatorial nomination, and the U.S. Supreme Court in an August special term considered whether Arkansas authorities had violated the Constitution. The governor won a landslide victory, and the Court decided against Arkansas public officials in *Cooper v. Aaron*. Rather than comply, Faubus closed the city's high schools. Not until local white moderates, informally aided by blacks, mobilized support for a special school board election in the spring of 1959 did the confrontation finally end. That same year, Martin Luther King, Jr., commented that Faubus's recalcitrance did more to unite northern public opinion in favor of African American civil rights than did Eisenhower's vacillation between inaction and decisiveness.

The federal government's inconsistent response to the segregationists' massive resistance in Arkansas revealed grim realities. In order to achieve significant support among northerners and elected officials, black protesters could ultimately depend only upon themselves, the northern media, a few federal judges, and the U.S. Supreme Court. Even so, after *Brown*, segregationists — politically secure within their own region — employed states' rights ideology and constitutional symbolism in attempting to maintain the South's traditional veto power over the passage of effective federal civil rights legislation. Thus, as civil rights historian George M. Fredrickson suggested, Little Rock revealed not only that African American "protesters faced a divided, fragmented, and uncertain governmental opposition" but also that the "most important division among whites that the [civil rights] movement was able to exploit was between northerners who lacked a regional commitment to legalized segregation and southerners who believed that Jim Crow was central to their way of life." The Supreme Court's forceful reaffirmation of *Brown* in *Cooper v. Aaron* showed King and other civil rights leaders, moreover, how best "to get the federal government on . . . [their] side and to utilize the U.S. Constitution against the outmoded states' rights philosophy of the southern segregationist."

Over the decades since *Brown*, public perception of the federal judiciary's role in the civil rights struggle was dynamic. During the 1950s and 1960s, opinion leaders either praised or condemned the federal judiciary and the Supreme Court as the nation's primary defenders of civil rights and liberties as the courts established a historic degree of racial equality under the Constitution. The Court's action favoring black litigants in *Brown* and its confrontations with southern white resistance in the Little Rock crisis, culminating in the *Cooper* decision, enlarged constitutional protection of individual rights in conjunction with the expanding reach of the post–World War II liberal state. Working through the channels of extended federal judicial, legislative, and administrative authority, the civil rights movement thus achieved significant social and constitutional reforms. This focus, however, underwent gradual change. By the 1990s the prevailing view among historians reflected growing public wariness of social policy outcomes won through court litigation. In particular, many historians of the civil rights struggle argued that African American consciousness-raising and community formation shaped the triumphs achieved through the nonviolent mass protest movement identified with Martin Luther King, Jr. Meanwhile, powerful historical scholars from C. Vann Woodward (1955) to Michael J. Klarman (2004) — although giving due recognition to black activist agency — focused more upon the influence of whites — either white southern elites advocating gradual change or segregationist proponents of massive resistance aggressively defending Jim Crow.

Historical interpretations that emphasized the effectiveness of reform activism over that of litigation had noteworthy limitations. First, concerning the civil rights movement as a whole, these viewpoints inadequately recognized that judicial action significantly influenced even "clear-cut" victories like the Montgomery bus boycott and the Selma voting rights march. Mark Tushnet in his incisive study of Thurgood Marshall and the NAACP Legal Defense Fund (LDF) observed that by 1955, when Rosa Park's refusal to move to the back of the bus sparked the historic Montgomery boycott, "the legal issues raised by Jim Crow ordinances [mandating racially segregated seating on public transportation] were not difficult, but it took a Supreme Court decision to end bus segregation in Montgomery." Thus, judicial action brought the Montgomery bus boycott to an end, benefiting black community activism. Although the emergence of Martin Luther King, Jr., as a national civil rights leader was clearly a more important outcome of the boycott, historians who focus on activism underestimate the degree to which within a decade King and others employed judicial action — in conjunction with the more conspicuous strategy of nonviolent protest — to bring about passage of the Civil Rights Act of 1964 and the Voting Rights Act of 1965. The interpretation of the civil rights struggle that prevailed by turn of the millennium either downplayed or ignored this use of litigation.

However, King, Julian Bond, and other civil rights leaders acknowledged how central judicial sanction of constitutional rights was in overturning the South's Jim Crow apartheid system. Indeed, the favorable outcomes of litigation before sympathetic lower federal court judges such as Judge Frank Johnson of Alabama represented a strategic aim to raise the most effective possible challenge to every facet of the racial oppression institutionalized in segregation. Since most southern federal judges, like their state counterparts, acted haltingly until the Supreme Court specifically settled a given desegregation issue, civil rights advocates' choice to resort to a few selected federal judges was instrumental to the success of the nonviolent resistance campaign. Taylor Branch's and David J. Garrow's monumental studies of King and the civil rights movement noted the pivotal role Judge Johnson played in the Montgomery boycott, the Freedom Rides, and the Selma voting rights march. Johnson and a small number of other federal judges thus enabled the civil rights movement, Branch observed, to "institutionalize its major gains. . . . Legal segregation was doomed. Negroes no longer were invisible." This book argues that the decision by the Little Rock NAACP to initiate the case of *Aaron v. Cooper* in 1955–1956, as well as its subsequent appeals throughout the protracted confrontation culminating in the Supreme Court's decision of *Cooper v. Aaron*, facilitated the judicial strategy later refined by civil rights activists.

This emphasis on the *Cooper* litigation as a progenitor of later civil rights judicial activism challenged an enduring faith in gradualism. Like Harry Ashmore, whose prize-winning moderate editorials in the *Arkansas Gazette* did much to define for a generation the meaning of the Little Rock crisis, leading southern historian C. Vann Woodward endorsed gradualism. Earlier historians of the South had accepted the premise that slavery, its racialist roots, and its influence upon the emergence and life of the Jim Crow apartheid system reflected a historical process of institutional and cultural continuity. Through a brilliant reevaluation of the so-called New South era that followed the Civil War and Reconstruction, however, Woodward argued convincingly that Jim Crow had arisen from historical discontinuity. Thus, during the first postbellum generation a real possibility existed that some southern whites and African Americans might create a genuine liberal democracy, Woodward believed. According to him, during the late nineteenth and early twentieth centuries, the "strange career of Jim Crow" had submerged but not destroyed southern liberal democratic tendencies. Woodward acknowledged that African Americans could shape their own destiny but he was nonetheless convinced that the "gradualism" instituted by a new generation of moderates was the only realistic course southern whites would embrace in order to surrender a social order based on terror, legally mandated racial discrimination, black second-class citizenship, and white supremacy.

Shortly after the *Cooper* litigation reached its denouement in 1959, historian Georg Iggers published an assessment rejecting such gradualism. A white Jewish émigré who as a child had fled Nazi Germany, Iggers was an active member of the Little Rock NAACP during the mid-1950s; he was involved deeply in initiating the *Cooper* litigation. While teaching at a predominately black college in New Orleans in 1960, Iggers published an essay arguing that the dramatic Little Rock confrontation that began in August 1957 originated from the local NAACP branch's successful effort to mobilize black community support against the weakening of the school board's initially rather progressive school desegregation plan following *Brown*. Accordingly, he asserted, "I find it difficult to escape the conclusion that the crisis . . . was not the result of premature integration but the breakdown of authority and the weakness of a false sort of gradualism." The Little Rock School Board believed, Iggers wrote, that "by progressively weakening its own plan and by emphasizing its own reluctance to follow the Supreme Court's [*Brown*] decision it would make the bitter pill more palatable." This gradualist strategy, however, "actually helped to consolidate extremist opposition."

Iggers's emphasis on the link between African American agency and the weak enforcement of racial desegregation in Little Rock presaged later historical interpretations. The popular television documentary *Eyes on the Prize* and accompanying book published in 1987 depicted the Little Rock confrontation as arising from litigation aimed at mobilizing the local black community's support for school desegregation in the wake of *Brown*. Also, John A. Kirk and Adam Fairclough considered the question "Was the Little Rock confrontation a success or failure for the NAACP?" Both historians supported the conclusion, in Fairclough's words, that the "NAACP's great achievement" in Little Rock and elsewhere was that its "legalistic strategy undermine[d] the legal foundations of segregation," paving the way for larger civil rights triumphs "at a time when the federal judiciary was increasingly sympathetic to the goals of the civil rights movement." Also, later commentators explored more fully the consequences of what Iggers described as state and federal elected officials' ambivalent reaction to the real and potential violence and disorder white segregationists pursued. As Michal R. Belknap has argued concerning Little Rock in particular and the civil rights struggle as a whole, federal authorities and "unreliable" state and local officials generally "evaded an obligation" to prosecute white "trouble makers," thereby "depriv[ing] blacks of rights guaranteed them by the U.S. Constitution."

African American use of litigation also facilitated black community mobilization in the face of white moderate vacillation. As Kirk and others have observed, the local NAACP court challenge in 1956 demanded resolution of its own internal divisions before the organization could promote unity among the wider black community. Yet the federal, state, and local government ambivalence toward or outright resistance to blacks' constitutional rights claims meant, David Goldfield concluded, that in Little Rock and other early civil rights confrontations of the 1950s, "blacks found themselves alone," and white moderates only responded "belatedly, primarily to hold down losses (economic and political) rather than to facilitate meaningful change." The members of the Little Rock NAACP held much the same view regarding the white moderates on the school board who readily diluted the school desegregation plan, thereby compelling them to resort to litigation in the first place. Moreover, the local NAACP and the black community had little reason to alter this view as the litigation encountered growing opposition until the moderates finally brought about the enforcement of *Cooper* in 1959. Meanwhile, the only initial allies Little Rock blacks found among government authorities were a few federal judges, including district judge Ronald N. Davies (a Republican appointee from South Dakota who, as a result of a routine temporary assignment, found himself at the center of the Little Rock confrontation), his colleagues on the Eighth Circuit Court of Appeals, and the justices of the U.S. Supreme Court itself.

The continued African American court challenges inspired by *Brown* engendered divided resistance among Arkansas whites. Historian Anthony Badger has observed that Arkansas moderates such as U.S. Senator William J. Fulbright and U.S. Representative Brooks Hays signed the Southern Manifesto of 1956, which employed states' rights principles to claim that *Brown* was unconstitutional. The document advocated any and all "lawful" resistance; just what that meant, however, was left vague. Ultimately, such ambiguous constitutional rhetoric played into the hands of Governor Orval E. Faubus. An economic liberal without racial prejudice, Faubus gradually shifted from a moderate desegregation stance to espousing an extreme segregationist states' rights position. Badger notes correctly that Faubus initially attempted to stay in office by exploiting the moderates' ideological pragmatism, which at once justified compliance with *Brown* on the ground of opportunistic submission to federal judicial supremacy even though they might disagree with desegregation itself. However, faced with Arkansas segregationists' increasingly aggressive states' rights campaign — and its potential for exacerbating many white southerners' deep-seated propensity for racial violence — Faubus embraced the extremists' constitutional perspective in order to justify his defiance of federal authority. Thus, Badger concludes, Faubus recognized that it was "difficult to . . . convince people that there was no alternative to obeying the law of the land when leading politicians in the state were proclaiming that there was an alternative."

Meanwhile, the U.S. liberal state's economic policies exacerbated social class and political divisions that Faubus and other southern leaders exploited in the desegregation struggle. Postwar Arkansas exemplified the eroding dominance white southerners maintained over African American labor and economic opportunity as a result of New Deal liberalism's labor and credit policies. Nevertheless, such liberalism provided incentives for both resisting and accommodating an end to Jim Crow. Blue-collar, middle-, and lower-middle-class southern whites faced increasing market and racial identity competition from blacks; hence these whites provided the rank-and-file for the extreme segregationists' campaign of racist violence and disorder associated with their claim of constitutional states' rights. Wealthier white business and civic groups generally benefited, however, from the larger economic transformation New Deal liberalism and its postwar incarnation brought about; they were the chief advocates of gradualism and tokenism based on expedient deference to constitutional federal supremacy identified with the Supreme Court and the *Brown* decision.

8

Faubus and other southern leaders effectively exploited the classist and racist identity politics embedded in the conflicting symbolism of states' rights versus federalism, which federal authorities' inconsistent enforcement efforts ultimately exacerbated.

The subtle yet powerful psychology inherent in opposing constitutional perspectives was revealed by two commentaries. In 1958, as Faubus's gubernatorial bid unfolded and the Supreme Court considered the appeal of *Cooper v. Aaron,* Harvard law professor Paul Freund wrote, "It would be idle to look for a sudden miraculous reconciliation. For one thing, resistance to integration flows from a deep spring of primitive, subrational fears, summed up by the frightful 'mongrelization' of the races. To exorcise this image is not the work of a day or a year." Moreover, in "districts where the Negro populace exceeds that of whites, the consequence of desegregation is that the white children in effect will be attending colored schools." Freund's academic assessment of southern whites' underlying racial animosity contrasted markedly with the view voiced by former U.S. Supreme Court justice and South Carolina governor James Byrnes. During the Little Rock confrontation, Byrnes's criticism of the *Brown* and *Cooper* decisions appeared in many periodicals. His article in the *Alabama Lawyer* of October 1959 stated, "It is our duty to let the people of other sections know the attitude of the South is due not to racial prejudice but to the firm belief that the court has arrogated to itself the power of a third legislature and if not curbed by Congress, will destroy local governments."

Byrnes knew, of course, that in private and public discourse segregationists often advocated states' rights as a surrogate for racist rhetoric and the defense of white supremacy. Yet as a former Supreme Court justice involved in early race opinions, he undoubtedly also knew that some liberal constitutional experts criticized the Supreme Court's *Brown* decision as an unwise exercise of judicial activism. Moreover, Byrnes surely was aware, too, that certain prominent liberal lawyers as well as noted northern members of the American Bar Association not only held these same critical views of *Brown* but also voiced those views before congressional committees that for decades had stalled efforts to enact civil rights legislation. In addition Byrnes clearly knew, too, that within the Republican majority that controlled Congress from 1953 to 1954, there were conservatives who proposed

legislation aimed at curbing the Supreme Court's activism. These critics claimed that the Supreme Court threatened local governments and
states' rights. Nevertheless, outside the South the cold war liberal
resistance to pronounced racist appeals was also strong. Thus, Byrnes
admonished fellow southern leaders to avoid expressly racist rhetoric;
he urged resorting to the same constitutional imagery being employed
by northern legal elites and many congressional Republicans. Essentially, Byrnes advocated a conservative reversal of the convergence
strategy then emerging among civil rights leaders.

Freund and Byrnes also examined how southern elected officials
used the segregationist states' rights platform to resist *Brown*. Northern constitutional experts like Freund considered the segregationist
states' rights theories merely to be masks for deep-seated racism. Yet
such experts' criticism of the Court's judicial activism shared with
segregationists the presumption that, despite the expansion of liberal
constitutionalism since the late 1930s, many fields of law that addressed family relations, marriage, community welfare, criminal justice, and education — generally dubbed police powers — remained
directly within local and state governmental control. For generations,
moreover, southern whites believed that through police powers local
and state control of race relations was fundamental to a way of life
grounded upon white supremacy. These attitudes were manifested in
the fact that only in the most exceptional circumstances would local
or state authorities punish violence whites perpetrated against blacks.
Thus, it made tactical political sense for Byrnes and Faubus to resort
to states' rights constitutional symbolism in order to win over segregationist leaders. More importantly, for most southerners that constitutional imagery was no mere symbolic abstraction; it embodied a
traditional way of life threatened by a pernicious Supreme Court,
black activists, and other evil outsiders. Thus, the Little Rock confrontation revealed to Faubus and other southern officials that
although southern moderates were impotent and federal enforcement
inconsistent, the states' rights ideology provided maneuvering room
to achieve at the least political risk the greatest political gain.

Indeed, President Eisenhower's ambivalence in the Little Rock
confrontation epitomized the federal government's inconsistent
enforcement of *Brown*. Notwithstanding his dramatic dispatch of

the 101st Airborne to enforce the federal court's desegregation order against the mob outside Central High, Eisenhower's general dislike of the *Brown* decision was public knowledge. In part this was so because the Eisenhower administration pursued a "southern strategy," seeking to win northern black voter support while at the same time cultivating conservative southern Democrats dissatisfied with the liberalism that had dominated the nation since Franklin Roosevelt. In addition, regarding the southern desegregation struggle and the cold war propaganda battle with the communists, Mary L. Dudziak and others have argued that one of the Eisenhower administration's major foreign policy concerns was strengthening the democratic image of the United States in African, Asian, Latin American, and European nations. The intrinsic justice of furthering the cause of racial equality in the South was of secondary importance. Moreover, Dudziak concluded: "To the extent that safeguarding the image of America was behind Eisenhower's involvement [in Little Rock], he got what he needed with *Cooper v. Aaron*. At this juncture, the cold war imperative could be addressed largely through formal pronouncements about the law. More substantive social change would await another day."

In the Little Rock confrontation, African Americans eventually overcame southern defiance of constitutional civil rights the Supreme Court affirmed. The images of overwhelming U.S. military force obscured African American resistance channeled through federal litigation. An emphasis upon equivocal outcomes resulting from federal coercion reduced the struggle for constitutional rights to a test of political will, primarily pitting white southerners not only against the federal government but also against one another. This book argues, by contrast, that litigation culminating in the Supreme Court's decision in *Cooper v. Aaron* (1958) revealed how the constitutional principles of federal-state relations and separation of powers remained dynamic and contestable as the civil rights struggle unfolded. African Americans increasingly linked the constitutional legitimacy the Supreme Court gave their rights claims to the cold war liberal consensus reflected in the national media and the Eisenhower administration's association of the propaganda battle with communism. Confronting the most powerful threat to the southern way of life since Reconstruction, southern white leaders mitigated the white supremacy

underlying Jim Crow by advocating states' rights ideology and rejecting judicial supremacy. Southerners' tendency toward racial violence
inherent in that same imagery nonetheless brought about the South's
political isolation as the interests of African American activists and
federal authorities converged in support of token enforcement of civil
rights. Thus, *Cooper v. Aaron* presaged civil rights struggles to come.

The Little Rock NAACP
Decision to Sue, 1954–1956

The decision of the Little Rock branch of the National Association for the Advancement of Colored People (NAACP) to bring the school desegregation suit in late 1955 reflected a wide context. Since Reconstruction in Arkansas, generally, and in Little Rock particularly, there existed a resilient tradition of black protest; after World War II this activism became centered increasingly in the local branches of the NAACP. As was true elsewhere in the South, the Arkansas local branches were not directed by the NAACP national office, but represented a genuine indigenous activism. Indeed, the local NAACP decision that litigation against the Little Rock School Board was necessary in order to enforce meaningful compliance with the Supreme Court *Brown* decision demanded significant mobilization of the city African American population. The decision to sue nonetheless aggravated divisions within the larger black community and the local NAACP itself; it also engendered resistance from white moderates and segregationists alike. In addition, the suit occurred amidst other racial desegregation efforts within Arkansas and across the South, which in turn fostered inconsistent responses among Arkansas elected officials and their counterparts in other southern states. Similarly, at the federal level the Eisenhower administration pursued an uneven policy toward civil rights as it confronted conflicting political exigencies in Congress and throughout the nation, as well as in the cold war propaganda battle abroad.

The federal system encouraged indeterminacy toward complying with *Brown*. Although the Supreme Court declared unanimously on May 17, 1954 (*Brown* I) that regarding elementary and secondary public education the long-established doctrine of separate but equal was now held to be "inherently unequal," the Court remedial decree (*Brown* II) handed down the next year equivocated, leaving local federal district courts to decide whether school boards were complying "with all deliberate speed." Publicly, the Court ascribed its flexible standard to the enormous difficulties inherent in enforcing uniformity across hundreds of local school boards. Privately, however, the justices expressed concern that local resistance could result from requiring immediate desegregation. Even so, the Little Rock School Board, like many of its counterparts across the upper South, responded to *Brown* I with a comparatively progressive, if tentative, proposal for desegregation; but by *Brown* II school officials publicized a plan seeking only minimal compliance. With this switch, the Little Rock NAACP reversed course: whereas it had supported the school board good faith effort initially, the NAACP decided to sue in response to the minimalist plan. Meanwhile, the Supreme Court authorization of a locally centered compliance process in *Brown* II enabled both Arkansas governor Orval Faubus and the Eisenhower administration to eschew enforcement responsibility. Only a local federal district court decision against the school board or public disorder precipitating intervention by state and/or federal chief executives could upset the tenuous balance of diffused authority.

Conflicted images of racial identity exacerbated these issues of official responsibility. At the start of the twentieth century, W. E. B. Du Bois predicted that the "problem of the color line" would define twentieth-century U.S. democracy. During World War II, Gunnar Myrdal focused upon the dilemma the southern Jim Crow racial apartheid system created for U.S. opposition to the racist nationalism of Nazi Germany and militarist Japan. Moreover, many southern blacks moved to northern and western industrial centers seeking wartime jobs, thereby establishing new voting blocs that supported racial justice. Yet outside the South, blacks did not comprise a large enough proportion of the population to call into question the rule of the white majority. Thus, although racial tensions undeniably existed in northern and western states, the political system accommodated them on a circumscribed, de facto basis. The unswerving commitment to white supremacy imposed through Jim Crow in the South, however, drew its force from the fact that blacks comprised a much larger proportion of the population than was the case in other regions. In many places throughout the South, the black population constituted a majority. Accordingly, in the postwar era, white racial identity politics dominated the South but not the rest of the nation. By the time of *Brown*

I, elected officials in Arkansas and its capital city nonetheless avoided racist appeals in favor of a program promoting economic liberalism; following *Brown* II, however, proliferating states' rights measures reflected whites' heightened racial antagonism.

This chapter locates the Little Rock NAACP decision to bring a school desegregation suit within the context of the diffuse political and legal accountability of the federal system, conditioned by racial politics in Arkansas and elsewhere. Disappointed hopes resulting from *Brown* I divided local NAACP leaders regarding Little Rock School Board good faith in formulating a desegregation plan. A switch occurred among local NAACP leaders — engendering the decision to sue — as a result of the weakened desegregation plan promoted by school board racial moderates, as both groups confronted *Brown* II. The resistance movement among segregationist extremists coalesced around the states' rights ideology promoting popular and congressional opposition to federal civil rights measures, as well as surreptitiously condoning violence. President Eisenhower's equivocation toward civil rights reinforced the school board moderates' and Governor Faubus's shifting claims of responsibility for enforcing *Brown*, encouraging the extreme segregationists' "massive resistance" and isolating the Little Rock NAACP desegregation efforts.

Brown I and Disappointed Hopes

The Little Rock NAACP, the city school board, and Governor Faubus responded to *Brown* I unevenly. Within days following the Court decision in May 1954, Arkansas local NAACP branches arranged meetings to inform black communities about school desegregation. During the summer, Daisy Bates of Little Rock, president of the Arkansas NAACP State Conference of Branches, actively participated in programs led by the national organization: delegates targeted September 1955 as the date for implementing the Court desegregation decision. In August, Bates and Wiley Branton of Pine Bluff, chair of the Legal Redress Committee of the state conference, met with NAACP national office field representative Mildred Bond to discuss litigation options. Accordingly, Branton mailed a petition to Little Rock School Board president William G. Cooper, declaring that as long as the board moved expeditiously, without seeking federal court direction, the branch would not sue to bring about compliance. Even so, as early as May 21, 1954, the *Arkansas Gazette* reported that the Little Rock School Board had affirmed, "It is our responsibility to comply with federal constitutional requirements and we intend to do so when the Supreme Court outlines the method to be followed." Meanwhile, Faubus — who over the summer was the surprise winner in the Democratic gubernatorial primary — avoided taking a firm position toward school desegregation; it was, he said, a local issue with which he intended not to interfere.

Bates's and Branton's leadership in the state NAACP provided a broad perspective encouraging hopefulness. On May 21, the same day that the Little Rock School Board expressed its intent to comply with *Brown* I pending further direction from the Court, the school board in Fayetteville, a northwest Arkansas community, voted to open its high school in September on a racially desegregated basis. By August 1954, Bishop Albert L. Fletcher of the Diocese of Little Rock also announced in local Catholic churches that some of the states' parochial schools would be desegregated in the fall. Clearly, *Brown* applied to public, not private, schools. Nevertheless, Bates and Branton could view the bishop's action — in conjunction with the Fayetteville School Board desegregation decision — as indicating that the state's record of racial moderation was prevailing, despite simmering racial animosity in certain localities. Also, Faubus's stance of no interference with local school boards concerning the desegregation issue reinforced the image of local control. Bates and Branton clearly were aware, too, that across Arkansas' seventy-five counties, in only six, located in the Mississippi Delta, did whites constitute a minority. In more than half of the state's counties, moreover, blacks comprised less than 10 percent of the population, as was the case in Fayetteville, located in the Ozark mountains. As the state's largest city, with a population of just over 100,000, Little Rock had a black population of roughly 22 percent. In Mississippi, by contrast, of the state's eighty-two counties, in thirty-one whites were a minority.

The NAACP petition to the Little Rock School Board thus reflected wary hopefulness that voluntary compliance with *Brown* I was possible. The Little Rock petition was like those Branton sent to at least ten other school districts throughout Arkansas. The petition fit the form suggested by the national office and the NAACP Legal Defense Fund (separate from the larger NAACP), which had orchestrated and won *Brown*. However, neither national organization controlled the actions of local NAACP branches. Also, since the local NAACP had no official standing before the school board, it arranged for eighteen residents of the city, who were parents of children attending the segregated public elementary and secondary schools, to sign the petition. The petitioners urged from the board "immediate steps" to "reorganize the public schools" on a racially desegregated basis in accordance with the Supreme Court *Brown* decision. Requesting to appear before the school board, the petitioners offered aid in order to bring about an orderly transition to desegregated schools. The petition also asked the board to give notice of the next meeting date; at the end of August, Superintendent Virgil Blossom informed Branton that the meeting was set for September 9, 1954.

Little Rock NAACP members' prior experience working with the school board concerning school desegregation had been mixed. Two years earlier, Georg Iggers, a white history professor and Jewish émigré teaching at the black, Protestant-affiliated Philander Smith College in Little Rock, who chaired the local NAACP Education Committee, had coauthored a report suggesting a strategy for remedying the unequal educational opportunities the black students endured. Compiled by Iggers and his wife, Wilma, the report appealed for limited school "integration" based on a factual demonstration that black facilities were grossly unequal to white schools by any reasonable standard, especially that of recent Supreme Court decisions that had eroded the separate but equal doctrine. Focusing on growing postwar activism by African Americans countenanced by Little Rock white moderate leadership, the report declared that "segregation in public facilities is bound to pass." This was not because of a wholesale transformation in the South's commitment to its way of life, but rather because, "with the increasing social and political awakening of the Negroes in the South, increasing pressure is being brought upon this system and is finding increasing sympathy among enlightened white citizens." Like the sentiments prevailing among the local NAACP members preceding the school board hearing on September 9, 1954, a cautious hope that moderate action might succeed underpinned the report proposals in 1952.

Still, the Little Rock NAACP and the school board response to the

1952 report provided conflicted precedent. The local NAACP leadership and several school board members embraced the observation that in Arkansas relative racial progress had come primarily through "mediation" rather than court action. Even so, the report continued, "full integration may come in two ways: either suddenly through court action or gradually through planned integration." The "likelihood" of court action "becomes greater as planned integration is pushed into a distant future or rejected." Litigation, moreover, engendered "social tensions . . . resentment on the part of pupils and teachers . . . and unemployment for many Negro pupils and teachers." The preferred alternative was "planned integration" beginning with black Dunbar High School students having limited access to facilities they lacked that were being "underutilized" at Little Rock Central High. Initially, the gradualist strategy seemed effective because the school board agreed to discuss confidentially the feasibility of implementation. Three board members seemed to be favorably disposed, whereas the superintendent was hostile. A breach of confidence, however, ended these exchanges. The *Arkansas Gazette* reported that NAACP branch president and attorney Thaddeus D. Williams had publicly announced an impending meeting with the school board to discuss gradually ameliorating blacks' limited educational opportunities under segregation. The story contrasted such moderation with the example of U.S. Tate, an NAACP attorney in Dallas who called for litigation seeking "immediate and complete abolition of segregation!"

For Bates, Iggers, Williams, and other members of the Little Rock NAACP executive committee, the 1952 encounter with the school board thus provided ambiguous lessons. Immediately following the *Gazette* story comparing Williams's and the Dallas NAACP lawyer's visions of desegregation, the school board cancelled the planned meeting; soon thereafter, it formally rejected allowing black students restricted access to the white high school. The reaction indicated that the school board moderates' support for even limited racial desegregation was tenuous when publicity resulted that might aggravate racial feelings among the white majority. More particularly, the episode suggested that the school board formed policy on the presumption that the majority of Little Rock whites remained relatively uninvolved unless some truly explosive issue aroused their attention. Initially, the proposed limited use by blacks of selected facilities at Central could be perceived as relatively unthreatening, especially given the Little Rock record of comparatively positive race relations since World War II. The *Gazette* story, however, fostered a contentious public image in which the distinction between selective access to and wholesale integration of Central was lost to most white peoples' overriding animosity toward the notion of race mixing itself. Bates, Williams, and Iggers, who remained a member of the Little Rock NAACP branch from 1952 through 1956, understood that white moderates' willingness to cooperate with the NAACP was highly conditional.

The 1952 episode also resulted in disagreement among the local NAACP branch members themselves. Privately, some executive board members expressed amazed dismay when Williams publicized the meeting with the school board, displaying as it did insensitivity concerning the quiet practicality blacks and white moderates customarily employed in order to maneuver within the Jim Crow system. Nevertheless, although Williams's personal motives remained obscure, his announcement clearly reflected a contrasting approach to dealing with white moderates. Although some NAACP members willingly cooperated with the moderates as long as they proceeded in good faith, Williams undoubtedly knew that the Legal Defense Fund was preparing the litigation strategy targeting the separate but equal doctrine. Certainly in 1952 no one could be realistically confident that the LDF strategy would prevail. The Dallas lawyer's pronouncement that the NAACP was seeking cases to challenge the separate but equal doctrine nonetheless publicized an idea that was common currency among black civil rights lawyers such as Williams. Given these considerations, it is possible that Williams was attempting to place the school board in a public position that would force it either to allow blacks limited access to Central or, by refusing to do so, provide grounds for litigation. Indeed, after the school board rejected the limited desegregation proposals, the branch executive committee for the first time seriously considered bringing a desegregation suit to achieve its modest objectives. But the LDF urged delaying the suit pending the outcome in *Brown;* the branch complied.

The split within the Little Rock NAACP was reinforced in a meeting with Superintendent Blossom soon after the *Brown* decision in 1954. In February 1953, Blossom took over as the superintendent of the Little Rock School District. Originally from Missouri, Blossom possessed significant teaching, administrative, and coaching experience in Okmulgee, Oklahoma, and Fayetteville, Arkansas. During World War II, as superintendent of Fayetteville schools, he formulated what was then considered a moderate plan to maintain racial segregation by busing from the city the few black students residing in the area. Blossom took the position in Little Rock amidst high expectations among blacks and whites alike that he would maintain its moderate reputation regarding race relations. In the days following the announcement of the *Brown* decision, Blossom met with a black delegation that included Daisy Bates's husband, L. C. Bates, a leading member of the local NAACP branch. When it became clear that Blossom's approach to desegregation amounted to nothing more than preparing studies until the Supreme Court handed down a remedial decree stipulating clear terms of compliance, L. C. Bates left the meeting in protest. Although most of the others in the delegation heard Blossom out, L. C. Bates's action was consistent with the position of those in the NAACP branch that had wanted to sue as a result of the collapse in negotiations with the school board in 1952. Blossom's wait-and-see approach to implementing *Brown* revealed that the division among the NAACP members persisted, though a majority was willing to give the school board the benefit of the doubt.

For the three local NAACP LDF lawyers, the outcome of the September 9, 1954, meeting with the school board was consistent with the two previously frustrating encounters. Branton, a Pine Bluff resident, focused on the mandate of *Brown*, which, though formally binding only upon the parties who originally sued under it, nonetheless set a clear precedent guiding Arkansas compliance. "We hope," Branton said, "that we can solve all our problems without the necessity of a lawsuit. Since the basic [constitutional and legal] problem has already been settled, we feel there is just one question now and that is how integration shall be put into effect. That is our purpose here today." Jackie L. Shropshire, a young black lawyer still at an early stage of practice in Little Rock, focused upon the deplorable conditions certain black schools endured compared to those for whites. "If you integrated," Shropshire told the board, "you would not have those problems." The third black lawyer present was Williams. He undoubtedly perceived some continuity between school board vacillation in 1952 and 1954. Indeed, notwithstanding the willing attention given the NAACP LDF lawyers, the board position, stated at the September 9 meeting through its counsel, was that despite the *Brown* decision the Supreme Court had issued no remedial order applying to Arkansas, and until it had done so "this board is not under a legal duty to immediately abolish segregation."

In a separate meeting on the same day, Branton and Williams received a similarly disappointing message from Superintendent Blossom. Noting the school board official announcement in May of its formal obligation and willingness to comply with the *Brown* decision, Blossom emphasized that studies were necessary before any racial desegregation plan could be formulated. As of September 9, he said, this work was still not under way; once initiated, such studies perhaps would require months to complete. Blossom assured Branton and Williams that these efforts did not represent delay but were instead essential in order to accommodate the Supreme Court mandate to the realities of a complex logistical and social transformation involving 10,000 children in the Little Rock School District. Branton pointed out, however, that although St. Louis and Baltimore were larger cities, initial steps toward school desegregation had already taken place. "Is it the intention of the Little Rock School Board to work honestly toward a program of desegregation," Branton asked, "and to announce that program as soon as possible without any outside influence from anyone?" Blossom initially equivocated, insisting that such difficult issues required study. When Branton pressed him, Blossom stated, "It is not clear as to what will be the policy of this board." Without complete study, he insisted, "We would be foolish to set any timetable now."

Branton thus learned what Williams already had discovered. In the area of school desegregation, Little Rock School Board expressions of good faith were contingent on forces beyond its control. Local and state public officials' general unwillingness to pursue compliance with *Brown* unless publicly known to be bound by a federal court order became apparent when the *Arkansas Gazette* reported on September 26 the policy enunciated by the Arkansas commissioner of education. In response to the U.S. Supreme Court solicitation of opinions from southern state officials through amicus (friend of the court) briefs, both the commissioner of education and the state's own brief stated that the policy "will be a recognition of the decision by the Supreme

Court and will be an effort to point out proper ways of implementing it in Arkansas." Meanwhile, the commissioner of education urged, Arkansas school districts should take no action until the Supreme Court handed down its remedial decree stipulating terms governing compliance with *Brown* enforceable in federal court. Within a month, the Arkansas conference of the NAACP voted a resolution "deploring" the delay. During the period from fall 1954 through spring 1955, the state NAACP also followed the policy the national office advised: cooperate with local school boards until September 1955. Litigation might then be filed against school boards making no meaningful effort to comply with the Court remedial decree.

Brown II and the Decision to Sue

From late 1954 through early 1956, the Little Rock NAACP eventually switched from opposing to supporting litigation. This gradually emerging course resulted from continuing divisions within the branch since 1952; it revealed, too, lost faith in the good will of white moderates on the school board and in Little Rock generally. Still, the single most important event precipitating the change was *Brown* II. At the same time, Little Rock NAACP members' eroded confidence in the white moderates fostered new acceptance of the organization in the black community, despite mild opposition from some blacks. The local NAACP decision to bring a desegregation suit to compel school board compliance with *Brown* II thus heightened the significance of the branch within the black community and thereby broadened the black activism that had emerged earlier in Arkansas, especially since World War II. Moreover, the move to a stronger protest stance exposed the white moderates' circumscribed support for weakening the Jim Crow system, coinciding as it did with growing national and international publicity given racial protest and violence occurring over the same period in Mississippi and Alabama. Initially, however, the convergence of these events within and outside Arkansas with the Little Rock NAACP decision to litigate encouraged faith that Faubus could resist pressure from extreme segregationists to side against racial desegregation. Meanwhile, the Eisenhower administration attempted to remain uninvolved directly in desegregation even as it struggled to redress a deteriorating image of U.S. democracy abroad.

Superintendent Blossom's plan evolved at both public and private levels prior to the Supreme Court *Brown* II decision. From fall 1954 to spring 1955, the superintendent's public effort focused on what seemed to be clearly formulated objectives. Nevertheless, that effort also may be understood as an attempt to provide Little Rock citizens with flexible terms that could be publicized pending announcement of the Supreme Court remedial decree. The Arkansas Commission of Education had advised taking no firm steps toward desegregation until the Court handed down its order. Thus, before the Court announced its decree, any desegregation action was tentative. The distinction was significant because privately and publicly Blossom presented different motivations. In private, Blossom assured whites the desegregation goal he pursued would result in the "least amount of integration over the longest period of time." Moreover, in Blossom's private papers a three-page statement without date bearing the title "Plan of School Integration — Little Rock School District" noted that desegregation should await completed construction of three high schools and twice as many junior high schools, as well as until "specific decrees have been formulated by the U.S. Supreme Court in the pending cases." Desegregation would then begin at the high school level as the first of three phases. "Following successful integration at the senior high level, it should then be started in the junior high schools." Desegregation of the elementary schools would be the final phase. Parenthetically, he wrote: "Present indications are that the school year 1956–1957 may be the first phase of this program."

Blossom's readiness to discuss privately his expected goals reassured Little Rock white leaders that the desegregation plan would constitute minimal compliance with the Supreme Court reversal of the separate but equal doctrine. More particularly, these leaders could believe that Blossom's minimalist approach was consistent with the desegregation of law and graduate programs at the University of Arkansas and state colleges and the desegregation of Fayetteville public schools that already had taken place without serious racial difficulties. It also seemed in accord with other successful desegregation efforts, including granting blacks access to the Little Rock Public Library, the removal of racial designations in some city public facilities, and hiring a few black police officers to patrol Little Rock downtown areas that generally served blacks. Moreover, although lynching, police brutality, and other racial violence periodically had occurred in Little Rock and other localities up to World War II, since 1945 the city and the state record of race relations were nationally recognized among the best in the South and the border states. At the same time, Blossom and other public officials repeatedly publicized that their primary justification for pursuing school desegregation in the first place arose solely from the duty to comply with federal court orders mandated by the Supreme Court. Such pronouncements shifted the public images of moral responsibility and political accountability to outside federal authority.

In addition, Blossom's public presentations were sufficiently vague that most on the Little Rock NAACP executive board supported his ostensible plan. During the months before the Supreme Court decided on the remedial decree in *Brown* II, Blossom publicly highlighted factors that to members of the executive board seemed to be relatively progressive. What most of the executive board understood to be Blossom's plan, Iggers described later, was that "two new high schools under construction, Horace Mann on the east side and Hall on the west side, would be opened upon completion, projected in fall of 1956, without racial designation. With the opening of these schools, all the high schools in the city would be desegregated. There would be three attendance zones, including Little Rock Central." By 1957 the junior high schools were to be integrated, with elementary schools following over a three-year period ending in 1960. Notwithstanding the "somewhat gerrymandered school zones," the result would have been genuine desegregation along the moderate lines suggested by Iggers's 1952 report. After studying for some months the potential for school desegregation in Arkansas and its capital city, an NAACP LDF fieldworker encouraged the belief among the local executive board members that their trust in Blossom's plan was reasonable. Although white resistance was inevitable in certain locales, the LDF official declared, the "brightest prospect among the southern states for integration" was Arkansas.

Other factors reinforced the trust most local NAACP executive board members had in the Blossom plan. Iggers recalled that prior to

Brown II there was "consensus in the branch that the plan was acceptable, good faith in the intentions of the [school] board, and a relative optimism that the Little Rock community would accept this stage-by-stage plan of integration." Correspondence from 1954 to 1955 between Iggers and Mrs. Franz Adler, a spokesperson for a desegregation group in Fayetteville, suggested that the Blossom plan was consistent with moderate opinions shared by accommodationist whites and most members of the Little Rock NAACP executive committee. Adler "agreed" with Iggers that "informal negotiations should be the approach employed in changing the pattern of segregation as long as there is hope of success by that means." In addition, some local NAACP members possessed informal connections with some liberals in the Urban League, Southern Regional Council, and organized labor, and among significant professional, business, and civic leaders. These whites, in turn, influenced the business elite residing in the affluent Pulaski Heights, who through their control of the suburban Fifth Ward — and in conjunction with black voters — determined school board elections because voting participation in the other four Little Rock wards was usually light among blue-collar, lower-middle, and middle-class residents. The informal and indirect contacts between black voters and the white civic elite fostered the comparatively moderate record in race relations the Arkansas capital had achieved since World War II.

Nevertheless, this trust was tenuous. On the executive board, L. C. Bates opposed the Blossom plan from the beginning; he considered it "vague, indefinite, slow-moving, and indicative of intent to stall further on public school integration." By contrast, Daisy Bates disliked the plan's vagueness but otherwise maintained a wait-and-see attitude. The black lawyers who usually represented the branch were similarly uncommitted. As a result of their work during the petition hearings in September, Williams and Shropshire had good reason to be skeptical of school board good faith. Still, until the Supreme Court acted, they were willing to await the outcome of events. Another black lawyer, J. R. Booker, had a long-term perspective on these issues. Locally known as a "black Republican," Booker's early partner was Scipio Africanus Jones, an African American lawyer who had effectively represented Arkansas blacks before the U.S. Supreme Court; he had also won extraordinary support from the state's white legal establishment, briefly serving as an appointed local judge. Before his death in 1944, Jones, along with Booker and Thurgood Marshall of the NAACP LDF, eventually won before the U.S. Court of Appeals black schoolteacher Sue Morris's lengthy litigation seeking salary equalization. From such experiences Booker learned caution in dealing with the white power structure. Still, pastor of Mount Pleasant Baptist Church, Rev. J. C. Crenchaw, newspaper reporter Ozell Sutton, and white professors at Philander Smith College Georg Iggers and Lee Lorch supported the desegregation plan Blossom initially publicized before *Brown* II.

The division within the NAACP executive board reflected wider divisions in the Little Rock black community. In Little Rock and elsewhere across Arkansas, although the local NAACP took the strongest stance against the Jim Crow system, it relied primarily upon litigation rather than direct public challenge. The number of members actively involved in branch work was small; nearly all were on the executive committee. Militancy based on legal action was nonetheless central to the African American protest tradition reaching back in Arkansas at least to Reconstruction. Most notably, from 1889 to 1944 Scipio Jones was prominent among a small number of African American lawyers who had confronted racially discriminatory jury selection, voting, and criminal justice administration. Moreover, especially since the 1940s, the Supreme Court began deciding cases against southern racial discrimination in voting maintained through the white primary voting system. Black activism achieved growing numbers of African American voters throughout Arkansas who were independent of the exploitive labor practices white planters employed in the Delta to control black voting. Still, in Little Rock, Pine Bluff, and a few other urban areas, many of these independent black voters included more affluent African Americans carrying on the accommodating traditions of Booker T. Washington, for whom the dual racial society possessed certain personal and employment benefits. Although these blacks clearly favored improved racial equality, they believed that NAACP activism in Arkansas was counterproductive in light of the state's comparative racial moderation.

Thus, the split on the Little Rock NAACP executive board represented disagreement about moderate whites' good faith and what account should be taken of the divisions within the wider black community. Two practical points were particularly contentious. First, to finance any litigation, the local branch would have to rely on its own resources to pay fees to attorneys like Williams, Booker, and Shropshire. Second, the NAACP could not, of course, initiate suit on its own — clients had to come from the families harmed by the school board failure to comply with the *Brown* decision. Regarding the first issue, the more affluent blacks were best situated to cover the litigation costs, but this group was also the most skeptical of pursuing such a course, especially led by the NAACP. On the second issue, affluent black parents were more able than their blue-collar counterparts to survive white intimidation through employment blacklists or violence. Yet many of these blacks were unwilling to jeopardize their standing through identification with the NAACP. Moreover, an especially pressing concern to many of these same black parents, teachers, and administrators was what would become of Dunbar High School. Despite the unequal resources the white school board allocated to it under segregation, Dunbar possessed a well-deserved reputation for academic excellence among black as well as white educators, a reputation sustained by strong teacher-parent commitment to the welfare of each student. Would white teachers and administrators in desegregated schools sustain this same level of commitment and excellence, particularly if compelled through litigation?

In conjunction with *Brown* II, the Little Rock School Board brought events to a turning point. On May 31, 1955, the Supreme Court announced its remedial decree. The Court allotted to federal district courts in each state the primary responsibility to determine — on the basis of school desegregation plans reportedly shaped by particular local conditions — whether school boards were complying "with all deliberate speed." Just days prior to *Brown* II, the school board published a revised Blossom plan titled the Little Rock Phase Program. The proposals Blossom had publicized during the preceding year allowed for desegregation to a sufficient degree that the local NAACP executive board trusted school board good faith. The phase program, however, evidenced no such faith. Desegregation would not begin until September 1957, at which time only the nationally distinguished Central High School would admit black students. A highly selective screening process ensured that only a few black young people could enter Central. Moreover, a transfer procedure permitted any child whose race was in the minority to attend a school in which his or her race constituted the majority. As a result, the new Horace Mann High School would be virtually all black when it opened. A second phase embracing the junior high schools would start in 1960; although the date desegregation might come to elementary schools was left open, it was unlikely to begin earlier than 1963. Additionally, seeking to mollify increasingly vocal extreme segregationists, the school board ceased public discussions with black leaders, though informal private contacts persisted.

These events aggravated the split among the local NAACP executive committee members. *Brown* I had quieted the disagreement over whether to bring suit; but it was revived once Blossom announced the phase program, which seemed to conform closely with *Brown* II. Now, however, the executive committee "militants" and the "moderates" switched places. According to Iggers, the "conviction was growing among those of us who previously opposed a suit from the standpoint of community relations that without a court order the board would never integrate a single school." Williams and Booker, however, the two black attorneys who usually did branch legal work, no longer supported bringing a case. At least two factors influenced their opinions. First and most importantly, they argued, the phase program seemed consistent enough with the Court "all deliberate speed" standard that federal judges in and outside Arkansas might readily uphold it. A bad precedent for the desegregation cause would be the inevitable result. Second, since *Brown* II seemed to create a presumption favoring phase program constitutionality, the amount of legal work required to challenge it would raise the legal fees to more than $1,000, roughly three times the amount such litigation usually cost. Thus, instead of targeting what Williams called the "phony" Blossom plan, the two lawyers advised joining a suit already under way against the Pulaski County Special School District, which had made no attempt to comply with *Brown* II. Finally, if the executive committee still desired to sue in Little Rock, Williams advised the place to begin was the elementary schools, where the phase program set no clear starting date.

Other factors fostered hesitation regarding the decision to sue. Whether the Little Rock black community in general supported litigation remained problematic throughout 1955. Although the *State Press*, edited by L. C. and Daisy Bates, favored such action, its more moderate black competitor, the *Southern Mediator*, stated in an editorial two months following *Brown* II, "Integration will come here in the South, but we still believe that persuasion, intelligence, and sound judgment are far better than the use of force." A significant proportion of the city blacks apparently agreed, considering litigation not worth the financial cost, especially given that the phase program had announced a starting date some two years away. As late as January 1956, the *Southern Mediator* editorialized about "some sort" of disagreement within the branch over the question of bringing suit. In fact, some local NAACP members, working through a sympathetic white attorney, attempted to avoid litigation by urging the school board to return to the desegregation proposals Blossom had discussed in the fall of 1954. But this effort went nowhere. In addition, from February 1955 on, the white citizens' councils became increasingly vocal in Little Rock and elsewhere across Arkansas, including in Hoxie, where council intimidation directed at local school desegregation efforts threatened to turn more violent. The confrontation received national press attention; even the federal government for the first time considered involvement in a desegregation case.

Members of the Little Rock NAACP undoubtedly were aware of escalating white violence against blacks outside Arkansas. During 1955, African American activists in Mississippi and Alabama encountered Ku Klux Klan violence, with at least one shooting death. Blacks expressing public support for desegregation were the object of blacklists that resulted in job loss and death threats forcing them to move from their communities. Although the national media reported such events episodically, they did not form a composite public image until the Emmett Till tragedy. A fourteen-year-old boy from Chicago visiting family in Money, Mississippi, Till reportedly spoke too informally to a white female store clerk. Her claim that his language had sexual overtones led local whites to abduct Till and brutally murder him. After an arrest and trial, an all-white jury acquitted the killers. Till's mother, however, publicized the murder. Proclaiming her desire that the "world see what they did to my boy," she had the casket holding Till's beaten body opened to public viewing in Chicago. Over three days some 50,000 people saw the body; *Jet* magazine published photographs circulated nationally and internationally. Some months after their acquittal, and in return for payment of $4,000, the whites revealed how they murdered Till in a story *Look* magazine published. This combination of publicity aroused national and international indignation against the South, subsequently influencing such people as singer Bob Dylan, writer Maya Angelou, and boxer Muhammad Ali.

The murder of Emmett Till, along with other nationally reported civil rights stories, was significant for Daisy Bates and Wiley Branton. From the vantage point of the NAACP state conference they could relate desegregation efforts in and out of Arkansas to particular communities experiencing organized white resistance. Till's death occurred in Leflore County, Mississippi, about fifty miles from the Arkansas Delta area, the center of agitation for states' rights legislation against *Brown* and the place where the state citizens' councils first organized. From the Delta the council moved upon Hoxie in 1955. Branton had family in Leflore; the area's proximity to Pine Bluff made him especially sensitive to the violence Till's murder portended elsewhere. Similarly, Daisy Bates could be directly concerned about the widening circle of white resistance because the founder of the Little Rock Citizens' Council, Amis Guthridge, was active in Hoxie. Nevertheless, these local black leaders and their colleagues could see in the Arkansas record of racial moderation reasons for hope that growing white resistance would be contained. From late 1955 to early 1956, discussions seeking desegregation of public transportation progressed in Little Rock, Pine Bluff, Fort Smith, and Hot Springs. In these cities desegregation occurred peaceably in April 1956. Over the same period in Montgomery, Alabama, however, amidst a nationally publicized bus boycott, Rev. Martin Luther King, Jr., and his followers encountered white leaders' threats of violence. Ultimately, King and the boycott prevailed only after LDF lawyers won from the federal judiciary the favorable decision of *Browder v. Gayle* (1956).

Internal and external events shaped the Little Rock NAACP executive committee decision to sue in December 1955. Blossom's publicity campaign for the phase program garnered sufficient support within the white community that near the end of the year city officials named him "Man of the Year." By that point, however, the Little Rock NAACP executive committee understood that the school board would assign only black teachers to the new Horace Mann High School, ensuring that it would open in February 1956 as a segregated institution. Of further concern was the likelihood that under the proposed

{ *Chapter 1* }

transfer guidelines, only a few black children would be able to attend Central High. Most black children living near Central would have to walk past the school to reach Horace Mann, some two miles away. Finally, no date had been announced for the desegregation of the rest of the Little Rock public schools. Within the context of potential citizens' council resistance, moreover, the picture was mixed. In Hoxie the federal court intervened effectively to allow desegregation to proceed peacefully, imposing an injunction against citizens' council intimidation that named Guthridge among others. Unlike the threatening situation emerging from the Montgomery bus boycott in late 1955, the attempt to desegregate public transportation proceeded peacefully in Little Rock and three other Arkansas cities. Thus, the executive committee members took notice of the escalating citizens' council activities in Arkansas, but the positive developments in Little Rock, Hoxie, and elsewhere suggested that the local record of racial moderation remained strong despite the Emmett Till tragedy.

These ambiguous pressures encouraged unprecedented reliance upon the city black community itself. Lacking support from their own lawyers Williams and Booker, the executive committee sought advice from U. Simpson Tate, a Dallas-based attorney affiliated with the NAACP LDF. Iggers discussed with him the advisability of seeking an injunction against opening Horace Mann as a segregated school. Tate counseled against this, urging instead that the children living near Central petition for admission there. By January 1956, the executive committee endorsed a litigation plan Iggers proposed. Litigation depended upon black parents attempting to register their children at one or more of the city schools and school officials refusing to register them. Then parents could apply for legal aid. With executive committee approval, Iggers and Lorch proposed a plan for getting the black parents involved as plaintiffs. When Horace Mann High opened, parents would attempt to register children in their neighborhood schools. To locate interested parents, four separate teams (including Georg and Wilma Iggers, Lorch, Reverend Crenchaw, and Daisy and L. C. Bates) visited homes throughout middle-class and blue-collar African American residential areas. The groups found parents supportive of the litigation idea and willing to become parties to it. Parents agreed to gather with their children on the stipulated date in January at several collection points and attempt to register them.

This positive response indicated a change of attitude among the city blacks, most of whom had not given the NAACP much attention in the past.

Effective mobilization of black litigants nonetheless depended upon funding attorneys' fees and legal aid. Neither the NAACP nor the LDF national headquarters supplied direct input regarding the suit; the NAACP field representative played virtually no role, although the branch informed him of its actions. The LDF agreed to review legal briefs prepared by local attorneys provided that the local branch pay for its own lawyer and bear all other costs. Moreover, the successful organization of plaintiffs undoubtedly derived at least in part from the fact that these parents were not being asked to pay. Accordingly, to find funding the executive committee relied upon the Iggerses. Georg and Wilma solicited contributions from family members and friends in the United States and Canada in order to finance the litigation. Their letters declared that "public opinion on the whole is moderate" in the city, and it "is likely that school integration can be accomplished with little social tension." But, the appeal emphasized, "School board officials, for political and other reasons, are generally unwilling to move unless directed by court order." Even though the school board had announced its formal willingness to comply with the *Brown* decision, the local NAACP considered the board plan "so vague as to appear more like circumvention than like compliance." A move to file suit thus was under way because of the impending opening of Horace Mann, "originally announced to be integrated but now restricted to Negroes. As a result. . . . several dozen Negro children will be passing the white high school, which at present has no space problem, on their way two miles farther to the new Negro high school."

Iggers's central role in the decision to sue suggested the pressures buffeting the executive committee. Despite resistance from both their own attorneys and white moderates, the executive committee switched from opposing to deciding in favor of litigation. Iggers's idea to organize the litigation around a group of black families rather than an individual black plaintiff required more involvement from the black community than the branch had before attempted. Taken together, these factors revealed the comparative marginalization of the NAACP branch within the Little Rock black community, especially in relation to the accommodationist approach toward desegregation epitomized by the *Southern Mediator* editorial position. Indeed, neither the adamant opposition nor the frustration with vagueness L. C. and Daisy Bates espoused, respectively, in condemning the phase program were sufficient in and of themselves to garner support in the city black community. Amid these conflicting currents, Iggers and Lorch were comparative outsiders. As such, they were able to argue that the retreat of the white moderates in implementing the phase program potentially might be used to foster greater popular support for a more activist litigation strategy than Williams had urged. Iggers later wrote that he and Lorch "played a crucial role in the organization of the suit. We did not steer the branch into a direction it would not have followed otherwise. There was a broad consensus behind the decision to challenge the school board retreat from the original Blossom plan. But in making this decision, the branch followed our advice" in "consultation" with Ozell Sutton, Reverend Crenchaw, and the Bateses.

With the necessary funding in hand, the executive committee faced squarely the need to hire an attorney. The unwillingness of its two experienced black lawyers to challenge the phase program undoubtedly involved a disagreement over tactics rather than principle. Still, it was noteworthy that the LDF lawyer reviewing the committee proposed suit observed that Williams's suggested fees amounting to $1,000 were much too high. Offering the more customary fee of about $300, the executive committee procured the services of Wiley Branton. Having represented the Little Rock NAACP in the September 9, 1954, hearing before school board officials, Branton was of course well known to the executive committee. Also, his work for the state conference Legal Redress Committee took him throughout Arkansas and Mississippi, providing him a broad perspective on racial issues. Branton's family had lived in Pine Bluff for several generations, was well-established there, and was on good terms with members of the white community. He was one of the first blacks to graduate from the University of Arkansas School of Law, which had been desegregated in 1948. Since returning to Arkansas from military service in World War II, Branton had been involved in various civil rights cases against Jim Crow; by the mid-1950s he represented black plaintiffs in several NAACP-affiliated suits. Thus, Branton had good reason to be optimistic that, compared to Mississippi, Arkansas provided more favorable conditions in which to bring the Little Rock litigation.

The Segregationist Extremists to Early 1956

The Little Rock NAACP executive committee change of heart toward litigation, like Branton's hopefulness, underestimated the segregationist extremists. The Supreme Court central policy presumption in *Brown* II was that legitimatizing local control of the school desegregation process was the surest means to promote gradual accommodation over resistance. Underlying this presumption were several expectations. First, in the name of gradualism, local white moderates could control the desegregation process sufficiently to garner general black support, while at the same time undercutting extreme segregationists' attempted radicalization of southern whites. Such success by white moderates, in turn, could diffuse political pressures felt by governors and other state officials resulting not only from the extremists' demands for solidarity based on white supremacy but also from northern outsiders' support of blacks' call for immediate compliance with the constitutional principle of racial equality. Balancing political and racial accountability at the local and state levels also minimized the need for federal intervention. Even so, the local NAACP decision to sue revealed that black activists had lost faith in the white moderates. By early 1956, further difficulties emerged in and outside Little Rock, raising doubts about whether the extreme segregationists could be held at bay. During the initial months of the local NAACP litigation, it became apparent that segregationists were pursuing a strategy aimed at forcing Faubus to abandon his political reliance on the moderates' constitutional pragmatism, favoring instead a states' rights ideology that subordinated federal authority to state police powers.

The school board vulnerability to extremists' criticism emerged gradually. On behalf of its clients, the Little Rock NAACP filed suit on February 8, 1956, in the U.S. District Court for the Eastern District of Arkansas. Beginning with the name of John Aaron, the plaintiffs were thirty-three black children ranging in ages from six to twenty-one, who as city residents had been refused registration in several local schools. School board president William G. Cooper, a well-

{ *Chapter 1* }

known physician and civic leader, the Little Rock School District, its secretary, and Superintendent Blossom were the defendants named in the case styled *Aaron v. Cooper*. By the time the case was decided in August 1956, the extreme segregationists had seized upon a profound flaw underlying the Blossom plan. Blossom's reshaping of his original proposals into the phase program provided grounds for the plaintiffs to argue that limiting desegregation to a few black students qualifying for admission to Little Rock Central effectively maintained racial segregation in the other city schools. In publicity and the defendants' trial argument, Blossom and the school board, like the city moderates, focused upon how minimal was the racial desegregation resulting from the phase program. The Little Rock Citizens' Council railed against the Blossom plan, however, not just because even the smallest breach of white supremacy was too much, but because it seemed unfair, the council emphasized, that only the white families residing in the attendance zone for Central High were being exposed to race mixing. The claim accentuated the fact that the schools located in affluent Pulaski Heights would remain racially segregated.

Unintentionally, the local NAACP litigation reinforced the segregationists' assault. The media reports of the impending trial regularly noted that the school board constitutional rational for complying with *Brown* disclaimed support for the principle of desegregation itself. The board justified the phase program primarily on the basis of pragmatic deference to Supreme Court authority. This media imagery conveyed the presumption that gradualism would diffuse resistance from the majority of Little Rock white residents. Given its impressive record of racial moderation since World War II, this presumption was reasonable. The confidence that moderation would prevail encouraged Blossom, however, to alter his original proposals that desegregation would include not only Central High, but also the new Hall High School, located in Pulaski Heights. In the phase program, Blossom's decision to remove Hall High School from the desegregation scheduled to begin in 1957 enabled the citizens' council to assert that the change reflected the purposeful decision of the school board to exempt Pulaski Heights elites from race mixing. This politicized social class imagery suggested that the affluent elite was unwilling to endure the breach of white supremacy, but had no qualms about forcing it upon blue-collar, lower-middle, and middle-class white families forced to attend Central High. Thus, media reports of the school board response to the litigation inadvertently popularized segregationists' assertions not only that any breach of white supremacy was disastrous, but just as significantly, that poorer whites were the object of class discrimination.

Lawyer and Little Rock Citizens' Council leader Amis Guthridge exploited these race and class antagonisms. Amidst the publicity surrounding the pretrial proceedings of *Aaron v. Cooper* in early 1956, Guthridge employed states' rights ideology to garner popular support for the segregationists' program. Grounded upon white supremacy, the program called for state legislation authorizing local school officials to "assign" white and black young people to separate schools. If such legislation failed to pass, he insisted, opposition to desegregation could reach the "point of destroying the public school system" through the election of school board members who would "reduce the millage rates to nothing . . . [thereby ending the] public status of the schools, permitting the buildings to be rented, leased, or sold to private corporations to operate." Guthridge couched these legalistic arguments, moreover, in terms of a larger ominous "conspiracy, and this race mixing is part of it." This conspiracy, he claimed, had aimed to "sidetrack the people . . . ever since Franklin D. Roosevelt was inaugurated." As a result, the "Communists actually took over the operation of the government of the United States from the inside. . . . And they have been determining our policies . . . ever since." These overtones of racial conspiracy and symbolic states' rights appeals also reflected a pervasive distrust of outsiders, along with a conservative Christian view that communists and liberals were employing desegregation to subvert God's law. Fundamentalist Protestant ministers preached these views among those same people Guthridge urged to join the citizens' council.

Guthridge often collaborated with statewide segregationist leader James Johnson. Elected to the state senate representing southeastern Arkansas while still in his twenties, Johnson was already a viable gubernatorial candidate in the 1956 summer primary. Johnson shared with his friend U.S. Senator James Eastland of Mississippi a firm commitment to the southern massive resistance against racial desegregation instituted by *Brown*. Like Guthridge's, Johnson's political discourse shifted from disclaiming violence to such assertions as

"Arkansas people didn't start integration, but Arkansas people are going to stop it in Arkansas." Influenced by James J. Kilpatrick's editorials on the states' rights theory of interposition in the Richmond *News Leader* of 1954, Johnson promoted through the state initiative procedure a constitutional amendment. If passed in the November 1956 general election, the Johnson Amendment would force the state legislature to "take appropriate action to pass laws" aimed at the "evasion" of *Brown;* it also imposed upon state officials possible criminal penalties for failure to enforce such legislation. Johnson proclaimed that his amendment would "absolutely guarantee segregation in the public schools of Arkansas and in other phases of Arkansas society." A letter to Senator Eastland further explained Johnson's opposition to the Supreme Court desegregation decisions: they displayed the intent "to rule against states' rights to ban intermarriage of whites and nonwhites." Noting that certain decisions were delivered "on the day that Russia was . . . commemorating the advent of communism in that country," Johnson urged "prayerful investigation of [Eastland and] the U.S. Senate."

Johnson later explained the assumptions underlying the Little Rock Citizens' Council opposition strategy. The symbolic imagery of interposition aroused southerners' popular feelings identified with states' rights ideology overwhelmed but not forgotten as a result of Civil War military defeat. That same imagery, moreover, symbolized the southern success in using violence to win from the northern Republican Congress and the U.S. Supreme Court nonenforcement of civil rights legislation and the Thirteenth, Fourteenth, and Fifteenth Amendments, which in turn ended Reconstruction and paved the way for imposing the Jim Crow racial apartheid system of southern white supremacy affirmed in *Plessy v. Ferguson* (1896). Thus, Johnson's rationale for interposition proclaimed that the Court *Brown* I decision was unconstitutional because it "made" rather than interpreted law only Congress could constitutionally enact. Of course, since Reconstruction the South virtually always blocked any such congressional action. He also condemned the Court decision because it relied upon "social facts" evidence, even though such evidence had been routinely used in federal courts at least since it was introduced by Louis Brandeis's famous brief in *Muller v. Oregon* (1908). Nevertheless, upon these constitutional and historical images depended a pervading if rarely articulated presumption that violence in the name of preserving white supremacy was an acceptable form of public action. The Emmett Till tragedy confirmed how rooted in southern culture and law was the presumption that the white legal establishment would rarely if ever penalize white violence against blacks.

Johnson's opposition strategy amounted to civil disobedience. Assuredly, he claimed, *Brown* II was "gutless" because a Court decree could not become "gradually constitutional." The "all deliberate speed" standard nonetheless offered segregationists an opportunity to combine traditional southern congressional resourcefulness against civil rights legislation with violence in order to defeat the Supreme Court. Johnson and fellow citizens' council leaders believed that the Truman administration had achieved its surprising 1948 victory largely because, touting civil rights, it won over northern urban black voters. During Eisenhower's first term, some Republicans were attempting a similar strategy by supporting the strongest civil rights bill since Reconstruction, promoted by U.S. Attorney General Herbert Brownell. The citizens' council interposition amendment, however, was part of southern congressional Democrats' efforts to join with conservative Republicans to enact legislation stripping from federal judges and the Supreme Court jurisdiction over civil rights cases. From the 1930s on, this "conservative coalition" had repeatedly defeated a federal antilynching bill; from 1955 to 1956 the same coalition targeted Brownell's proposal. Thus, Johnson and his fellow segregationists believed that the surest way to defeat the Supreme Court was to have *Brown* II vigorously enforced, fostering still more popular resistance. Given that there were "not enough jails to punish all resisters," the clamor would force Congress to respond with legislation either supporting or opposing federal judiciary civil rights jurisdiction; Johnson believed that the opposition would prevail.

This strategy found national expression in the March 1956 "Southern Manifesto." At the time and since commentators described the manifesto, signed by the large majority of the southern congressional delegation, as a clarion call to "massive" yet "lawful" resistance against *Brown* and the Supreme Court. Less conspicuous was southern officials' rarely articulated but clear understanding that the citizens' councils privately authorized violent disorder, confident that even if brought to trial, conviction of white supremacists was quite unlikely in southern state courts. Receiving even less attention was the congressional political context of the manifesto, which included mobilizing southern Democrat and conservative Republican opposition to Brownell's civil rights bill, as well as that same coalition support for measures limiting federal jurisdiction over civil rights generally. Accordingly, the Southern Manifesto aimed not only at compelling southern moderates to take a public stance condemning racial desegregation generally, and the Supreme Court in particular, it also reached out to conservative Republicans who since the New Deal had joined with southern Democrats to denounce the growing liberal state, especially the new directions taken by the Supreme Court in the area of civil rights and liberties. This context, then, gave wider political meaning to the manifesto words: "We regard the decision of the Supreme Court in the school cases as clear abuse of judicial power. It climaxes a trend in the Federal judiciary undertaking to legislate, in derogation of the authority of Congress, and to encroach upon the reserved rights of the states and the people."

During this period, the citizens' council considered how best to pursue its strategy within Arkansas. Johnson, Guthridge, and their supporters especially feared racial desegregation in counties where blacks outnumbered whites, such as those in the east Arkansas Delta. In addition to the obvious "population pressures" reflected in white identity politics, council leaders knew that the NAACP was already active in the Delta black communities, which for decades had been dominated by white planters who manipulated black voting to control the Arkansas legislature. Mounting their own anti-integration campaign, the councils hoped either to win over or replace the planters' traditional rule. At the same time, activism in the Delta could arouse opposition along class and race lines in moderate strongholds such as Little Rock, as well as those few smaller communities where some white leaders had voluntarily accepted a few blacks into public schools for economic reasons. The councils also wanted to intimidate free black voters in places such as Little Rock, Pine Bluff, and smaller towns, one of which had elected a black alderman. Finally, and most importantly, council leaders targeted Faubus's success in avoiding a political stance expressly demanding white supremacy preceding the

1956 gubernatorial primary election campaign. "Pretty soon we're going to tell Faubus," Guthridge exclaimed, "he's either for white folks or the NAACP, and we don't want any smart remarks."

The desegregation confrontation in Hoxie, Arkansas, revealed the ominous potential for the council strategy. The struggle in the small rural hamlet on the edge of the state's Delta region occurred over the same period as the national, state, and local events described above, including the initial phases of the Little Rock desegregation case. The Hoxie School Board received national attention in *Life* magazine, particularly in a photograph of two elementary school children — one white, the other black — walking peacefully along, holding hands. The council turned the publicity to its own ends. Employing late night phone calls, knocks on doors, and a boycott, council leaders fomented local resistance to the school board voluntarily opening, as a cost-saving measure and in compliance with *Brown* II, Hoxie white school to some black families whose school was publicly known to be in deplorable condition. At rallies inflammatory speeches were commonplace; threats were made repeatedly that "someone might get hurt" unless the school board reestablished separate schools. One segregationist speaker attacked the Fourteenth Amendment as a fraud, predicting that "blood would run knee-deep all over Arkansas" unless firearms and "grass ropes" were used to keep the "nigger out of the white bedroom." Lynching affirmed that the "power of government was with the people." Guthridge called the Hoxie School Board a tool of the Supreme Court "revolutionary plot." He accused the Methodist Church of favoring racial desegregation and exclaimed that if anyone committed violence against a school board member, the FBI would be powerless to intervene.

Hoxie revealed that the council strategy had mixed results. A state-wide leader active during the confrontation, Johnson publicized the interposition amendment as the answer to integration, alluding to the "lynching" of a black man in Mississippi and predicting the "mongrelization" of both races should integration occur. Guthridge, too, used Hoxie to arouse council support in Little Rock. The Hoxie School Board nonetheless overcame the intimidation campaign, receiving from the federal court an injunction against any illegal action by segregationist leaders. Although a local segregationist, Herbert Brewer, continued to agitate electoral politics, the school board desegregation decision prevailed. Amidst the gubernatorial reelection campaign, however, Faubus altered his moderate stance toward desegregation. He publicly supported interposition measures put forward by Delta politicos that they claimed were distinguishable from Johnson's proposed amendment. Faubus's shift revealed that, although the symbolic identity politics of interposition were coming to dominate the contending factions among Arkansas Democrats, there was not yet any popular consensus regarding the practical effect of the issue upon the enforcement of *Brown*, nor most importantly, who should lead the opposition. For its part, the Little Rock NAACP took heart from the federal court imposition of injunctive relief to enforce desegregation in Hoxie, though whether the moderates on the Little Rock School Board were as willing as their Hoxie counterparts to take the lead in response to intimidation was unknown.

Federal Equivocation

The Eisenhower administration equivocated on civil rights issues. In his first presidential campaign, Eisenhower promised to end racial segregation in public accommodations throughout the District of Columbia. As president he fulfilled this promise. For decades southern Democrats used congressional committees to block enforcement of Reconstruction-era laws requiring equal access to district public facilities. Over their opposition, Attorney General Herbert Brownell won a court decree ordering compliance with the old laws. The Eisenhower administration also enforced the Supreme Court decision ordering desegregation of district public schools. Regarding the enforcement of *Brown*, however, Eisenhower expressly avoided involvement; privately, he criticized the Supreme Court and Chief Justice Earl Warren for the decision. During the same period, the Emmett Till murder was the object of cold war contention from western and communist news media alike, questioning the U.S. government refusal to intervene. As a result of Hoxie school officials' request, by contrast, Brownell authorized a FBI investigation and filed an amicus brief in the federal appellate court supporting local officials and the federal courts against the citizens' council intimidation. The Till and Hoxie episodes aroused northern media criticism of southern racial violence. The Eisenhower administration responded to demands for action with an assertion that federal laws did not clearly empower federal intervention where state sovereignty traditionally prevailed. In conjunction with the lassitude toward *Brown*, such claims rang hollow to critics of the South even as they emboldened the segregationist extremists.

Attorney General Brownell was at the center of these policies. The chief U.S. government legal official, he advised the president and all federal officials on their obligations under national law and the Constitution concerning domestic and foreign affairs. He was also responsible for national law enforcement, for federal government arguments before courts, and for drafting administration bills introduced into Congress. Brownell was among those from the "moderate wing" of the Republican Party soliciting Eisenhower's candidacy in 1952 in order to regain control of the presidency after twenty years. He and Eisenhower became close friends. Thus, Brownell was fully equipped to assess the legalities, politics, and personal loyalties influencing administration civil rights policies. He understood the president's deep regard for constitutional separation of powers, which explained the readiness to desegregate the District of Columbia, where federal authority was absolute, but also the hesitancy to become involved with state police powers enforcing Jim Crow. Eisenhower did not prevent Brownell acting in school desegregation cases such as Clinton, Tennessee, and Hoxie, where local authorities confronting violence enjoined by federal courts requested federal intervention. However, when the University of Alabama surrendered to violence preventing Autherine Lucy from attending class, and, because of a technicality, the federal court did too, Brownell insisted that the U.S. Department of Justice was powerless to act. He took the same position when Texas governor Allan Shivers blocked school desegregation in Mansfield, employing the Rangers.

Of course, Eisenhower was duty-bound to reject state sovereignty where federal law was supreme. The problem, however, with federal authorities taking the lead in enforcing the *Brown* decision and against the violence occurring in the Till, Hoxie, and other cases, was that southern Democrats and their conservative Republican allies had succeeded in limiting federal legal authority over the states' Jim Crow laws. Moreover, although *Brown* epitomized the Supreme Court reversal of the legitimacy it had conferred upon the racial apartheid system from Reconstruction to the 1920s, the constitutional status of Jim Crow and federal executive authority over it remained quite unsettled between the 1930s and the 1950s. Moreover, from Secretary of State John Foster Dulles, Brownell knew the difficulties Jim Crow created for the administration's propaganda battle with the communists among western allies in Europe, in nonaligned nations such as India, and with emerging nationalist leaders in Africa, the Middle East, and East Asia. Such cases as the Emmett Till murder gave the communists an easy propaganda advantage, gained without any necessity to lie about the apparent hypocrisy of proclaimed U.S. commitment to the democratic ideal of equal justice. Foreign affairs clearly were within the president's primary constitutional powers. Yet because of the constitutional and political tensions involving longtime state sovereignty over the southern Jim Crow system, Brownell could not advise Eisenhower on an unequivocal civil rights policy unless and until either a Court order or congressional legislation provided stronger constitutional grounds.

Eisenhower and Brownell considered *Brown* an uncertain constitutional basis for executive action. As a result of Supreme Court solicitation of justice department amicus briefs prior to its decision in *Brown* II, Eisenhower himself contributed suggestions leaving wide discretion to local federal judges over what constituted compliance with desegregation decrees. Accordingly, the U.S. government brief advocated a remedy that, eschewing immediate enforcement of *Brown* I, favored federal judges employing a flexible process accounting for diverse local circumstances, proceeding steadily toward orderly compliance. Also, under Brownell's direction the justice department briefs included the proviso "that school districts should be required to submit a plan within a period of ninety days. Thereby the executive branch would be empowered to step in as soon as a court approved the plan to enforce desegregation." The Supreme Court "all deliberate speed" standard was consistent with Eisenhower's position; the Court did not accept the second point of the justice department, however, which would have authorized more immediate enforcement action from federal authorities in desegregation cases. Publicity presented Eisenhower and Brownell as being at odds over *Brown*. Indeed, Brownell recalled, preceding the president's 1956 reelection bid the Republican platform committee proposed including a "plank crediting Eisenhower for

Brown." The president expressly rejected the idea, insisting that he had declined any public stance concerning the decision and his administration was not responsible for the Supreme Court opinions.

The administration internal tension over the enforcement of *Brown* suggested the interaction between political contingencies and constitutional imagery. Dominated by "moderate" Republicans like Brownell, the platform committee for Eisenhower's 1956 reelection campaign reasonably could have concluded that claiming credit for *Brown* would appeal to black voters in northern and western cities. Eisenhower's denial of that strategy, by contrast, was consistent with an understanding that southern Democratic support for his first election in 1952 was unlikely to be repeated if he publicly defended *Brown*. The president's noncommittal approach to the decision, although in private he criticized the Court, was framed in terms of adherence to "separation of powers," thus turning constitutional imagery to political purposes. At the same time, his ready enforcement of desegregation in the District of Columbia attracted northern black voters' support, even as it conveyed sincere respect for the same separation of powers principle, since the district was directly subject to federal authority. Perhaps more significantly, Eisenhower's public affirmation of separation of powers, along with avoidance of public comment on *Brown*, focused southern public attention upon the Supreme Court as the agent of the decision. Moreover, as a result of the *Brown* II decree — including the "all deliberate speed" standard that tracked Eisenhower's own position expressed in the government amicus brief prior to the decision — the federal courts rather than the executive primarily were responsible for enforcement, further deflecting political responsibility from the Republican administration.

Eisenhower also was ambivalent toward Brownell's draft of new civil rights legislation. The most significant civil rights measure presented to Congress since Reconstruction, Brownell's proposal called for establishing a civil rights commission (Title I) as well as remaking the justice department small civil rights section into a stronger division headed by an assistant attorney general (Title II). More controversially, Title III enlarged the definition of conspiracy among private persons, establishing justice department jurisdiction over criminal or civil violations such as those occurring in the Emmett Till or Hoxie cases, including the power to seek injunctive relief from federal judges; that same power would include voting rights cases (Title IV). Eisenhower opposed Title III; indeed, when the U.S. cabinet discussed the proposed bill in December 1955, Brownell and Secretary of State Dulles, more or less alone, supported that provision. Accordingly, Brownell and Republican committee members employed parliamentary maneuvers to retain Title III in the bill that subsequently passed the House, but southern Democratic and conservative Republican senators blocked its enactment, insisting upon the guarantee of jury trial in all cases arising under the controversial provision. During his reelection campaign Eisenhower publicly supported the voting rights sections of the bill, but ignored Title III. The ploy worked. Although Senate southern Democrats and Republican conservatives prevented passage, blacks gave Eisenhower more votes than ever. Until after Eisenhower's reelection in November 1956, however, the fate of the bill was in limbo.

Brownell's and Dulles's advocacy of Title III revealed the tensions underlying the Eisenhower administration civil rights stance. The Supreme Court *Brown* decision had ameliorated the national propaganda image in 1954; southern racial violence occurring in the wake of *Brown* II, however, once more presented the communists a propaganda advantage. Even so, Brownell stated, "Secretary of State Dulles generally supported our propos[ed civil rights bill], citing the difficulties encountered by the State Department because of our domestic condon[ement] of segregation." Similarly, as Hoxie and Mansfield revealed, although some school desegregation cases but not others could foster demands for federal intervention, neither *Brown* II nor preexisting federal law provided an unambiguous basis for federal intervention, leaving the outcome ultimately up to southern state courts and juries, which virtually always favored white malefactors. Brownell's proposed Title III would have given justice department officials wider jurisdiction over individual conspirators in civil rights cases before federal judges, much like that argued for in the department brief prior to *Brown* II. The Court nonetheless rejected that authority in its remedial decree, and a conservative coalition in the U.S. Senate blocked inclusion of a similar power in the civil rights bill. Ironically, both Eisenhower and Chief Justice Earl Warren appealed to the separation of powers in order to justify their criticism of one another as a result of difficulties arising from southern opposition to *Brown*. Eisenhower employed the same principle to resist Title III.

Brownell later assessed such outcomes positively. He observed that as "head of state," the president "governed a nation made up of people and of geographical regions with fiercely opposing views on segregation. The southern rhetoric about the race problem was as strident as in the pre–Civil War debates over slavery. The president endeavored to keep the trust of both sides so that when he acted he would be supported by both sides." Eisenhower believed too, said Brownell, that "changes in the law may be part of the process in moving the nation to full equality, but change in the hearts and minds of many white Americans was also required, change that would not come immediately or by legal fiat." Finally, "for Eisenhower, his duty, first and foremost, was to see that the Constitution, and by implication the Supreme Court interpretation of it, was upheld." In the short term, Eisenhower's vacillation over *Brown* and the civil rights bill garnered black votes in his 1956 reelection, and it facilitated the Southern Manifesto blaming desegregation solely upon the Supreme Court. Such results reinforced Orval Faubus's efforts to avoid responsibility for enforcing school desegregation as well as the minimalist rationale for desegregation of Blossom's phase program. Moreover, the president's vacillation also fostered the extreme segregationists' strategy combining real and imagined violence with longstanding congressional maneuvering against measures like Title III. Accordingly, the Little Rock NAACP decision to sue in order to bring compliance with *Brown* soon became isolated within local, state, and federal authorities' equivocation.

CHAPTER 2

Aaron v. Cooper
Rights at Bay, 1956–1957

Like the Little Rock NAACP decision to sue, the trial, appeal, and immediate outcome of *Aaron v. Cooper* were embedded in a conflicted political context. During early 1956, the local NAACP executive board pursued a litigation strategy that mobilized less affluent black community support for their organization. This successful community-oriented strategy, in conjunction with Wiley Branton's handling of pretrial proceedings, heightened white school authorities' and their lawyers' erroneous perception that the NAACP New York headquarters had targeted the Little Rock phase program as a test case, all of which exacerbated racial tensions. The trial and decision of *Aaron v. Cooper* in August 1956 by Federal District Judge John E. Miller followed Governor Faubus's successful primary reelection campaign, which had been hotly contested through white identity politics reflected in states' rights appeals to interposition. Miller's affirmation of the school board argument for minimal desegregation within local control permitted by *Brown* II resonated with Faubus's political maneuvers linking the same constitutional principle of localism to a more moderate interposition program than radical segregationist Jim Johnson's. These developments coincided with southern congressional segregationists' efforts to garner conservative Republican opposition to Title III of the civil rights bill and Eisenhower's equivocation on civil rights issues amidst his reelection campaign and cold war pressures.

By early 1957, the federal appeals court upheld Miller's decision and Little Rock moderates won a school board election against segregationists. Despite the moderates' victory, segregationists effectively used interposition politics to intimidate their opponents. The black plaintiffs' defeat enabled Superintendent Blossom to ensure that few blacks would desegregate Central High. Miller's decision provided a constitutional basis for token desegregation. By the summer, however,

Blossom's private contacts with local law enforcement, the justice department, and Faubus confirmed that school officials were feeling more pressure than ever from the segregationists' growing interposition protests. These claims gained public force because segregationists exposed a profound flaw in the phase program, which augmented the race issue with class tensions pitting the Little Rock affluent elite against poor whites. The segregationists' interposition arguments received further legitimacy during the fateful summer of 1957. In the U.S. Senate, conservative Republicans and southern Democrats blocked passage of Title III, and Eisenhower's stance on civil rights remained weak. Finally, although Faubus in public statements continued to espouse local control of racial desegregation, privately he established contacts with Little Rock segregationists, tying his political fortunes to their constitutional claims that interposition and states' rights superseded federal authority. From 1956 to 1957, then, the *Aaron v. Cooper* litigation meshed with political opportunism, giving segregationists' constitutional rhetoric both legal legitimacy and popular momentum.

Aaron v. Cooper: Pretrial Misperceptions and Racial Tensions, 1956

As the Little Rock NAACP lawsuit unfolded during spring and summer 1956, each side misperceived the other's underlying motivations. The local NAACP executive committee decided to sue the school board only after overcoming disagreement with their own attorneys. Georg and Wilma Iggers raised from family and friends the money required to hire Pine Bluff attorney Wiley Branton. Despite skepticism among black middle-class opinion leaders, executive committee members recruited litigants among black families whose children had been denied admission to neighborhood schools for reasons of race. The executive committee succeeded in this effort largely because working-class black families perceived a means to redress the profound deficiencies in their children's segregated education. Branton filed suit on February 8, 1956; depositions were taken in May in preparation for a trial the following August before Judge Miller. Thus, on their own initiative and for their own reasons the Little Rock NAACP and the local black litigants carried through with their suit without significant involvement of the national offices of either the NAACP or its Legal Defense Fund (LDF). In response, Blossom organized an attorney group representing a cross-section of Little Rock moderate whites concerning racial desegregation, who nonetheless shared the conviction that minimal compliance with *Brown* was necessary. From the beginning, these lawyers worked from the assumption that the national NAACP had instigated the suit. That argument was central to the defense they raised before Judge Miller, and its influence was evident in the judge's decision in *Aaron v. Cooper.*

The local NAACP executive committee motivation for bringing suit reflected a new opportunity to mobilize black community support. Since it first considered school desegregation litigation in 1952—and notwithstanding the *Brown* decision—the executive committee faced the reality that it had limited influence among Little Rock blacks. The executive committee switch from opposing to supporting litigation followed Blossom's institution of the phase program, which not only established the beginning date of desegregation solely for the three city high schools but also insured that the new Horace Mann High School would be all black. A *Southern Mediator* editorial suggested that the middle-class black community willingly accommodated this change because it at least *began* desegregation at Central High in 1957. The executive committee nonetheless knew from contacts throughout the wider black community that poor families feared the change signaled creation of even more impediments to the already limited educational opportunity segregation imposed. Thus, soliciting financial support from their family and friends, the Iggers's letters stated that the local NAACP sought to bring suit because Horace Mann was "originally announced to be interracial, but now restricted to Negroes. As a result . . . several dozen Negro children will be passing the white high school, which at present has no space problem, on their way two miles farther to the new Negro high school." Some blacks believed, moreover, that the school board would refuse to fill essential teaching positions remaining open from previous years.

The class divisions within the black community became more apparent as the executive committee sought litigants. When Horace Mann High School opened, the local NAACP, parents, and children implemented a registration strategy. The parents—many more than had been approached by executive committee members—gathered at collection points in their neighborhoods and walked to the schools. Only a few of the children were from professional or middle-class families. Most children were from black working-class backgrounds. Because some of these parents were employed as service personnel by the school board and so were particularly vulnerable to recrimination, they were dissuaded from participating. After attempting to register their children and being turned away, the parents formally appealed to the local NAACP branch for legal aid. The unexpected numbers of parents seeking to participate indicated growing support in the black community for a more activist role by the local NAACP. After Branton filed *Aaron v. Cooper*, local blacks contributed about $1,000 in support of the litigation, another indication of a change of mood among city blacks. Shortly before the filing, however, the president of Philander Smith College intervened. President M. LaFayette Harris had come to "understand" that professors Iggers and Lorch had "been visiting Horace Mann High School in the act of soliciting students to transfer. This would certainly seem to be improper." Harris acknowledged that "faculty must have academic freedom," but "freedom always entails responsibilities."

Iggers's clash with his employer focused on immediate considerations. Harris told Iggers "you will take the consequences of anything which follows as a result of your action." The president denied any desire to interfere with Iggers's "community activities. The College will tell you in rather definite terms if the consequences of your action affect the Institution adversely. Therefore, I am not arguing the merits of the case either way." Harris felt that the only permissible course was to visit the students' parents. "After all," he concluded, "the parents must file the suit." In a handwritten reply, Iggers agreed with Harris that "academic freedom also entailed responsibility" and that "it would have been highly improper to have solicited students on any public school campus to transfer." He explained, accordingly, that "Mrs. Iggers, Dr. Lorch, and I visited Negro parents in their homes; each time we were accompanied by a prominent person in the Negro community." He did not identify such persons as fellow executive committee members Reverend Crenchaw, Daisy and L. C. Bates, and Ozell Sutton. Iggers closed by asserting "I fully understand your concern about this matter and am glad to be able to refute the allegation made to you about me." Harris's firm stance condemning solicitation upon public school property undoubtedly reflected pressure from white leaders. He specifically acknowledged that the school board was "within its right" to "object to any deliberate interference from outside" with "activities on its campus." Still, Harris clearly underestimated the willingness of poor black families to receive Iggers and his colleagues into their homes.

The episode suggested how locally rooted was the suit. Given the predominantly black middle-class character of the college faculty, Harris was probably aware of the disagreement within the local NAACP branch concerning the decision to bring suit, editorialized in the *Southern Mediator*. He probably also gave in to white pressure aroused by images of Iggers and Lorch soliciting black students to register. Nevertheless, those same whites revealed a limited understanding of the Little Rock black community consistent with the presumption that "outsiders" were initiating contacts with black students, something "respectable" blacks would not do. Although Harris willingly rationalized school board authority, he allowed Iggers to remain involved as the desegregation suit proceeded, displaying equivocation concerning the merits of the litigation itself rather than mere deference to whites. At the same time, Harris's acceptance of Iggers's explanation of the facts of the situation concerning the black family visits displayed his own misperception of the local NAACP bid to mobilize support among working-class black families whose children would bear the brunt of a phase program, aimed as it was at the most minimal compliance possible with *Brown*. Ultimately, Iggers wrote later, the "attempt to test the segregation patterns in January 1956 apparently had the support of large numbers of the black population. After that support of the NAACP action became a matter of pride. This pride also expressed itself in financial support of the litigation. Once the suit was filed, almost all the money . . . came from [Little Rock] blacks."

Branton's leading role in the litigation further confirmed its local character. As one of the few black lawyers in Arkansas, Branton's civil rights work continued a long tradition reaching back to Scipio Africanus Jones of Little Rock. His contribution to the Arkansas Conference of NAACP branches, especially as chair of the Legal Redress Committee, involved him regularly in the Little Rock branch activities, including its resistance to the reformulation of the Blossom plan from 1954 to 1955. Thus, it was not surprising that the executive committee hired him following the disagreement with its own attorneys regarding the issue of bringing suit. Meanwhile, Branton's affiliation with the NAACP LDF suggested that organization's *disinterest* in the Little Rock case. Like the relatively few other black civil rights lawyers then working throughout the postwar South, Branton routinely reported to the main office in New York any civil rights cases he filed. Usually, Thurgood Marshall and Assistant Counsel John L. Carter reviewed such filings and arguments in order to avoid legal or constitutional wrong turns, but the LDF offered no funding and would not be further involved unless and until the case was appealed. Indeed, in February 1956, the same month Branton filed *Cooper v. Aaron*, the national office selected eight states for particular litigation efforts where resistance to enforcing desegregation was most aggressive. Little Rock received notice that its suit presented no problems, but the case was not otherwise considered important enough to be among LDF targets. At the outset, then, Little Rock blacks were on their own.

Branton did have some assistance. U. Simpson Tate of Dallas, Texas, was one of several southern black civil rights lawyers whom the national LDF office considered qualified to advise and otherwise aid local lawyers such as Branton. The Little Rock NAACP executive committee periodically consulted Tate, most recently following the split with its regular attorneys. When Branton filed suit, the executive committee paid for both his and Tate's services, even though Tate remained only indirectly involved until the trial in August. Thus, Branton alone represented Crenchaw and Daisy Bates at the May deposition hearing. Most importantly, although Branton and Tate corresponded from February on, Branton did virtually all the pretrial work, including preparation of the complaint. Following an LDF-approved model, the complaint alleged that the school board had failed to comply with "all deliberate speed" requiring a "prompt and reasonable start" because, by altering its original plan, desegregation would embrace only a small number of blacks at one high school beginning in fall 1957, and the dates for completing the later "phases" of desegregation were vague. The complaint requested a hearing before a three-judge panel, which federal rules stipulated in order to enjoin the school board from employing "unconstitutional" state laws or police power regulations to block plaintiffs from attending public schools nearest to their residences and otherwise discriminating because of race. Although Branton considered himself junior to Tate, the Dallas lawyer's lack of attention to the complaint framed by Branton would have profound consequences.

Although the complaint was consistent with Branton's clients' desires, it also reflected significant uncertainties. Clearly, *Brown* I left open the question of when compliance should begin. Although it was not publicly understood at the time, Chief Justice Earl Warren had gained Court unanimity in its 1954 opinion in return for satisfying Justice Felix Frankfurter's desire to avoid stipulating a particular timetable — such as that urged in the justice department *Brown* II brief — employing instead the open-ended standard of "all deliberate speed." Coincidentally, Arkansas and other southern state lawyers had called for just such indeterminacy in their arguments submitted to the Court as part of the *Brown* II proceedings. Applying that standard to the complex process of deciding whether school boards were complying with *Brown*, Frankfurter and these southern lawyers sought vague discretion in Supreme Court exercise of equity powers. As the justice department brief suggested, the scope of discretion governing this equity power was unsettled. Indeed, during the postwar period such discretion had been disputed in complex antitrust cases. Even so, Attorney General Brownell and Thurgood Marshall had asked the Court to prescribe the scope of discretion so as to give reasonable preference to enforcing the rights of black litigants sooner rather than later. Branton's Little Rock complaint followed the same logic; given the change in the school board plan from broad to minimal desegregation, his argument was reasonable. The difficulty was, however, that as a result of Frankfurter's insistence, *Brown* II permitted as "reasonable" a more vaguely defined discretion.

Like all civil rights lawyers in trials of desegregation cases, Branton faced a particular federal judge. As a result of a preexisting vacancy in the federal district including Little Rock, the chief judge of the U.S. Eighth Circuit Court of Appeals assigned *Aaron v. Cooper* to Judge Miller of Fort Smith, Arkansas. Southern federal judges fell broadly into one of three categories when it came to exercising the equity discretion *Brown* II permitted. Some judges were truly obstructionist, and a few others acquired a reputation for being liberal; most, like Judge Miller, however, simply applied the equity power conservatively.

Thus, Miller's approach to equity relief was consistent with that of one of the first federal court decisions construing *Brown* II — *Briggs v. Elliott* (1955). It stated that what the Supreme Court "has decided, and all that it has decided, is that a state may not deny to any person on account of race the right to attend any school that it maintains. This, under the decision of the Supreme Court, the state may not do directly or indirectly; but if the schools which it maintains are open to children of all races, no violation of the Constitution is involved even though the children of different races voluntarily attend different schools, as they attend different churches."

Briggs thus applied the narrowest exercise of equity authority consistent with the language of *Brown* II. The same reasoning enabled Miller and like-minded southern federal judges to deny black plaintiffs' pleas for equity relief, such as the injunction requested in the Little Rock blacks' complaint, unless they met a heavy burden showing that school boards intentionally conspired to discriminate because of race. Thus, following the language of *Brown* II, Judge Miller could refuse to enjoin the implementation of the phase program if the school board refuted the black plaintiffs' allegations by showing that it had displayed "good faith" by making a "prompt start." *Brown* II, of course, also stated, "But it should go without saying that the vitality of these constitutional principles [proclaimed in *Brown* I] cannot be allowed to yield simply because of disagreement with them." Nevertheless, in *Aaron v. Cooper* the black plaintiffs carried the burden of proving that the school board September 1957 deadline for desegregation to begin was not a meaningful "start," and that the shift occurring from 1954 to 1955 from substantial to limited numbers of blacks being admitted to white schools over a vague period of time expressed intentional "bad faith." Put another way, Little Rock blacks began with the minimal results the phase program implemented and alleged that those results were not consistent with the remedy called for in *Brown* II; the school board position was, however, that efforts merely seeking such results — rather than numbers of blacks actually attending formally segregated white schools — were enough to constitute lawful compliance.

The local NAACP and its black clients thus faced broad public misperceptions regarding their affirmation of equal rights. The school board chief attorney, A. F. House, in part shaped the defense of the phase program around the assumption that the New York headquarters of the NAACP had singled out Little Rock as a test case. "It seems to me," he wrote fellow defense counsel, "that when [the] NAACP comes to a community like Little Rock and starts dictating what is a reasonable time to accomplish integration, it may be opening itself to criticism." Noting that no Little Rock civil rights lawyers had signed the complaint, he interpreted the *Southern Mediator* editorial concerning a "disagreement" within the local NAACP to mean that city black lawyers generally disapproved of the "precipitancy of the NAACP." Though Branton had been involved regularly in Little Rock NAACP legal work, city blacks as well as whites encountered his name in press reports identified as a resident of Pine Bluff. More damaging still, the other lawyers' names appearing on the complaint were Tate, Carter, and Marshall of Dallas and New York, respectively, representing the NAACP. Of course, local NAACP autonomy was unknown to all but a few Little Rock citizens, white or black. Moreover, commenting upon Branton filing the *Aaron v. Cooper* complaint, the *Southern Mediator* as well as the two major city dailies, the *Gazette* and *Democrat*, presented readers the distinct impression that the NAACP organization was directed from New York.

House summarized one prong of the school board defense accordingly, although he fundamentally misconceived the motivations engendering the local NAACP suit. He assumed that local blacks were in a better position to determine the reasonableness of the phase program than was "an aggressive national organization." Depositions would probably show, he stated, "a diversity of opinion as to the timing of the suit . . . [and] that local conditions have been subordinated to the aggressiveness of the national leaders." Demonstrating the existence of such diversity, House concluded, could show the federal court that "reasonableness is on our side." When the pretrial proceeding got under way, he could point also to a *Southern Mediator* editorial that appraised somewhat positively the Blossom plan. In addition, as the school board attorney, House could well have been aware of those whites who had asserted to President Harris of Philander Smith College that his white faculty members — Jewish immigrants fitting the stereotypical image of outside agitators and members of the local NAACP — were recruiting litigants on school premises. As discussed above, each of these perceptions was in error, founded on a misunderstanding of local branch autonomy from the national NAACP, the local executive committee decision to sue despite the break with Little Rock black civil rights lawyers, Branton's central role in filing the *Aaron v. Cooper* complaint amidst LDF denial of targeting Little Rock in its litigation campaign, and above all, the new local NAACP engagement with poor blacks as the principal litigants in the case.

Although House altogether misconceived black motivations for bringing suit, those misperceptions informed a defense strategy that comported well with the logic of *Brown* II. Prior to the deposition hearing, Branton grasped the depth of erroneous white understanding. House mistakenly sent Branton the earlier version of the Blossom plan, which the Little Rock NAACP executive committee originally had approved. Branton told House that it was "a reasonable one" and the "NAACP might go along with it." House replied that the plan had been revised into the one now at issue in the suit. Discussion between the two attorneys regarding this mistake should have affirmed for House, as Branton wrote Tate, that blacks sought "a more definite plan." Branton wrote further, however, that House was "all wet on the policy of the NAACP as he had the idea that our New York office sent people down into Little Rock, which had been selected as part of a planned move for the sole purpose of filing a lawsuit." Nevertheless, unshaken in the assumption that "outsiders" had instigated the challenge to the changed school board plan, House circulated among fellow defense attorneys a memo explaining his strategy. The "basic question" for the federal court would be whether *Brown* required "slow and orderly" racial desegregation or "prompt action with a disregard of the economic educational factors involved and the possibility of violence." House believed that the federal court would be "realistic and will look with favor upon any program which will prevent violence and obtain for both negro [*sic*] and white the best educational opportunities."

As the trial proceedings began, each side was entrenched. Little Rock NAACP executive committee member Lorch wrote Tate requesting advice regarding whether the branch should seek negotiations over the school board cancellation of an auto mechanics course at Horace Mann High, a major blow to Little Rock black educational opportunity. Lorch's action affirmed that the basic concern of the local branch was the educational needs of black young people, especially given new working-class family support for bringing *Aaron v. Cooper*. Replying for Tate, Branton "strongly recommend[ed] that the NAACP not carry on any negotiations with the board or school officials concerning" such "matters . . . unless further advised by counsel." Branton resisted interjecting into the suit new issues not covered directly by his side's complaint. Meanwhile, Blossom recruited four additional law firms to join House in the school board defense. As race and interposition increasingly agitated Arkansas politics during spring and summer 1956— especially Faubus's second-term reelection bid— Blossom endeavored to establish solidarity among Little Rock moderate whites by hiring lawyers publicly known to have different views on racial desegregation. One lawyer favored complying with *Brown* in part to improve race relations, another took the opposite position because of contrary racial feelings, and the others occupied the middle ground out of pragmatic deference to Supreme Court authority. Blossom won the group's support, exclaiming, "philosophies don't make any difference. I only want to preserve a fine school system."

The May 4 deposition hearing crystallized these contrary underlying motivations. Over Branton's objection, Judge Miller granted defense counsels' plea to interrogate local NAACP leaders. Concerned not only about attorney-client privilege, Branton preferred not to reveal that Tate, who did not attend the hearing, actually reflected the LDF New York office disinterest in the suit. Indeed, when Branton had queried Tate about House's mistake regarding the two plans before the depositions, the Dallas lawyer responded only in general terms stating the federal court jurisdiction. Perhaps, too, the younger Branton was unwilling to imply disrespect for Tate's senior status in the LDF, an organization already beleaguered amidst southern massive resistance. Thus, Branton objected to exposing the local NAACP internal process to public scrutiny in court, but not for the reasons the defense believed. The defense lawyers chose to call Rev. J. C. Crenchaw, the local NAACP branch president, and Daisy Bates, president of the Arkansas NAACP Conference. House urged Leon Catlett, his colleague assigned to do the questioning, to offer "no criticism whatsoever" of the NAACP. House emphasized that the organization "seems to be sacrosanct in the eyes of [Justices] Douglas, Warren, et al., and any skirmish might be viewed in the appellate court as an indication of a reluctance on the part of the district to integrate at a reasonable pace." House nonetheless was certain that questioning that focused on the reported local "disagreement" with the Little Rock black attorneys would "prove helpful" in demonstrating NAACP aggressiveness.

The depositions reinforced each side's conviction. Branton's objections asserting attorney-client privilege generally kept private local NAACP discussions about initiating suit. As Branton stood alone against the multilawyer group representing the school board, however, the four out-of-state lawyers' names listed on the blacks' complaint facilitated the conclusion among whites that outsiders were targeting the Blossom plan as a test case. Initially, Catlett's interrogation simply revealed Bates's and Crenchaw's beliefs regarding desegregation. Whereas Crenchaw admitted never having seen a copy of the Blossom plan, he insisted that any such plan should desegregate "now." If, Crenchaw said, "you start with all on one level and they all know the same thing . . . nobody is being put to any particular disadvantage, but if you push one group forward and one group back, somebody is hurt there and as a National Association for the Advancement of Colored People, we figure we were [*sic*] the ones being hurt." Bates went further. Conceding that the school board dealt courteously and cooperatively with the local NAACP, she emphasized that solely because of race many black children were "being denied . . . the right to attend the school nearest their home." Finally, Catlett asked Bates directly to explain the *Southern Mediator* editorial addressing the executive committee disagreement with the Little Rock black attorneys and whether it directly concerned *Aaron v. Cooper.* Branton repeatedly objected and Catlett rephrased the question until Bates denied any connection. Branton then asked to question Blossom; to the plaintiffs, the defense refusal seemed to show bad faith.

The hearing also strongly confirmed racial feelings of whites and blacks. As Catlett questioned Bates, he sometimes mentioned the NAACP "nigger" leaders; he also referred to Bates by her first name. When she objected, Catlett stated he would not address her by name at all. The local NAACP considered Catlett's conduct insulting. Responding to their request about whether redress might be possible, Branton could only reply that he was "quite surprised and embarrassed at the conduct of a fellow lawyer," which clearly violated the Canons of Legal Ethics requiring "fairness and due consideration" toward "adverse witnesses." The executive committee issued a public statement protesting Catlett's "boorish, rude, impertinent, and unethical conduct" as "an insult to every Negro. It shows clearly the contempt in which he holds us and the determination with which he would relegate us to second-class citizens." Following the *Gazette* account of the incident, an East Arkansas businessman wrote Catlett that the "stand" concerning Bates "amused" him, except that "you answered her too mild, make it stronger next time." Thus, though it was only a small part of the pre-trial proceedings, the incident drew conflicted responses, exposing the depth of racial feelings regarding the issues at stake in *Aaron v. Cooper*.

The Decision: In the Shadow of Interposition Politics, 1956

When the trial commenced on August 15, 1956, both sides knew what to expect from Judge Miller. As a young attorney he had prosecuted black sharecroppers charged with "riot" in Phillips County, Arkansas, one of many racial disturbances occurring throughout the nation in autumn 1919. The Supreme Court decision in this case, *Moore v. Dempsey* (1923), was among the few victories against Jim Crow the NAACP and Little Rock black lawyer Scipio Jones won prior to the 1930s. Miller's fateful prosecution nonetheless presaged a successful political career resulting in election to both the U.S. House and Senate. Having never lost an Arkansas Democratic Party race, Miller had been nominated by Franklin Roosevelt to be a federal district judge. In 1955 news reports regarding *Brown*, Miller frankly said that although the Supreme Court should not "impose its sociological beliefs on others," federal judges and southern lawyers had "no attitude to take other than to enforce the law as it was declared by the High Court." A confidential NAACP memo from about the same period confirmed, moreover, that the "rather consistent trend of Judge Miller's decisions on integration ha[s] caused many white Southerners to see the handwriting on the wall . . . a factor which will keep down violent expression." Those familiar with Miller also knew that upon appeal his opinions usually were upheld.

As part of their arguments, Miller asked the lawyers for citations to precedents concerning racial desegregation. Although each side of course cited *Brown*, House asserted that the "only" question was whether the phase program was reasonable given local circumstances. That line of reasoning conformed not only to *Brown* II but also its minimalist interpretation by recent lower courts in decisions such as *Briggs*. Accordingly, during the trial Blossom and Little Rock School Board president Cooper testified that their plan resulted from voluntary initiative, which the NAACP had originally supported; it thus had made a "prompt start." Blossom's various public presentations also could be understood as reflecting a sincere effort to shape local public opinion. Moreover, though racial desegregation was to develop over a vague time period, the phase approach nonetheless could be said to comport with the moderate race relations so often identified with the public image of Little Rock. The plaintiffs' arguments, however, had to address these points by reconciling *Brown* I absolute affirmation that separate-but-equal schools were "inherently unequal" with *Brown* II equivocal "all deliberate speed" standard permitting reasonable delays defined by particular local circumstances, as long as evidence did not show that the reason for minimal progress was race. Thus, the NAACP lawyers were asking Miller to apply the discretion inherent in equity relief to affirm the black plaintiffs' rights because the change from meaningful to minimal desegregation demonstrated bad faith on the part of the school board and was therefore unreasonable. Miller's background did not suggest receptivity to this reading of *Brown* II.

Tate's conduct aggravated the black plaintiffs' difficulties. Throughout the pretrial proceedings Tate was not engaged, replying only in general terms to Branton's various direct questions involving the case. Tate also did not attend the May 4 deposition hearing and otherwise left case preparation to Branton. His same lack of attention continued at the trial. Tate arrived in Little Rock the night before the plaintiffs' day in court. He discussed the case with neither Branton nor the members of the local NAACP executive committee, preferring instead to retire. In court, Tate emphasized the *Brown* ringing affirmation of racial equality as the measure of whether the school board was acting in good faith, making a prompt start. He did not otherwise address the challenging remedial issues raised by *Brown* II. Tate thus did not confront directly the phase program vagueness and the hardships it imposed upon black young people. Branton's arguments attempted to emphasize these points within a reasonable reading of *Brown* II. In keeping with the real needs of the local black litigants stated in the original complaint, he endeavored to present the local NAACP leaders' hopes that litigation would compel the school board to return to the 1954 version of the desegregation plan. Tate's oral argument was thus at odds with the local NAACP purpose. Inferentially, too, the ambivalence of Tate's and Branton's arguments reinforced the doubts the depositions aroused concerning NAACP motivations in bringing suit and the bearing that had on demonstrating reasonable good faith on the part of the school board.

The consequences of Tate's actions became apparent in Miller's decision of August 28, 1956. Addressing the oral argument of the plaintiffs' "learned counsel" that the defendants "had not made a prompt and reasonable start toward full compliance" with the 1954 *Brown* decision, and that "additional time should not be allowed" the school board, Miller cited *Briggs* in reasoning that desegregation need not mean immediate or even eventual mixing of races. He then interpreted "start" to mean that the "objective [of desegregation] cannot be obtained in an orderly manner until a variety of obstacles have been removed. The defendants are making every effort to remove those obstacles in this case, and the court thinks they have made a prompt and reasonable start toward full compliance with the requirements of the law," as "declared" by the Supreme Court. Convinced of the defendants' good faith by Blossom's testimony concerning the phase program, Miller held that school officials "are seeking and have been seeking ways and means of effectuating a transition from a segregated to a nondiscriminatory system without destroying the fundamental objectives of the system itself." Regarding the plaintiffs' request for injunctive relief, Miller declined to exercise discretionary equity powers that would place the court in the position of substituting its judgment for that of the administrative officials possessing direct knowledge of local conditions. Finding the phase program to be reasonable under *Brown* II, Miller denied the relief the plaintiffs sought.

Miller retained the court jurisdiction over *Aaron v. Cooper* amidst shifting state and national politics concerning desegregation. House conceded in a letter to the judge that the phase program failure to prescribe specific dates for desegregation of junior and elementary schools was a "weak spot." In order to "deflect attack" claiming "bad faith" on appeal, Miller would review subsequent modifications of the program. "In following this suggested plan," House wrote, "we have nothing to lose and much to gain in the way of winning appellate court approval." As he had with the defendants' argument generally, Miller incorporated House's idea into his opinion, insuring that the federal district court would continuously monitor implementation of the Blossom plan. Accordingly, disappointed but hopeful that the Eighth Circuit Court, which was not dominated by southern judges, would be more responsive to arguments focusing on the desegregation plan vagueness than Miller had been, the Little Rock NAACP executive committee appealed. No decision was expected until spring 1957, leaving the case in the shadow of state politics. During the intervening months, moderate race relations in Little Rock along with Faubus's faith in their continued viability were subject to mounting political pressure from the proponents of states' rights interposition. Although a split between East Arkansas politicos and citizen council extremists weakened the interposition campaign, the consequences of this rift remained unclear to both Faubus and the Little Rock white moderate leadership. Meanwhile, the Eisenhower administration remained ambivalent on the desegregation issue.

Miller's decision thus indicated how racial tensions were aggravating politics within and outside Arkansas. The two major Little Rock daily newspapers, though often disagreeing on desegregation matters, were optimistic about the outcome of *Aaron v. Cooper.* The *Arkansas Democrat* asserted that the decision was a "momentous victory. . . . Common sense, social order, and local school authority stand triumphant [upholding] . . . gradual integration." The *Arkansas Gazette* suggested that "extremists" both for and against *Brown* I were "fated" to "attack" the Little Rock plan because it provided "a minimum of integration" spread out over a period "that may run as long as ten years." In the face of such extremes, Miller upheld a desegregation plan receiving the "support of a considerable majority of the citizens of Little Rock of both races, who accept it as a practical solution to a difficult problem." Court approval of the phase program also might "well set a pattern for the Upper South and point a way out of the dilemma that now faces many Southern communities." Affirming the indeterminate remedial approach *Brown* II established, Miller's opinion thus "takes into account the social problems inherent in any such transition, and the emotional climate in which school officials must function. But it turns away from the futile course of defiance of legal process . . . which is being urged across the Deep South." The *Gazette* was hopeful, then, that the Little Rock desegregation efforts would escape the disorder the citizens' council perpetrated in Hoxie, the more violent racial clashes occurring in Mississippi and Alabama, and the inflammatory resistance incited by the Southern Manifesto.

Little Rock newspaper commentary suggested more directly the implications of Miller's decision for the burgeoning issue of interposition. Miller affirmed the school board claim that the phase program was "peculiarly fit and suitable for the defendant district," but the plaintiffs "unreasonably insist on a hasty integration which will be unwise, unworkable, and fraught with danger." Miller's logic coincided not only with the school board argument but also with Faubus's equivocal stance toward local control the preceding August during the Hoxie confrontation, resisting the citizens' council demand that he take their side. "Whatever could be done might only aggravate the situation," he had said, identifying the council with "out-of-Arkansas" forces. By the time Miller handed down his decision in August 1956, Jim Johnson had unsuccessfully challenged Faubus in the gubernatorial primary campaign on a platform inspired by the Southern Manifesto, calling for a constitutional amendment establishing interposition. Although Faubus handily defeated Johnson, the so-called Johnson Amendment passed during the general election of 1956; it required the legislature during the session of early 1957 to enact laws empowering local authorities like the Little Rock School Board and state officials such as Faubus with the means to "evade" compliance with *Brown*. Johnson's interposition campaign thus politicized the Little Rock School Board defense of local control — the same defense Miller had affirmed, the *Gazette* espoused, and Faubus employed to avoid being drawn into Hoxie.

Interposition politics nonetheless forced Faubus to stake out a position. Prior to the southern congressional delegation introduction of the Southern Manifesto, the Arkansas U.S. House and Senate members requested and received Faubus's assessment of the political risks; as the elected official most attuned to grassroots politics across Arkansas, he predicted defeat in the impending 1956 state Democratic primary elections for anyone who failed to sign the document. Concerning his own reelection campaign against Johnson, moreover, Faubus felt that

Eisenhower's public silence on *Brown*, although perhaps gaining southern votes for the president's reelection bid, also placed state officials like himself in the unfair position of having to deal with a federal issue that was not of their own making, especially given the explosive racial tensions associated with the citizens' councils' interposition demands. Accordingly, Faubus turned to East Arkansas proponents of interposition at odds with Johnson's campaign. The East Arkansas leaders perceived their traditional dominance of black voters — which in turn was essential to maintaining Delta influence within the legislature — to be threatened by Johnson and the citizens' councils. For these long-established Delta politicos, Johnson and the citizens' councils were one brand of "outsiders." At the same time, in response to the citizens' councils' efforts, members of the state NAACP braved the danger of local retaliation to work among Delta black voters. Faubus thus sided with those like a Delta county sheriff suspicious of Johnson who reportedly declared, "We're getting along fine without anybody stirring up trouble."

Faubus had cultivated the Delta leaders' support since 1955. During his first term as governor, a tax increase Faubus proposed to support a liberal economic program, including funding for education, was defeated by East Arkansas legislators. Thus, prior to his 1956 reelection campaign, Faubus appointed East Arkansas leaders J. L. (Bex) Shaver and Marvin K. Bird to key positions in his administration. In addition, Faubus polled the East and Southeast Arkansas counties, determining that Johnson was the candidate to beat. Faubus did not publicly disclose that the poll focused solely on the areas in the state where the proportion of the black population was largest, ensuring that the racial desegregation issue was most important to white voters. Faubus did announce that the poll demonstrated that 85 percent of Arkansas opposed school desegregation. He then stated that if the state ever achieved desegregation, it would be only after a "slow process." Declaring further that a "court edict" could never alter "centuries-old customs," he firmly rejected being "a party to any attempt to force acceptance of change to which the people are so overwhelmingly opposed." The implied deference to local control enabled Faubus to avoid involvement with places where desegregation was already under way like Little Rock or Hoxie. In addition, Faubus formed a committee chaired by Bird that included Shaver and other East Arkansas leaders, especially R. B. McCulloch, a Harvard-trained lawyer credited with drafting the Arkansas amicus brief for *Brown* II. Faubus charged Bird's committee to prepare a set of interposition measures that would comply with *Brown* II even as it preserved states' rights.

The Bird committee provided the basis for Faubus's interposition stance. Shaver knew about Virginia interposition proposals and the state's efforts to avoid the radicalism identified with Georgia interposition measures. The Bird committee's first recommendation copied the Virginia call for solicitation of voter opinion toward racial desegregation. Couched in high-sounding states' rights phrases, it did not call for direct action or state power to block the enforcement of *Brown*. McCulloch termed the measure no more than a resolution of principle. The committee's second recommendation was legally enforceable, calling for the enactment of a pupil placement law stipulating eighteen factors (formally excluding race) that could be employed to assign students to schools. Following the approach taken in his *Brown* II brief, McCulloch crafted the proposal so as to comport with laws lower federal courts had already upheld. As the Bird committee did its work, Johnson presaged his gubernatorial campaign with the call for a special legislative session to enact interposition. Faubus refused, announcing instead the Bird committee efforts. A *Southern School News* headline proclaimed, "Governor of Arkansas Inclines to Segregation." But Faubus proceeded cautiously, asserting that desegregation was a "local problem . . . best . . . solved on the local level according to the peculiar circumstances and conditions of each local school district." Thus echoing the local control language McCulloch's brief affirmed and *Brown* II upheld, Faubus pleaded for "the cooperation of all the people in upholding law and order and in preserving . . . peace and harmony."

Faubus's reported "tilt" toward segregation missed political imperatives interposition unleashed. A clear division existed between racial moderates identified with the Little Rock School Board victory in *Aaron v. Cooper* and the East Arkansas defenders of segregation controlling the Bird committee. Both groups, however, felt threatened by Johnson's and the citizens' councils' interposition imagery, which seemed little more than a rationale for violent resistance. The moderates responded by disclaiming any belief in racial desegregation as a matter of principle, instead justifying it solely out of deference to

Supreme Court authority. By contrast, Shaver and McCulloch blended states' rights ideology and deference to local control inherent in *Brown II* to provide a version of interposition that possessed powerful political symbolism, and it ensured interminable litigation testing purportedly race-neutral pupil assignment policies administered so as to maintain segregation in fact. Johnson's gubernatorial campaign, following the much-publicized Southern Manifesto, made interposition a political surrogate for racial politics in Arkansas and across the South. Accordingly, in order to insure reelection, Faubus shifted from the racial moderate stance that had failed to win legislative support for his economic liberalism during his first term to the Bird committee version of interposition. The political advantages of this version of interposition were that it enabled Faubus to contrast himself with the "radical" Johnson, which attracted the racial moderates' support, and it captured the East Arkansas leaders who opposed Johnson as an outsider.

Arkansas gave Faubus a landslide victory in the Democratic primary election. Johnson claimed that Faubus was "pussy-footing" on desegregation. Such assertions were no match for Faubus's reelection strategy. He offered state legal assistance to any school district seeking to resist desegregation through court litigation, declaring, "No school district will be forced to mix races as long as I am Governor." Stating that "I am convinced that the surest way to safeguard our public school system at present for all citizens — both white and Negro — is to preserve our segregated schools," Faubus also left to local control those school districts such as Hoxie or Little Rock where desegregation was under way by court order. Meanwhile he pushed a liberal economic program, secretly winning East Arkansas support for a tax increase in return for Faubus's endorsement of the Bird committee interposition proposals. In the primary election, Faubus received 180,760 votes to Johnson's 83,856, with another 45,000 votes scattered among several minor candidates. Faubus won votes from all groups, including independent black voters in Little Rock. Still, core support received among the state's southwestern and east central counties was enough to give Johnson one of the highest vote counts for a runner-up against an incumbent in Arkansas history. Blaming defeat on election fraud, Johnson formed a states' rights party in order to fight Faubus on a radical interposition platform enshrined in a constitutional amendment.

Although Faubus had shown remarkable skill in using the interposition issue, whether he could continue to avoid capitulating to the segregationist extremists remained an open question.

The political clash over interposition in conjunction with the decision in *Aaron v. Cooper* revealed how racial desegregation projected a regional public image by late 1956. Over the years immediately following *Brown* I, the national media publicized episodically the succession of racial disturbances from Emmett Till's murder to blacks' diverse desegregation efforts in public education and public transportation. Presented as being "a southern problem," such incidents clearly were most newsworthy when disorder resulted, readily associated with popular culture imagery conveyed in movies such as *Tobacco Road* and William Faulkner's novels. The *Southern School News*, a publication supported by northern philanthropy at Vanderbilt University in order to provide factual and objective analysis of southern racial issues and law, reinforced the regional focus by suggesting, as had the *Arkansas Gazette* commentary upon Miller's opinion, that the Blossom plan could well offer a model for desegregation efforts outside the deep South. Arthur B. Caldwell, a lawyer from Arkansas in the U.S. Department of Justice civil rights section, probably conveyed to Brownell much the same assessment of Miller's affirmation of the phase program, as the attorney general grappled with obstruction of the administration civil rights bill by the southern congressional delegation.

The *Aaron v. Cooper* litigation coincided with Eisenhower administration ongoing political adjustments to the desegregation issue. Brownell experienced personally the intensity of white southern racial animosities at a social gathering when a southern state attorney general's wife denounced him as a "nigger lover." By contrast, northern blacks both praised and voted for Eisenhower simply as a result of administration attempts to pass the civil rights bill. Yet consistent with his constitutional separation of powers rationale, Eisenhower publicly declined to endorse *Brown*. For the same reason, he rejected the Republican reelection committee efforts to identify him with the *Brown* decision, which appealed to southern Democratic supporters like James Byrnes. Meanwhile, he did promote the voting rights principles of the civil rights bill, but eschewed the hotly contested enforcement authority incorporated into Title III. Against the cold war propaganda background, moreover, the administration explained the desegregation issue as a southern problem within U.S. federalism. Even so, the freedom of U.S. democracy would ameliorate the problem. That this claim seemed persuasive was suggested by a U.S. Department of State dispatch received in early 1956 from the U.S. consul in Madras, India, declaring the "hope of most South Indians that the conflict will be resolved quickly and relatively painlessly, in compliance with the ruling of the Supreme Court." The Soviet brutal suppression of the Hungarian uprising in October 1956, following weaker claims from Yugoslavia and Poland for increased independence, reinforced this sanguine view.

Aaron v. Cooper Appealed amidst Segregationists' Mounting Pressure, 1956–1957

Segregationists politicized racial desegregation and the Supreme Court along separate channels as *Aaron v. Cooper* was appealed from 1956 to 1957. As the Eisenhower administration and the national media addressed racial desegregation as a "southern" matter, segregationists used the issue to increase the political heat on elected officials like the Little Rock School Board and Governor Faubus. Southern congressional leaders also attempted to unite conservatives outside the South, especially Republicans, by attacking the Supreme Court. Even so, among southerners these assaults were synonymous with opposition to racial integration. Although southern congressional leaders endeavored to mobilize national conservative support by employing states' rights symbolism and cold war analogies to criticize the Court, they also claimed that race was a distinctly southern issue. Thus, although the interposition constitutional amendments Arkansas voters passed in the November general election of 1956 were expressed in legal language, whites and blacks alike knew that they reflected racial feelings. The amendments nonetheless imposed a divided political mandate represented by the Bird committee measures and Johnson Amendment, which Faubus hoped would enable him to fend off mounting pressure from segregationist extremists in the legislative term beginning in early 1957. Meanwhile, Arkansas' racially charged interposition politics provided the context for the Little Rock NAACP appeal of its case; as yet, however, the appeal had no direct connection with the southern congressional delegation rallying national conservatives against the Supreme Court.

In November 1956, the passage of divergent interposition amendments raised questions for Blossom. Arkansas voters passed the Johnson Amendment to the state constitution 185,374 to 146,064. Johnson declared that when the legislature enacted the measures the amendment mandated, state and local officials could prevent school desegregation until Congress acted to limit Supreme Court authority over cases such as *Brown*. The less confrontational proposals Faubus sponsored passed by a larger margin. The voters approved the mandate for a pupil placement law by 214,712 to 121,129, and the interposition resolution 199,511 to 127,360. In the Pulaski County wards, which included Little Rock, voters approved the Johnson Amendment 27,325 to 16,660, the pupil assignment measure 27,325 to 16,666, and the interposition resolution 23,038 to 17,808. Shortly after the election, Blossom wrote school board attorneys House and Catlett seeking advice as to whether the interposition measures would influence Judge Miller's order in *Aaron v. Cooper* and its appeal scheduled for decision in spring 1957. Blossom's questions reflected the technical issues of administrative discretion raised by the pupil assignment provision, as well as the vague but potent implication that states' rights could supersede federal court orders.

House replied for Catlett and himself, suggesting that the impact of interposition on the school board desegregation plan was unclear. He concluded that neither the interposition resolution nor Amendment 47 should affect court affirmation of the city desegregation plan. As a matter of constitutional principle, House stated, even if the Arkansas legislature passed laws seeking to interfere with the federal court desegregation order, such laws could have no *legal* effect, given the Supremacy Clause of the U.S. Constitution. House assessed the pupil assignment measure differently. Any law enacted under this constitutional provision would apply to all school districts throughout Arkansas. As long as such a law remained technically faithful to various administrative reasons — expressly excluding race — for assigning students to different schools, it might affect the federal court order, since *Brown* II authorized federal judges to grant extensive discretion to local school administrators. Nevertheless, House declared, "In our opinion, no pupil assignment law can displace federal court supervision. If, however, our conclusion proves to be incorrect, at the appropriate time we should ask that the supervision being given by Judge Miller be terminated."

The private exchange between Blossom and the school board attorneys suggested the conflicted images identified with racial desegregation. Notwithstanding the legal technicalities and states' rights phraseology defining interposition, Little Rock white and black citizens understood the racial tensions — including the propensity for violence — underlying the measures passed in the November election. Faubus displayed consummate political skill, garnering broad voter support among the full range of whites as well as independent blacks, for the position that his interposition measures, unlike those associated with the Johnson Amendment, could prevent desegregation in the majority of Arkansas white schools but at the same time not interfere with the few locales where it had already occurred or, as in Little Rock, had been sanctioned by court order. The ongoing clash between Faubus and Johnson nonetheless exacerbated for Blossom not only the practical legal questions addressed by House but also the uncertainties enmeshing the phase program in the volatile racial antagonism underlying the potent interposition imagery. House's reply affirmed federal judicial supremacy over states' rights symbolism as a matter of constitutional principle, although he recognized that legitimate constitutional questions remained concerning the reconciliation of the pupil assignment law to *Brown* II. Still, although House's response was clearly correct as a matter of law, it ignored the threatening interconnections between the legal constitutional formalities favoring the minimal *Brown* II desegregation remedy being appealed in *Aaron v. Cooper* and the larger conflict unfolding through interposition politics.

The gap between constitutional principle and states' rights symbolism soon became clear. Empowered by the Johnson Amendment, segregationist extremists demanded creation in the upcoming legislative session of a state sovereignty commission. Mississippi segregationists employed such a commission to investigate and publicize the names of blacks or white liberals known to be desegregation supporters. The publicity resulted in intimidation, which in turn forced many blacks to flee the state, and it constrained the few white liberals. Arkansas segregationists thus followed the Mississippi lead. In addition, the newly elected state attorney general, Bruce Bennett, sponsored related legislation imposing upon desegregation proponents, especially the local NAACP branches, the requirement that they register and publicize their membership lists. Republican Winthrop Rockefeller (Faubus's appointee to head the Arkansas Industrial Development Commission) condemned the bill creating the state sovereignty commission as a "dangerous" extension of state authority to create an "Arkansas Gestapo," leaving no organization "safe from embarrassment of an investigation; and behind closed doors, too." A private report from the local NAACP affirmed that although the federal courts would almost certainly strike down all these bills if enacted, the litigation would be costly and take years. Faubus, too, pushed forward the two measures he had advocated during the reelection campaign: one relieving children of compulsory attendance in racially mixed school districts, the other granting state-funded legal aid to school officials involved in desegregation litigation.

The rubric of interposition covered all these proposed bills, and recollections of the segregationists' intimidation in Hoxie and elsewhere compounded their contentiousness. During the months preceding the legislative session, Guthridge promoted interposition, asserting that the phase program and its affirmation by the federal court were contrary to states' rights. The school board responded by publishing the Blossom-House correspondence in the *Arkansas Democrat* and the *Arkansas Gazette*. Faubus nonetheless undercut the school board position. He suggested legitimately, as House had admitted to Blossom in their private correspondence, that the pupil assignment bill could receive constitutional sanction in federal court. When the legislative session got under way in early 1957, an estimated 900 persons attended the hearings for the interposition measures. Attempting to repeat his success during the earlier legislative session, Little Rock senator Max Howell employed parliamentary procedure to kill the bills; this time, however, these maneuvers failed. Insisting upon the comparative moderation of the Faubus bills in particular, Shaver and McCulloch defeated Howell's efforts, contending that the proposals were not inconsistent with the gradual desegregation already under way in certain Arkansas communities. Amidst the clamor for passage, Faubus supported not only his own proposals, but also the sovereignty commission and Bennett's bills. At the same time, he resisted, and subsequently vetoed, a loyalty bill the legislature enacted into law. Even so, the legislature passed the interposition laws by substantial majorities.

The clamor the interposition hearings unleashed obscured Faubus's private maneuvering to win a tax increase. During Faubus's first term as governor, the legislature failed to approve a tax package providing the necessary funding for an ambitious liberal economic program aimed at promoting Arkansas' progressive image favoring both public services and business development. Faubus's reelection campaign pushed this liberal economic program but downplayed the need for new taxes. Upon reelection, he asked the legislature to vote on a $22 million economic program requiring the largest tax increase in the state's history. In order to ensure victory, Faubus turned to William J. Smith, a lawyer recognized as one of Arkansas' most effective political powerbrokers. In previous races, Smith supported Faubus's opponents, but in fall 1956, after a lengthy exchange of views about the state's future, the lawyer became the governor's closest adviser. Accordingly, Smith led the way in privately negotiating passage of the economic program amidst the debate over the interposition bills. The East Arkansas delegation had defeated Faubus's earlier tax proposals; Smith, however, succeeded in winning delegation support for an even larger tax package in return for Faubus' support of the East Arkansas interposition measures. Despite strong opposition, the tax package passed, largely because the East Arkansas delegation voted in favor of it. Faubus later wrote that after the Delta representatives sided with him on the tax increase "I could not ignore them."

Entangling the liberal economic program in interposition politics had unpredictable ramifications. The East Arkansas delegation vote for the tax package in return for Faubus's endorsement of all the interposition proposals was, of course, not publicized. Yet Faubus's second-term inaugural address did link the tax package to the desegregation issue. The "problem" of "racial segregation," he stated, had "upset and confused the entire South." Southerners were not a "lawless people," but the Supreme Court was attempting to "wipe out generations of human attitudes, traditions, and customs." Faubus insisted that it was "folly . . . to expect judicial dictation to compel social adjustment." The race issue was, he declared, a "compelling reason for favorable consideration of the tax program" because "if all our people are given good service . . . there is less likelihood of discord and disorder in dealing with this or any other problem." Although the reference to disorder conveyed images of resistance identified with the interposition campaign, Faubus's promotion of a controversial tax package suggested an abiding faith that economic liberalism administered fairly to whites and blacks alike could diffuse racial antagonism. Indeed, Faubus could point to the votes reelecting him from segregationists and moderate whites as well as independent blacks in places such as Pine Bluff and Little Rock, which indicated the transcendent appeal of economic liberalism. Less conspicuously, however, economic liberalism was now tied to interposition, which in turn, linked Faubus's political fate more than ever to segregationists' demands that those measures be enforced.

In early 1957, segregationist pressure in Little Rock increased. As the legislature enacted the interposition measures, House wrote Catlett in February concerning preparation of briefs in the appeal of *Aaron v. Cooper*. "In view of what the legislature is doing," House said, "you should be prepared to explain to the Court how there can be an island of constitutionality in a sea of lawlessness." In effect, House admitted the wide gap between the constitutional principles at issue in the U.S. appellate court review of Judge Miller's desegregation order and the contentious symbolism aroused by interposition. Within Arkansas, moreover, the political and extralegal force of those images undercut public acquiescence to federal judicial authority and the constitutional principles it affirmed. Nevertheless, in March a citywide election for two school board positions suggested that segregationist extremists still could not successfully challenge moderates. A dentist, George P. Branscum, president of the states' rights Constitution Party, and Robert Ewing Brown, a radio and television businessman who was also secretary-treasurer of that party and president of the Capital Citizens' Council, ran for these seats on an interposition–states' rights platform. With the support of the Save Our Schools Committee, Branscum and Brown targeted Little Rock moderate-income and blue-collar white voters living around Central High who were the only ones facing actual race mixing. A low turnout among those same voters, however, enabled two moderate supporters of the phase program, lawyer Wayne Upton and businessman Henry V. Rath, to win with votes from high-income Pulaski Heights whites and blacks.

As the appeal of the Little Rock case was about to be decided, the Arkansas interposition politics and the moderate school board election victory sent a conflicted message. The *Southern School News* reported a vote count for the two school board seats of 4,340 for Upton over 2,398 for Brown and 4,267 for Rath over 2,455 for Branscum. Although the two moderates won by substantial majorities, the victory depended upon the combined vote of the Pulaski Heights elite and blacks as well as a low turnout among the majority of Little Rock poorer white voters. Thus, segregationist extremists deployed interposition as a surrogate for racial antagonism and condemnation of the Supreme Court in order to arouse middle-class and blue-collar white voters facing desegregation at Central High in September 1957. But since the phase program was vague as to when the other city public schools would face the same fate, the white majority felt no immediate threat. At this point, then, the minimalist approach to desegregation Blossom had carefully incorporated into the phase program — which judge Miller had affirmed — effectively divided not only wealthy and poor whites but also won support from more affluent blacks who countenanced the minimalist approach, and isolated the large numbers of working-class blacks identified with the black litigants in *Aaron v. Cooper.* However, the growing contentiousness of interposition between 1955 and 1957 implied that political momentum steadily was shifting against racial moderation. Viewed in this light, the school board election of March indicated repeated struggles ahead.

House's letter to Catlett distinguishing "constitutionality" from "lawlessness" during the appeal of the Little Rock case suggested this larger struggle. The U.S. Circuit Court of Appeals in St. Louis heard arguments in *Aaron v. Cooper* on March 11, 1957. On behalf of the black plaintiffs, Wiley Branton, joined by Robert L. Carter from the LDF headquarters in New York, presented arguments based on briefs signed by Thurgood Marshall and U. Simpson Tate. Catlett and House argued for the school board, following briefs signed by Richard C. Butler and two other attorneys. Branton had taken the lead in preparation of the appeal itself. Carter's and Marshall's involvement nonetheless indicated the LDF regular policy of participating at the circuit court level in cases the Supreme Court conceivably might choose to accept on final appeal. Nevertheless, the Little Rock case was only one of several school desegregation orders working their way through the federal courts in the wake of *Brown* II. Accordingly, Branton remained the principal advocate for the local NAACP and black plaintiffs' desire to test the phase program; the case clearly did not reflect a national campaign targeting Little Rock. Like Blossom and the school board, however, House and his fellow attorneys remained convinced that the New York NAACP had singled out the Little Rock case in order to test the limits of the equity relief mandated by *Brown* II. Given how firmly held was this conviction amidst the ever mounting concern about interposition politics, white moderates readily dismissed the inequities perceived by the black litigants.

The U.S. Circuit Court of Appeals decision on April 26, 1957, enforced the minimal remedial standards of *Brown* II. Among the states comprising the Eight Circuit, Arkansas was exceptional in imposing Jim Crow. Indeed, the three judges — from Nebraska, Iowa, and North Dakota, respectively — who decided *Aaron v. Cooper* were unaffected by direct southern cultural influences as they applied *Brown* II deference to the discretionary local control of federal district judges like Miller. It was "on the second and implementing decision of the Supreme Court . . . that the controversy here centers," the Court stated. The "local courts, in passing on the plans of school authorities and formulating their decrees, [should] give weight to certain equitable principles and administrative problems, while at the same time requiring a prompt and reasonable start toward full compliance with the original *Brown* decision declaring segregated schools inherently unconstitutional." Excluding the reason of race or any opposition expressly associated with race, the "courts may consider problems related to administration," such as "revision of school districts and attendance areas into compact units to achieve a system of determining admission to the public schools on a nonracial basis, and revision of local laws and regulations which may be necessary in solving the foregoing problems." Following Miller's findings, the court affirmed Blossom's "convincing and competent testimony to the effect that under existing conditions gradual integration of the schools was administratively advisable. Desirability of gradual as opposed to immediate integration was premised on factors referred to in the second *Brown* decision. The superintendent's testimony was not contradicted."

The circuit court rejected the LDF focus upon the vagueness of the Blossom plan. Unlike Tate's unhelpful arguments during the trial, the LDF appeal emphasized the harm done to the black litigants' educational opportunity resulting from the plan failure to specify dates of desegregation beyond September 1957. In order to counter this claim, of course, House had received Miller's agreement to maintain ongoing oversight of the plan implementation. The LDF lawyers cited cases from Kentucky, Virginia, and Tennessee enforcing desegregation orders more expeditiously than that occurring in Little Rock. The circuit court held, however, that such "decisions serve only to demonstrate that local school problems are 'varied' as referred to by the Supreme Court. A reasonable amount of time to effect complete integration in the schools of Little Rock, Arkansas, may be unreasonable in Saint Louis, Missouri, or Washington, D.C." Moreover, "local problems," including the "maintenance of standards of quality in an educational program may make the situation at Little Rock, Arkansas, a problem that is entirely different from that in many other places." In recognition of "such 'varied' school problems," the Supreme Court *Brown* II decision "remanded" desegregation cases "to the local district courts to determine whether the school authorities, who possessed the primary responsibility, have acted in good faith, made a prompt and reasonable start, and whether or not additional time was necessary to accomplish complete desegregation. The question of speed was to be decided with reference to existing local conditions." Thus, on each significant point the court affirmed Miller's decision.

Fateful Summer, 1957

During summer 1957, the desegregation issue in Arkansas and the nation took a fateful turn. Accepting the court defeat philosophically, the Little Rock NAACP supported a few black students preparing for admission to Central High in September. Unbowed by the March school board electoral defeat, the Capital Citizens' Council publicized the perceived racial inequity the phase program forced upon city poor whites compared to the Pulaski Heights elite. The citizens' council also goaded Faubus to abandon political equivocation and enforce vigorously the recently enacted interposition measures. Although publicly Faubus continued to espouse local control, he now pursued private contacts with his segregationist opponents. Ever faithful to the public image of racial moderation, Blossom threatened use of the pupil assignment law to pressure black parents who remained committed to entering Central; in addition, the school board steadfastly justified its phase program on the basis of pragmatic deference to the Supreme Court, eschewing the *Brown* I basic principle of equal justice. Privately, however, school officials more than ever felt the heat from segregationists. In June, House visited Arkansas native Arthur B. Caldwell in Washington, D.C., hoping that if disorder threatened, the justice department would intervene to enforce Miller's court order. Enmeshed in Brownell's losing fight for Title III of the civil rights bill, Caldwell discouraged House's inquiry. Caught between the blacks' demand for civil rights and extreme segregationists' demands for interposition, then, local, state, and federal officials sought to avoid responsibility for desegregation.

The appellate court loss in *Cooper v. Aaron* forced the Little Rock NAACP to reconsider its options. By bringing suit, the executive committee had hoped both to increase NAACP influence within the black community and to compel the school board to return to its earlier desegregation proposal. Prosecution of the suit in and of itself was enough to win over many working-class blacks to the cause of greater activism, at a time when more affluent blacks were satisfied to accept the minimal desegregation the phase program established. The appellate court defeat left undiminished the increased visibility of the NAACP in the black community, but it did force the executive board to decide whether an appeal to the U.S. Supreme Court was advisable. Meanwhile, the executive committee aided the few students who remained committed to entering Central High after Blossom persuaded other black families that attending Horace Mann was in their best interest. Significantly, Blossom pursued this process amidst the growing citizens' council clamor. Thus, Branton wrote to House that the U.S. appellate decision at least provided blacks a "cloak of protection against some die hard anti-integration groups who might still try to delay integration." Declaring that the "plaintiffs feel just as strongly about the issues," he nonetheless was optimistic that "time has made many of the problems moot and the opinion of the appellate court clarified some of the issues more favorably for us." Some room remained for "give and take" encouraging "a spirit of good will and harmony among the students and patrons in the initial phase of school desegregation at Little Rock."

By midsummer, the Little Rock NAACP course of action was clear. After much consideration the executive committee decided against an appeal to the Supreme Court. A practical reason was that the school year was scheduled to begin within just a few months: further litigation could easily provide the school board reasonable justification for delaying desegregation of Central until the Court reached some decision. Privately, too, both Branton and the New York LDF lawyers expressed concern that the Supreme Court might follow the circuit court reasoning in *Aaron v. Cooper*, thereby establishing the Little Rock desegregation plan as a model for meeting the remedial standard of *Brown* II. Although such concerns clearly were well taken, the outcome nonetheless was that the Little Rock NAACP had in effect aligned itself with the more affluent black opinion leaders' acceptance of the phase program articulated by the *Southern Mediator*. Reluctantly, the local NAACP now accepted the very same minimal desegregation plan it had challenged since late 1955. The executive committee was compelled to do so largely because the federal courts had affirmed the reasonableness of the phase program within the minimal desegregation remedy *Brown* II mandated. As a result of the court decision, moreover, the local NAACP had little choice but to cooperate with Blossom, despite threats that unless black parents voluntarily countenanced an arbitrary screening process and attendance zones he would use the new pupil assignment law to pursue the same result. "I know it is undemocratic, and I know it is wrong," Blossom warned local NAACP leaders, "but I am doing it."

Notwithstanding the tension between the local NAACP and Blossom, between nine and thirteen black youths persisted in their efforts to attend Central. Amidst the growing pressure from the Capital Citizens' Council during the early summer, Blossom worked within the flexible standards Miller and the appeals court had upheld to determine how many black students out of some two hundred might want to transfer from Horace Mann High or Dunbar Junior High to Central High. The initial number was seventy. When in private meetings

NAACP executive committee members objected to apparent intimidation directed at the black families requesting transfers, Blossom justified his actions on two grounds. First, he said, "I feel that for this transition from segregation to integration in the Little Rock system, we should select and encourage only the best Negro students to attend Central High School — so that no criticism of the integration process could be attributed to inefficiency, poor scholarship, low morals, or poor citizenship." In response to assertions that many blacks who clearly met these standards nonetheless felt Blossom had intimidated them to remain in black schools, he replied frankly that Judge Miller, privately, had condoned the process. Ultimately, Blossom succeeded in limiting the number seeking transfer to Central High to nine — Minnijean Brown, Elizabeth Eckford, Ernest Green, Thelma Mothershed, Melba Pattillo, Gloria Ray, Terrance Roberts, Jefferson Thomas, and Carlotta Walls. Ultimately, despite the gauntlet they faced, the nine students' decision to enter Central was neither Blossom's nor that of the NAACP; it was each young person's individual choice.

The nine did not meet as a group until August 1957. Still, they all shared two basic motivations, influenced by other common factors. Each student lived within ten blocks of Central High, whereas Horace Mann was at least two miles away; thus, the desire to attend the school closest to home was the first reason they shared for pursuing admission to Central. In addition, each student combined individual fortitude and a strong sense of independence with intellectual ambition, facilitating the confident assumption that an education at Central, which possessed a national reputation for academic excellence, would enhance attainment of high career goals. All were aware that their desegregation of Central was historic, but compared to the two leading practical motivations, this was at most a secondary factor. Moreover, with one exception, the family of each student proudly supported her or his independent judgment as to the benefits and risks involved in the choice of attending Central. Only Gloria Ray's parents firmly rejected her decision, though she pursued her choice anyway. Cartelyou Walls, by contrast, most encouraged his daughter Carlotta. A decorated combat veteran of World War II, he declared himself to have "fought as hard as anybody else. . . . So I don't see why my child should be barred from a school for which I fought. The Constitution of the United States gives her as much rights as anyone else." The families of all nine young people were longtime Little Rock residents and were comparatively affluent; they all had, too, various friendly personal contacts among whites.

Blossom's efforts to limit the number of blacks transferring schools played into the hands of the Capital Citizens' Council. During late June and early July, Amis Guthridge presented before the school board a case for white parents whose children would attend Central. Citing the reasoning of the *Briggs* precedent Miller had cited in *Aaron v. Cooper*, Guthridge claimed that the Supreme Court *Brown* I decision did not compel "compulsory integration." He declared that the new interposition laws authorized the board to assign white students to segregated schools, which he insisted the citizens' council would fund if given the opportunity. Guthridge then raised various questions about likely interracial "social mingling" occurring at integrated school activities. Finally, he claimed, Blossom and the school board allowed blacks to choose their school, whereas white children were "trapped" into attending Central because they were unable to transfer to all-white Hall High in Pulaski Heights. Guthridge had exposed the underlying class inequity of the phase program. Clearly, Blossom had readily altered attendance zones to ensure that only a small number of blacks would be eligible to enter Central. The refusal to desegregate Hall, at the same time curtailing the transfer of whites in the Central zone, substantiated segregationists' social class rhetoric that "blue-stocking" Pulaski Heights residents received unfair special treatment over the "common people."

On July 11, Guthridge published his arguments in an open letter, to which the school board replied in its own published statement. The board reiterated its disagreement with the principle of racial equality affirmed in *Brown* I, but justified its desegregation plan out of obedience to the constitutional supremacy of the Supreme Court. It also intimated that racial mixing would not occur at school social activities. The statement pointed to the Constitution's Supremacy clause, Article VI, which made the Constitution and federal laws passed under it "the supreme law of the land . . . the Constitution or laws of any State to the contrary notwithstanding." The language was, the statement affirmed, "unmistakable and those who say State laws permitting segregation, directly or indirectly, are supreme simply refuse to read that which is plainly written." The school board statement emphasized, moreover, that two federal courts had upheld the phase program. The statement then challenged the citizens' council to test its states' rights arguments in court, the "traditional American way" of deciding disputes over state and federal power. Until segregationists pursued this means of redress, the school board urged no more "insinuations" that the phase program was contrary to state law, or that school officials were conspiring with the NAACP.

The citizens' council nonetheless stepped up its intimidation campaign. There "will never be integration in Little Rock public schools," Guthridge insisted, but if the school board carried through its plan, there would be "hell on the border." Robert Ewing Brown predicted "considerable and continuing protests against race mixing." Most Little Rock blacks were satisfied with their existing "ample and fine schools." The idea of racial desegregation resulted from "the aims of a few white and Negro revolutionaries in the local Urban League and the [NAACP]." A citizens' council guest speaker at one meeting was more explicit. Rev. J. A. Lovell of Dallas, Texas, exclaimed that if the Supreme Court and elected officials maintained their "weak-kneed" attitude toward desegregation "there are people left yet in the South who love God and their nation enough to shed blood if necessary to stop this work of Satan." Increasingly, the citizens' council targeted Faubus. Under the interposition laws, Brown claimed, Faubus could apply ordinary police powers to command the "two races" to attend separate schools in order to "preserve tranquility." Those same police powers, he asserted, made Faubus "immune to federal court orders." In July, Brown published a letter calling upon Faubus to block desegregation of Central by exercising these police powers in order to "avoid calamity." In a newspaper advertisement Guthridge increased the pressure, demanding to know why Faubus was allowing desegregation in Little Rock when Texas governor Allan Shivers had avoided federal intervention despite using Rangers to prevent desegregation after disorder in Mansfield.

Placed on the defensive, the Little Rock NAACP provided one measure of the effectiveness of the citizens' councils' campaign. Soon after the Arkansas legislature enacted the interposition measures early in 1957, Daisy Bates announced that the NAACP would challenge them in court. During the months that followed — as Brown's prediction of mounting protests was fulfilled — the local NAACP did not, however, initiate litigation. In conjunction with its decision against appealing *Aaron v. Cooper* to the Supreme Court, the failure to test the interposition laws confirmed the images of states' rights and police power legitimacy the citizens' council was concurrently publicizing. The laws Arkansas attorney general Brewer sponsored aimed at publicizing local NAACP membership lists further weakened the organization. Lee Lorch and his wife Grace were attacked as communists. Although resolutely committed to the cause of racial justice, the Lorches' known leftist sympathies nonetheless reinforced the public image of radical outside influences working within the local NAACP, undercutting organization credibility among its few liberal defenders in Little Rock, as well as strengthening Bennett's attack. In addition, the citizens' councils' increased protests occurred at the same time the Little Rock NAACP accepted the minimal desegregation plan Blossom imposed, which more affluent blacks also sanctioned. These factors combined to neutralize local NAACP activism.

Following the publicized exchanges with the citizens' council, the Little Rock School Board also reacted more quietly. By July, Blossom had sent his daughter to stay with relatives living elsewhere in Arkansas; he also established regular contacts with city police and Governor Faubus, seeking to learn about any racially linked disturbances. Most importantly, in June 1957, A. F. House visited Arkansas native Arthur B. Caldwell in Washington, D.C., in order to inform him about the growing citizens' council protests. Speaking for the school board, House expressed the hope that the justice department might be prepared to act. In charge of the department small civil rights section, Caldwell was enmeshed in Brownell's struggle to overcome the combined southern Democrat and conservative Republican congressional opposition to Title III of the civil rights bill. Caldwell was thus well prepared to explain how limited the justice department options were in a case like that House thought might be developing in Little Rock. As long as the conservative coalition continued to block the authority Brownell sought in Title III, the justice department could only depend on old laws from the Reconstruction era, which decades of southern resistance and Supreme Court decisions had eviscerated. Admittedly, since the 1930s the Supreme Court was slowly creating a constitutional basis for stronger federal action defending civil rights, but members of

Brownell's justice department were divided over how to enforce this as long as Title III remained in political limbo.

Caldwell's response to House's visit was not encouraging. He made a preliminary investigation, interviewing House, Blossom, Harry Ashmore (editor of the *Arkansas Gazette*), and Police Chief Marvin H. Potts in Little Rock, along with Judge Miller in Fort Smith. Caldwell's report of findings acknowledged that the U.S. Code and certain federal court decisions provided the legal basis to initiate an investigation of the Capital Citizens' Council activities, but concluded that more evidence was necessary before ordering federal authorities into action. Caldwell also emphasized that he had asked House whether the Little Rock School Board might consider litigation of the sort the Hoxie school officials had initiated to defeat segregationists, this time testing the constitutional and legal standing of the 1957 interposition legislation. House had declined, but suggested that black attorneys might "be persuaded" to try such a suit. Nevertheless, Caldwell's focus was significant in part because it indicated that the justice department was hesitant to conduct even an investigation unless it could claim to have been requested to do so by local authorities, which, indeed, had occurred in Hoxie. More broadly, Caldwell revealed how weak was existing federal legal authority in the face of the notorious presumption grand and petit jurors shared against prosecutions of southern whites for crimes involving black civil rights. Undoubtedly, Caldwell was keenly aware that in fourteen well-publicized black rights cases from 1955 to 1957, white defendants won before white juries in all but one.

Thus, by July 1957, Little Rock school officials, the local NAACP, and the justice department privately admitted the segregationists' threat, but were unwilling to challenge it. Why? The NAACP reasons were the most straightforward. Defeat in *Aaron v. Cooper* compelled local NAACP complicity with Blossom's minimal desegregation plan; in addition, the organization faced legal demands from state attorney general Bennett to reveal its membership lists. The defense against this measure would strain NAACP resources to the limit. Also, the newfound standing of the organization within the black community was buffeted by revelations of the Lorches' radical sympathies. These same problems confirmed the presumption among Little Rock whites that the NAACP New York headquarters was behind the local branch actions. In fact, however, meaningful support from the LDF for the desegregation litigation ceased when the local NAACP decided not to appeal it to the Supreme Court. The LDF did cooperate with local black lawyers in the legal fight against Bennett, but the local NAACP bore most of the expense. Given these pressures, litigating the interposition laws, as Daisy Bates had initially suggested, was out of the question.

The reasons for justice department and school board inaction were less clear. By July, Brownell realized that southern Democratic and conservative Republican senators had successfully blocked enactment of Title III of the civil rights bill. Meanwhile, Eisenhower equivocated, publicly supporting the modest voting rights provisions of the bill and the expanded funding for the new civil rights division, which received relatively insignificant conservative opposition. This outcome reinforced Caldwell's discouraging report that the justice department was prepared to assist Little Rock school officials only if they acted first. The analogy Caldwell drew with Hoxie indicated that without stronger congressional and presidential backing — and express pleas for help from local authorities — top justice department lawyers were unwilling to risk almost certain defeat before southern courts in civil rights cases. That being so, why were Little Rock school officials adverse to litigating the interposition laws the Capital Citizens' Council repeatedly employed as the basis for their provocative public protests? An initial answer was, as House told Caldwell, that in light of Daisy Bates's public statement, the NAACP might test the interposition laws. Still, by July, with no such case forthcoming, and Blossom's increased private contacts with city police and Faubus indicating no abatement of anxiety, why not act upon Caldwell's suggestion to follow the Hoxie example?

Although school officials' motivations regarding this question were obscure, several considerations suggest a plausible answer. Despite the moderates' lopsided victory in the March school board election, the outcome exposed the class inequity white parents at Central felt toward the Pulaski Heights elite whose children would attend all-white Hall High. The low turnout in the election belied the public anger this discrimination potentially could arouse among the Little Rock majority of middle-income and blue-collar white voters. Targeting this inactive white electorate, the Capital Citizens' Council hammered home the argument that blacks and affluent whites possessed a choice of schools whereas the majority of whites did not. The citizens' council protest campaign also linked this class agitation to the repeated claim that interposition — grounded as it was in states' rights and police powers — superseded federal authority, including the Supreme Court *Brown* decision and its implementation in the Little Rock phase program upheld in *Aaron v. Cooper.* In terms of propaganda effect, the citizens' council created a public image that interposition was a legitimate constitutional remedy for inequity thrust upon the Little Rock white majority by an affluent elite conspiring with blacks in conjunction with the Supreme Court. As this public image garnered force throughout the summer, school officials may have been reluctant to pursue Caldwell's suggested litigation challenging interposition, because to do so would only publicize further the class discrimination the phase program allegedly imposed upon the Little Rock white majority.

These contested public images pitting the racially moderate elite against the citizens' council aggravated Faubus's political position. During spring and summer 1957, as he had for the previous two years, Faubus continued to insist that desegregation should be left to local control. He avoided comment directly on Brown's and Guthridge's much publicized claims that states' rights and police powers enabled state governors to prevent desegregation. Faubus did announce after the federal appellate court decision in *Aaron v. Cooper* that desegregation in Little Rock was a "local problem," and that he saw no need to intervene. At the same time, he did nothing about the racial desegregation that had already occurred in the public schools and public transportation facilities of several Arkansas communities. On various occasions he also emphasized that Arkansas public colleges and universities had admitted some black students. He took credit, too, for the near equalization of white and black teacher salaries. As the segregationists' publicity campaign was in full swing by June, however, the press reported a statement from Faubus that, because of the large Little Rock black population, the city was perhaps not ready for school desegregation to begin in September. Thus, although preserving an image as the moderate alternative to extreme segregationists remained important to Faubus, he clearly was becoming aware that their protests demanded from him a more active political response concerning the impending desegregation of Little Rock Central High School.

Faubus also sought political accommodation on the interposition measures enacted earlier in the year. He delayed making appointments to the state sovereignty commission until compelled to do so by suit, whereupon his selections included his old East Arkansas confidant, Bex Shaver. At a press conference, moreover, Faubus brushed aside questions regarding segregationists' assertions that the commission could prevent desegregation, declaring, "Everyone knows that state laws can't supersede federal laws." Faubus also positioned himself against Attorney General Bruce Bennett, who, Arkansas politicos expected, would campaign for governor based upon vigorous enforcement of the interposition laws targeting the local NAACP membership. During the congressional hearings on the 1957 civil rights bill, Bennett's hard-line segregationist testimony received local publicity as the official position of Arkansas. Faubus countered this public image, dispatching Shaver, who focused upon the state's moderate and comparatively impressive progress in race relations, as his spokesperson before the same congressional committee. Thus, by spring and summer 1957, the segregationists' protest campaign demanded of Faubus a political calculus that more than ever adjusted the interdependencies between racial desegregation and the white identity images engendered by interposition.

During the summer, however, Faubus's secret initiative was at odds with his public image of racial moderation. A confidential NAACP report conveyed this public image, admitting that Faubus not only declined to defend desegregation in principle but also proposed to use all legal means to delay it legally if such were the "will of the people." Nevertheless, it stated, "the fact remains that he is not against integration and he is fairly certain that there is not legal means of preventing integration in the long run." Most importantly, unlike any probable successor, Faubus would "certainly do everything within his power to keep down violence . . . [fully recognizing] the significance of violence and agitation to people in other states, as well as its reaction on people within the state." Faubus's triumph over Jim Johnson suggested that Faubus remained committed to such a comparatively moderate stance, should it become necessary "to buck the extremists again." But in July

Faubus asked clothing store owner James T. (Jimmy) Karam to arrange a confidential meeting with Guthridge, Brown, and prosegregationist Baptist minister Rev. Wesley Pruden. With the three segregationists, Faubus and his legal adviser William J. Smith discussed in quite general terms the possibility of delaying or even preventing the desegregation of Central High, perhaps employing state police troopers. Some reference also was made to Faubus running for a third gubernatorial term, a rarity in Arkansas. Even though the discussion remained vague, the segregationists had reason to believe that Faubus might come around to their position. This private initiative thus eroded the public perception the NAACP report captured.

Faubus's contrary public and private actions suggested how the constitutional principle of local control shaped political accountability for enforcing *Brown*. The confidential NAACP report assessing the Arkansas governor's motivations as Central High desegregation loomed, as well as Wiley Branton's and other independent blacks' vote for him, confirmed the perception that Faubus was neither a racist nor a committed segregationist. Instead, Faubus's publicized "tilt" toward interposition reflected repeated maneuvers to preserve political images of racial moderation and local control, at the same time accommodating the growing force of extreme segregationist protest, appealing as it did in Little Rock to both racial hatred and class tensions. The black activists believed, then, that Faubus would enforce minimum compliance with *Brown* II, as upheld in *Aaron v. Cooper*, but strive to preserve order. Faubus's effective turn to the principle of local control to win two gubernatorial elections reinforced this expectation. Faubus's secret meeting with Little Rock Citizens' Council leaders revealed, however, that he was increasingly unwilling to risk the consummation of his liberal economic program — and his political future as well — on continued opposition to the extreme segregationists' radical states' rights and police powers claims. Thus Faubus faced a hard political question: How could he maneuver around Arkansas and Little Rock white voters' growing hope that interposition enabled the governor to prevent desegregation, even at the cost of violent protests?

Like Faubus, the other participants in the Little Rock desegregation struggle responded to constitutional principles. The defeat of *Aaron v. Cooper* left the local NAACP and black litigants little choice but to comply with the limited constitutional standard of *Brown* II. Meanwhile,

Blossom's private contacts with Faubus, like House's initiative resulting in the discouraging report by justice department attorney Caldwell, revealed that although Little Rock school officials increasingly worried over the segregationists' agitation, they were unwilling to take the lead in countering it. School officials relied upon the constitutional minimum imposed by Miller's court order, affirmed on appeal. Although the explanation for school officials' reluctance to follow the course of their Hoxie counterparts remained obscure, it likely involved concerns about publicizing the class tensions the Capital Citizens' Council had exposed regarding the failure to desegregate both Hall and Central High Schools. In any case, school officials were prepared to abide by, but not exceed, the limited constitutional duty under *Brown* II. Similarly, as Caldwell's report confirmed, the justice department was unwilling to counter segregationists' resistance unless Congress augmented federal powers, since southern state courts and juries virtually always employed constitutional authority to protect white defendants in civil rights cases. The impending defeat of Title III of the civil rights bill in summer 1957 confirmed this reality, as did Eisenhower's equivocation toward civil rights justified by insistent appeals to constitutional separation of powers. Accordingly, even though U.S. constitutional history discredited interposition, segregationists successfully used it to shape their opponents' actions.

CHAPTER 3

The Crisis Erupts, 1957

During September 1957, Little Rock drew the attention of the United States and the world. Governor Orval Faubus and the U.S. government projected opposing images of constitutional rights claims and the duty to preserve order, enmeshing nine black young people and the NAACP in intractable confrontation. The clear-cut public imagery, which reached a turning point in August 1957, arose from surreptitious maneuvers among school officials, Judge Miller, Governor Faubus, segregationist extremists, and, eventually, the U.S. Department of Justice. These clandestine exchanges evidenced ambiguous motivations belying the sharp public claims and counterclaims emerging from state and federal courts in the final days of August, precipitating Faubus's surprising announcement on September 2 that the Arkansas National Guard would indefinitely maintain racial segregation at Central High. The secret maneuvers preceding Faubus's defiance influenced the ensuing three-week crisis. Thus, Little Rock presented a stark clash between state and federal authorities' contrary constitutional rights claims, culminating in violence resolved though Eisenhower's dramatic dispatch of the 101st Airborne in the name of federal supremacy and cold war necessity. These powerful images reflected the constitutional obligations the federal courts repeatedly affirmed throughout the course of *Aaron v. Cooper*. The obscure actions fostering the crisis ensured, however, that the outcome of the case would be ambiguous.

Uncertainty encumbered Faubus's political calculations. Biographer Roy Reed quotes Faubus frankly telling a few supporters in 1954, following the first *Brown* decision, that should he discover the means to exploit racial conflict, "they'll never get me out of office." But amidst the growing tension of August, Reed also reports, Daisy Bates of the local NAACP believed Faubus was a follower rather than an instigator of political pressures unleashed by school officials and Little Rock Pulaski Heights elite, which, in turn, aggravated poor whites' racial antagonism. "He's against you and the people in the Heights," she told her friend, white lawyer Edwin E. Dunaway, "and I'm going to have to pay for it." Reed admits that he and other news reporters for the *Arkansas Gazette* and *Arkansas Democrat* were unaware of the private actions all principals — except the black litigants and NAACP LDF lawyers — pursued in the attempt either to avoid responsibility for or altogether block enforcement of the Little Rock desegregation plan. This chapter examines how public and private events resulting from clashing federal court orders and state laws brought on the August turning point; it then considers why this legal conflict shaped Faubus's choice of defiance, resulting in the crisis as well as Eisenhower's intervention as a resolution of the constitutional confrontation. Even so, the struggle over federal versus state authority steadily overshadowed the black students' constitutional rights.

August Turning Point

During August, the black students faced growing tension over the court-ordered desegregation of Central High. The Little Rock Citizens' Council public announcements repeatedly demanded that Faubus employ the recently enacted interposition measures — and the police powers upon which they rested — to block the federal court order. Faubus's private polling revealed that even though the constitutional form and substance of interposition and police powers generally remained abstract to most Little Rock and Arkansas citizens, he could not avoid addressing the political imagery of "lawful" resistance these principles conveyed. The political pressure became irresistible after Georgia governor Marvin Griffin and his fellow traveler, Roy V. Harris, claimed in a Little Rock segregation rally on August 22, 1957, that their state successfully deployed interposition to defy federal authority. That same night, a rock crashed through the window of Daisy and L. C. Bates's home, carrying a paper message that read: "STONE THIS TIME. DYNAMITE NEXT." Daisy Bates and the students were aware, too, that the Mothers' League of Central High had formed to "peacefully" oppose the desegregation order. Although the mothers' leaguers disclaimed any affiliation with the citizens' council, subsequent evidence confirmed what Bates and the students assumed — that the two white segregationist groups were closely aligned.

Thus, constitutional legal conflicts and simmering threats shadowed the black students just weeks prior to the beginning of school. Press reports repeated school officials' affirmations that desegregation would occur in an orderly fashion. Nevertheless, Superintendent Blossom's intense efforts to admit the fewest possible blacks to Central, as well as his repeated efforts to shun the young peoples' legal representatives, the local NAACP and Daisy Bates, aggravated the students' and parents' concerns. Even so, personal commitment to greater academic excellence and the opportunity for an improved future it represented sustained the students as they confronted the risks. Jefferson Thomas presented one example of such hope. Six of his seven older sisters and brothers had left Little Rock, including two sisters living in San Diego, one working as a nurse, the other attending a racially integrated public school. In San Diego, residential patterns determined that some blacks were to be found in most if not all secondary schools, and the one predominantly black high school also enrolled some white students. Thomas believed that the well-known academic quality of Central High would better equip him eventually to join in his sisters' West Coast experience. Still, the segregationist publicity campaign entwined states' rights appeals with what blacks understood to be racially charged antagonism.

Generally sharing a comfortable middle-class family life, the black students and their parents, to be sure, often had personal contacts with opened-minded whites. Notwithstanding such contacts, the students never were allowed to forget the enduring force of the racial divide separating the two communities. Moreover, the segregationist public announcements could not help but remind middle-class blacks that they were unwelcome as they moved into the formerly all-white neighborhoods surrounding Central High by the late 1950s. Thus, as she prepared to enter Central, Melba Pattillo experienced quite different racial feelings visiting her great uncle's family in Cincinnati. Years later she remembered how she had "lost that Little Rock feeling of being choked and kept in 'my place' by white people." She was "both frightened and excited when [her uncle's] white neighbors who lived across the street invited [her] for dinner. It was the first time white people had ever wanted to eat with me or talk with me about ordinary things." The memory remained vivid: "Over the dinner table, I found out they were people just like me. They used the same linen napkins that Grandma India favored. They treated me like I was an equal, like I belonged with them." At the same time, she imagined, "if [Little Rock] white mothers were fighting integration, it had little chance of success. I knew very well the power of my own mother and grandmother."

Meanwhile, the students' legal representative, the local NAACP, publicly identified with Daisy Bates, fought on several fronts. Press reports publicizing Blossom's efforts to limit the number of blacks admitted to Central invariably named Bates in conjunction with both the students and the NAACP. Although the local NAACP paid the legal costs of Wiley Branton of the LDF, representing the black students in the ongoing implementation of Judge Miller's court order in *Aaron v. Cooper,* the popular assumption prevailing among Little Rock and Arkansas whites was that the students were merely a pretext enabling the New York–based NAACP to disrupt the well-known moderate racial status quo of the city and state. This assumption received further fuel during August, as Arkansas attorney general Bennett initiated suit in state court to compel the local NAACP to publish its membership lists. As Bennett joined segregationists in linking the NAACP to a communist conspiracy, certain white politicians conceded that Bennett's motivations were aimed mainly at gaining electoral advantage in the gubernatorial race of 1958. These pressures strained limited local NAACP resources and created tensions between the branch and the New York office concerning Lee Lorch's reputed radicalism. Nevertheless, as the local NAACP fought Bennett in court, the appeals to cold war fears heightened its insistence upon projecting itself and the students as loyal U.S. citizens defending their constitutional rights.

Indirectly, the Little Rock NAACP was involved also in a private contest among national black civil rights leaders. During the first half of 1957, according to historian David J. Garrow, a group of Christian ministers identified with Martin Luther King, Jr. consolidated organizational efforts sparked by the Montgomery bus boycott into the new Southern Christian Leadership Conference (SCLC). NAACP leaders and the new "minister" group disagreed over principally relying upon nonviolent direct action versus litigation, voter registration, and legislative lobbying, especially concerning the civil rights bill then being debated in Congress. NAACP leader Roy Wilkins asserted that the organization "does wish to cooperate with the minister group." He nonetheless stated that "the particular form of direct action used in Montgomery was effective only for certain kinds of local problems and could not be applied safely on the national scale." King, by contrast, supported political efforts to enact effective civil rights legislation and the sort of litigation strategies culminating in Supreme Court cases like *Brown* I. He nonetheless believed that blacks "must not get involved in legalism [and] needless fights in lower courts," which was "exactly what the white man wants the Negro to do. Then he can draw out the fight. . . . Our job now is implementation. . . . We must move on to mass action . . . in every community in the South, keeping in mind that civil disobedience to local laws is civil obedience to national laws."

Although the separation between the Little Rock NAACP and black ministers was not contentious, it further strained the branch's limited resources. By mid-August, the pastor of the First Baptist Church of Little Rock, Rev. Roland S. Smith, lead ten black ministers in filing a federal lawsuit testing the constitutionality of the interposition laws the Arkansas legislature had enacted earlier in 1957. Supported by the local NAACP, the suit targeted segregationist extremists' assertions that state police powers enabled state authorities to block the enforcement of federal court orders mandating desegregation. The case reflected fundamental problems. As both King and moderate Arkansas segregationist R. B. McCulloch observed, litigation challenging the interposition measures faced protracted legal proceedings lasting years before the federal courts would likely strike down the statutes. Meanwhile, segregationist extremists and moderates alike could correctly claim that federal supremacy remained in doubt, engendering among the mass of white Arkansas citizens hopeful political support for defiance. Moreover, such delays emboldened southern Democratic and conservative Republican congressional efforts to limit federal jurisdiction in Title III of the civil rights bill, and even the Supreme Court power upon which the *Brown* decision depended. Thus, cooperation between the Little Rock NAACP and black ministers inadvertently fulfilled King's predictions about pernicious "legalism."

Yet such litigation efforts also fostered unity within the Little Rock black community. The federal appellate court affirmation of Judge Miller's decision in *Aaron v. Cooper* upholding the Blossom plan as reasonable under *Brown* II pleased black moderates because desegregation would proceed gradually. As a result, the local NAACP — which previously had seemed too activist — gained new credibility throughout the middle-class black community, which remained proud of how well teachers at Dunbar High School had served generations of black students notwithstanding the glaring inequities segregated facilities had imposed. The newfound willingness of the Little Rock School Board to measurably improve black schools symbolized by Horace Mann High was, these moderates believed, a direct outcome of white school officials' minimal compliance with *Brown*. This gradualism reinforced, too, the city's image of racial moderation then being tarnished by the militant segregationists. NAACP pragmatic acceptance of gradual racial desegregation further convinced black moderates that they would continue to receive the support of Governor Faubus, who not only publicly endorsed local control of black voting and the desegregation of schools and public facilities, but who also recruited moderate black leaders to Arkansas Democratic Party committees. Thus, although the NAACP litigation seemed inconsistent with King's mass action, it encouraged the community solidarity such action required.

By mid-August, black families encountered mixed signals from white authorities. At that point nine black students were firmly committed to entering Central, but at least four others were uncertain unless their safety could be ensured. During the same period, amid Blossom's public statements that trouble was unlikely, he met with a group of Negro parent teacher associations (PTAs) to discuss security measures. Also attending the meeting were Pulaski County sheriff Tom Gulley and Little Rock police chief Marvin H. Potts; the plan they presented to the group had been approved by Little Rock mayor Woodrow Wilson Mann. The plan provided for forty-eight police officers to maintain a presence at Central on the opening day of school. Two plainclothes officers would walk around Central itself. The number of police officers involved in the plan, out of the entire force numbering 175, suggested what the authorities believed necessary in order to prevent disorderly demonstrations. Neither law enforcement nor school officials nor the mayor publicized these precautions. During increasingly frequent contacts with Faubus, Blossom may well have referred to these preparations vaguely. Even so, although the city security plan may have reassured members of the black community that white authorities were serious about maintaining order, the preparations raised legitimate questions regarding Blossom's public assertions that all would be well.

During August the citizens' council expanded its campaign to control the images of desegregation and its consequences. The council purchased newspaper ads posing racially charged questions about potential black-white student interactions at Central High social events. Enlarging upon the lessons learned in the Hoxie confrontation, council members made repeated phone calls to white parents living in the Central High district designed to mobilize opinion against desegregation and gain new council recruits. The councilors also directed intimidating phone calls to Blossom and other officials. Reports of the Bates's rock-shattered window and its accompanying threat exacerbated the public fear of violence. The launch of the Mothers' League of Central High, followed by defiant speeches by the Georgians, Governor Griffin and Roy Harris, before some three hundred fifty council supporters in a Little Rock hotel on August 22 further agitated public perceptions. Meanwhile, council leader and mothers' league lawyer Amis Guthridge filed suit in Pulaski County Chancery Court seeking an order granting Kay Wilbern, the daughter of Eva Wilbern, admission to a segregated school authorized by the interposition legislation. In unrelated litigation, Attorney General Bennett sought from the federal court a delay in the trial of the ministers' case, which challenged the constitutionality of those same laws.

The Little Rock Citizens' Council main target remained Faubus. As late as July, Faubus stated publicly that federal law was superior to state law and that "if anyone expects me to try to use them [interposition laws] to supersede federal laws they are wrong." Yet during August, Faubus paid increasing attention to the council leaders. Through Jimmy Karam's efforts, Faubus held further secret meetings with Wesley Pruden, Amis Guthridge, and their associates, in which they discussed the effect of Central High desegregation on a third-term gubernatorial bid in the 1958 Democratic primary campaign, less than a year away. Faubus listened intently to the segregationists' claims that the interposition laws authorized him to block federal court orders as had Governor Shivers of Texas and, as well, to lease public schools to private groups — thereby privatizing them — in order to maintain racial segregation. The council leaders were, of course, encouraged by this private attention. They were emboldened also by Faubus's willingness to have Griffin and Harris stay at the governor's mansion during the council rally, though Faubus neither attended the rally nor discussed any controversial matters with his two guests. So formidable was Faubus's skill at reflecting the moderate center of Arkansas politics, the extreme segregationists were unsure of his final course of action, though they had strong reason to believe that segregation would continue.

The council leaders gradually realized that Faubus had two blind spots. He rarely reached outside his inner circle for advice, and he could be persuaded by extreme assertions if they were sincerely presented in ways directly bearing upon his political calculations. Pruden and Guthridge exploited these weak points by imagining ways to make Faubus believe that violence threatened Little Rock if desegregation proceeded. To further influence Faubus, they helped organized the mothers' league as a seemingly authentic movement among Little Rock white parents for nonviolent opposition to race mixing. Publicly, of course, both segregationist groups denied any affiliation with each other (only years later did the leaders of both groups admit their close involvement). During the weeks preceding the opening of Central High, mothers' leaguers contacted white parents by phone and visited them, urging peaceful resistance against desegregation. Published lists revealed the league membership to be about one hundred sixty-five. On August 28, the *Gazette* and *Democrat* each quoted Recording Secretary Mary Thomason as having provided conflicting membership figures of about one hundred versus two hundred. Historian Graeme Cope later estimated that the number of mothers with children actually attending Central was approximately thirty-one, or 18.8 percent of about one hundred sixty-five. Such limitations notwithstanding, President Nadine Aaron affirmed at an August 27 rally, "We are working as a group of Christian mothers in a Christian-like way. We do not approve of violence."

Indeed, the public discourse of the citizens' council and the mothers' league presented noteworthy contrasts. Although interposition and states' rights were the strategies both groups employed to justify resisting the federal court desegregation order, male citizens' council speakers readily resorted to crudities such as "a nigger in your school is a potential communist in your school." The mothers' leaguers, however, expressed themselves within the bounds of decorum associated with respectable southern white women, especially mothers committed to preserving their children's well-being. In September, amidst an unfolding crisis, Thomason stated succinctly what from the beginning had motivated the league members: "If this injustice of the states losing their rights continues, we will be losing everything that has made America a great and Christian nation. When the will of the people is ignored, then dictatorship sets in. . . . I do not believe the mothers in the league can ever accept integration in our hearts and it has never been the American way of life to sit and have something forced on us." At about the same time, Aaron told FBI investigators that the pernicious consequences of integration could include "interracial marriages and resulting diseases." Mothers' leaguer Margaret Jackson also expressed no animosity against blacks, but nonetheless believed that "God himself set us apart by boundaries and language."

The social class background the two segregationist groups shared with Central High parents reinforced the resistance rhetoric. The Blossom plan division of attendance zones between Hall and Central High Schools, which enabled wealthy Pulaski Heights parents to avoid racial desegregation, clearly created receptivity among many whites living around Central to the segregationist message. These same white families disapproved of the growing number of black middle-class homeowners throughout the neighborhood. Moreover, although many segregationists did not live in the neighborhood, enough did so to convey the impression of community unity threatened not only by the "race-mixing evil" but also unfair treatment favoring the city's social and economic elite. This elite, moreover, displayed little or no public sympathy toward Central High white parents; it also expressed considerable condescension toward citizens' council and mothers' league members as less than respectable people. By contrast, the segregationists could claim solidarity with the less-affluent white families living in the Central attendance zone. As historian Graeme Cope has shown, most of the white parents — like the segregationists themselves — were blue-collar or middle-class wage earners employed by large public institutions or private businesses, including many working mothers. These groups perceived their identities as diminished by both middle-class black homeowners and the better social standing of the Little Rock elite.

By the last week in August, then, the segregationists were more successful in influencing Faubus than white or black moderates realized. The Little Rock white elite remained so unaware of the immediate realities of desegregation that they continued to believe that the city tradition of racial moderation would diffuse the citizens' council racist and states' rights hyperbole, as well as the mothers' leaguers' softer Christianized rhetoric. White community leaders were confident, too, that this same moderation so bounded Faubus's political calculations that he would not collaborate with his political opponents, epitomized by Jim Johnson and the citizens' council. Similarly, although the segregationist threats most directly jeopardized middle-class blacks — especially the few students set to enter Central — these blacks had reason to trust in the same moderate tradition that had facilitated their own advancement. Faubus's consistent support for blacks' modest but real gains reinforced their faith that the governor would not surrender to the extremists' demands. Neither white nor black moderates realized, however, that Faubus's polling revealed the anger felt among whites in the Central High neighborhood, which in turn swayed them in favor of the extremists' constitutional claims that state police powers and the interposition laws provided a legitimate basis for state officials to prevent enforcement of federal courted-ordered desegregation.

The private pressures on Blossom and Faubus mounted. Throughout August, to be sure, some school board members perceived no real threat of disorder. Blossom and Faubus, however, faced covert opposition belying such confidence. Much later, Jim Johnson admitted that he orchestrated repeated anonymous phone calls to both men, claiming that the admission of blacks to Central High would arouse bloody violence perpetrated by armed people converging on Little Rock. According to journalist Roy Reed, Johnson later stated "We were dedicated to hustling . . . [Faubus]. Our people were phoning him from all over the state. Orval hid out, but our people in Little Rock got through to him." Johnson's people also inundated the superintendent's office with the same phone messages until "we had Blossom climbing the wall." Given these covert threats, in conjunction with the increasingly defiant segregationist rhetoric, the security plan school and law enforcement officials had prepared could be understood as a reasonable precaution. Nevertheless, Blossom's and other officials' comparatively sanguine public statements that desegregation would likely proceed in good order were inconsistent with the increasing personal anxiety Blossom expressed to Faubus. By contrast, Faubus's initial refusal to side publicly with the segregationist police powers advocates indicated that, well into August, he maintained a public image favoring local control of, and as much as possible his own noninvolvement in, desegregation.

Why Faubus Chose Defiance

School officials' willingness in mid-August to engage Judge Miller informally encouraged Faubus to change course. In his August responses to queries, Miller provided more direction than he had earlier. In June, school board attorney Archie House and justice department lawyer Arthur B. Caldwell privately had asked Miller about possible ways of dealing with the growing segregationist clamor. The judge replied that if in open court they, or the NAACP for its black clients, presented clear proof of a conspiracy to disrupt his order, he could issue an injunction against the malefactors. He also volunteered an opinion that if there was evidence that supported issuing such an injunction, he could likely issue a declaratory judgment holding the interposition laws unconstitutional. Given that Caldwell and House raised issues broadly fitting the Hoxie precedent, Miller's statements comported with the wide range of discretion left federal judges under the reasonableness standard of *Brown* II. That Miller's hypothetical offer of injunctive relief was problematic was suggested by the fact that House refused to proceed, describing it as a "sham." In June Caldwell had noted, too, that in any suit asking the court to enjoin the segregationists, they would likely raise a defense demanding strong evidence proving conspiracy. Failure to meet this high standard ensured inevitable acquittal before a white jury; the defeat of Title III of the civil rights bill undercut federal efforts to overcome this virtually inevitable result.

On August 13, Miller again entered into private discussions with a school board official. After appearing before the judge in unrelated court proceedings, lawyer and school board member Wayne Upton discussed with Miller the possibility that an unidentified individual, perhaps a segregationist extremist, might on the basis of the interposition laws seek a state court order blocking Miller's desegregation order. If such a state challenge arose, Miller observed, some respectable citizen, clearly not a segregationist, could bring a state suit testing the constitutionality of the interposition laws. The school board, he said, would then have reason to return to his court to seek a delay in the implementation of the desegregation order, pending a decision regarding the constitutionality of the interposition laws. Miller then informed Upton that, given such conditions, he would be favorably disposed to grant a delay. During the informal exchange in June the judge noted the need to present evidence in court subject to the opposing side's rebuttal; in the context of such litigation, he also expressed a willingness to decide the constitutionality of the interposition laws. The discussion could be understood as remaining within the bounds of a hypothetical case. In the August meeting with Upton, however, Miller expressed willingness to delay the implementation of his own order until a state court challenge was decided — which he undoubtedly knew would take at least a year — providing a clearer course of direction than he had in the earlier exchange.

Thus, in the August 13 meeting, Miller focused not upon the possible outcome of a public adversarial process in which each side presented evidence addressing an adjudicable question. Instead, to Upton, the representative of one of the parties upon whom his order was binding, the judge directly acknowledged a preference for granting a delay favoring the school board. Within days, the Miller-Upton exchange had strong ramifications. Returning from Fort Smith to Little Rock, Upton discussed Miller's comments with Blossom; the two school officials then met with Faubus over breakfast on August 15. According to Roy Reed's account of the meeting, Faubus expressed agreement with the idea of bringing a state case challenging the interposition laws; he also stated the belief that the laws were almost certainly illegal. In light of the governor's public statement just weeks earlier that federal laws "superseded" state laws, his comments left unstated an assumption that a federal rather than a state court decision would ultimately be necessary in order to establish such supremacy. Given that Faubus already had engaged in secret conversations with citizens' council leaders Guthridge and other segregationists, it is logical to conclude, as does Reed and others, that Faubus took away from his breakfast meeting an understanding that he need not worry about Miller's intervention with his actions. This reading neglects, however, that what Miller had volunteered to pursue was a *delay* in the implementation of his order.

This emphasis upon delaying desegregation may be contrasted with the alternative the segregationist extremists pressed upon Faubus by mid-August. At that point his clandestine contacts with Pruden, Guthridge, and other council members, as well as their public advertisements, challenged Faubus to do as Texas governor Shivers had done: employ state police powers to block desegregation. Faubus knew, moreover, as the council members confirmed, that neither the Eisenhower administration nor the federal courts imposed any consequence upon Shivers's actions, an outcome reinforced by the defeat of Title III. This result suggests that Faubus understood the segregationists' request of him to block Miller's order and thereby perpetuate segregation. But more practically, fulfilling this expectation would tie the fate of the third-term gubernatorial bid to Faubus's ability to continue to distinguish himself from Johnson and Bennett and their interposition position, including their more racist-oriented public rhetoric toward Arkansas blacks, something he had never countenanced. The possibility Blossom and Upton had presented to Faubus was, however, a delay that would end after the interposition laws were declared unconstitutional. Faubus — unlike the segregationist extremists — clearly believed that the federal courts would overturn the interposition laws, though the decision likely would not occur until after the gubernatorial primary.

This distinction between maintaining segregation versus delaying desegregation brings into focus the significance of proliferating court proceedings. During the evening following their breakfast meeting with the governor, Upton and Blossom met at the home of Faubus's attorney, William J. Smith. Notwithstanding disputed accounts as to what exactly transpired, the discussion clearly focused upon Blossom's rising anxiety about impending violence should desegregation proceed. He then pleaded for a public announcement from Faubus opposing violence and for Smith to initiate a state lawsuit testing the interposition laws. Although neither Faubus nor Smith agreed to Blossom's pleas, two court tests of the interposition laws followed. On August 16, Reverend Smith and his fellow black ministers brought suit in federal court seeking a decision that the interposition laws were unconstitutional and an injunction against the state sovereignty commission enforcing them, pending a decision by a three-judge federal panel. Attorney General Bennett immediately entangled this case in a protracted procedural maneuver. William F. "Billy" Rector, a Little Rock businessman with two children enrolled in city schools, also brought suit in the Pulaski County Chancery Court on August 17. As reported in the *Southern School News*, Rector's suit sought to address the "present conflict" raised by federal and state "laws," which because of "confusion and contention" threatened potential "civil commotion."

Other contingencies heightened Faubus's perception of the proliferating litigation. On August 18, Blossom and school board members Upton and Harold J. Engstrom went to Fort Smith to present Miller a copy of Rector's suit. Miller replied that regardless of the eventual outcome of this suit, he would not consider delaying implementation of the Little Rock desegregation order except to counter an injunction issued by a state court. Yet in order to prevail in such proceedings, Upton and Engstrom knew, the school board would have to stipulate formally, in conjunction with its request for a federal injunction against the state court, the reason for granting a delay. Back in Little Rock, school officials faced new tensions. On August 19, Guthridge asked the Pulaski County Chancery Court to order the school board to assign Kay Wilbern to an all-white school. Within the next three days, the mothers' league came into being and held its first public meeting; the widely publicized visit of Griffin and Harris also occurred. Against this background, Blossom reported to Faubus that the school board had decided against involving itself in a court test of the interposition laws and, most significantly, an attempt to delay desegregation. These events undoubtedly left Faubus with the strong impression that school officials were sufficiently anxious about potential disorder to discuss with Miller means of delaying desegregation; their anxiety was not so great, however, that the school board itself was willing to pursue an injunction.

The juxtaposition of litigation and escalating events pressed Faubus, but his course of action was undecided. Although contemporary and later commentators somewhat disagreed on how strong an impact the Griffin-Harris speeches at the citizens' council rally had on mobilizing opposition to the impending desegregation of Central High, Blossom affirmed that after the August 22 event, school officials found Faubus increasingly less responsive to their appeals. By contrast, Daisy Bates commented to her husband that their rock-shattered window was "a message from the Arkansas *patriots*," employing the same term Griffin used that same night to describe the members of the audience at the downtown rally. But neither the Bateses nor other blacks claimed that the Georgians had swayed Faubus from the path of moderation. Indeed, Griffin later said that although their stay at the governor's mansion would "ruin [Faubus] with the integrationists and the liberals," he also stated that the two considered him "so far on the other side that we didn't even speak about" desegregation when the three breakfasted together the morning after the rally. Perhaps the rally had a ripple effect in the days that followed, as the council had "taped Gov. Griffin's speech and ran it — over and over — on KARK radio."

Even so, earlier in August, Faubus had called the justice department requesting a meeting to discuss desegregation. The call occurred prior to the rally, but immediately following the series of lawsuits filed after Blossom had discussed with Faubus the possibility of bringing an injunction in order to delay desegregation. By the time Faubus met with Arthur B. Caldwell on August 28, the governor had sufficiently considered how best to exploit school officials' refusal to carry through on Miller's suggestion for delaying desegregation. No doubt Faubus measured the segregationist claims that the interposition laws and state police powers superseded federal authority in light of his own recently publicized affirmation that the opposite was true. In the future primary, would not a switch on such a basic claim of constitutional symbolism open Faubus to attack from Johnson (or even Bennett) that the governor was insincere — transparently opportunistic — especially compared to Johnson, whose segregationist credentials were impeccable? Faubus knew, too, that despite his covert contacts with the citizens' council leaders, neither Pruden nor Guthridge fully trusted that he would truly abandon his proven facility to undercut them by finding some middle ground within Arkansas politics. Moreover, Faubus was keenly aware that he was bucking the strong Arkansas tradition against third-term gubernatorial bids. Finally, Faubus was receiving the Johnson-orchestrated phone calls predicting violence.

Thus, by August 28, the political expediency of pitting straightforward defiance against a mere delay was for Faubus equivocal. During a private seventy-five minute conference, Faubus learned what he might expect from federal authorities. Noting that the order to desegregate Central High was scheduled to commence on the upcoming Tuesday, he asked Caldwell what the justice department options were should disorder occur. The lawyer explained that given the defeat of Title III of the Civil Rights Act of 1957, which Eisenhower shortly would sign, the justice department lacked clear authority to intervene. Admittedly, Title 18, Sections 241 and 242 of the U.S. Code provided the basis for criminal court proceedings, though a high evidence standard would have to be met. Caldwell then stated the limits of justice department authority. In the *Hoxie* case it had presented amicus curiae (friend of the court) briefs — detailing evidence the FBI had gathered — that the federal court used to enjoin from violence segregationists such as Guthridge. In Clinton, Tennessee, the justice department supported federal court contempt proceedings against segregationists found to have defied U.S. law. Essentially, Caldwell explained, employing the technical language of the criminal law, the federal government would have reason to intervene only *after* a court finding of some unlawful act.

Perceiving how limited were justice department options, the governor explained his own course of action to Caldwell. He affirmed that Governor Griffin's appearance in Little Rock on August 22 had pushed respectable people to join the "rabble-rousers" in opposing desegregation of Central High. As a result, more than ever before he was "on the spot" because the recently enacted interposition laws bound him unless and until a court held them unconstitutional. Caldwell reported to justice department superiors shortly thereafter, moreover, that Faubus declared "he could not tell the people that these Acts were unconstitutional although he admitted that a number of leading attorneys had privately confided in him that the statutes were probably unconstitutional." Caldwell reported further that Faubus admitted being so concerned about likely disorder and violence that he had "arranged" a suit to be filed in local chancery court in order to enjoin school officials from beginning the scheduled desegregation of Central. According to Caldwell, Faubus said that he hoped the state court injunction would compel school authorities to seek from Judge Miller an order delaying desegregation until the courts decided upon the constitutionality of the interposition laws. Caldwell told Faubus that the justice department would not countenance the governor's action; he informed Faubus, too, that local law enforcement authorities denied that violence was imminent or even likely.

Faubus's actions had immediate ramifications. The next morning, August 29, Caldwell attended the chancery court presided over by judge Murry O. Reed. In the case Faubus admitted to having "arranged," the plaintiff was the recording secretary for the Central High Mothers' League, Mary Thomason. The school board, with president William G. Cooper first named, was the respondent. Thomason testified, Caldwell stated, that the "mothers are terrified and afraid to send their children to Central High School." Under questioning, the witness "failed to bring out much evidence to support these fears of violence except that she had heard rumors from a filling station operator whose name she would not divulge, that there was a possibility of shotguns and shooting in Central High School if the colored children entered." Nevertheless, it was Faubus's testimony that received most attention. He testified that recently firearms had been taken from white and black students. The appearance of Georgia governor Griffin had contributed to a change in local attitudes from acquiescence to opposing the school board phase program. "People are coming to me and saying," a *Southern School News* story quoted Faubus as stating, "if Georgia doesn't have integration, why does Arkansas have it?" Leaving the stand as the courtroom erupted into "cheers and applause," reported Caldwell, Faubus "bowed."

Faubus's testimony had public and private impact. Following Faubus on the stand, Blossom, Cooper, and the city chief of police Marvin Potts all testified that they had no reason to believe that the scheduled desegregation of Central High would engender violence. Blossom added, moreover, that law enforcement authorities had assured him that the police were well prepared should unexpected disorder develop. The judge, whom Caldwell noted was a Faubus appointee, nonetheless granted the injunction to stop the school board from implementing the phase program on September 3. Chancellor

Reed declared that "in view of the testimony and the show of the threat of violence, riots, and bloodshed, and particularly in the opinion of Governor Faubus, I feel I can only rule to grant the injunction." As applause again filled the courtroom, the segregationists' claims that state authority was superior to a federal court order seemed to hold more weight. Because of the extensive clandestine maneuverings culminating in this moment, however, Faubus and Blossom gained still more conflicted understandings. Faubus knew that Blossom's testimony clearly contradicted the superintendent's covert actions during August, which revealed growing anxiety about impending violence. Blossom's and the other officials' assertions also placed them directly at odds with Faubus's public statements concerning the matter.

Even so, the *Thomason* case most directly revealed Faubus's course of action. Blossom's stated lack of concern about violence seemed truly to have surprised Faubus, contrary as it was to the superintendent's repeatedly stated fears during the preceding weeks. Nevertheless, Blossom's testimony under oath in open court also assured the governor that, notwithstanding the discussions about the need for procuring a court test of the interposition laws in order to get a delay from Judge Miller, school authorities were unwilling to pursue such a goal themselves. In addition, on August 26, in a private meeting with school board members, Faubus refused their request that he issue a public statement formally disclaiming support for desegregation, but — acknowledging the legal obligation of the board under a federal court order — also stated that as governor, he would do all in his power to maintain order in the community. Faubus rejected making such a public statement, he said, because of the conflicting federal/state legal claims, which he feared might engender violence. Thus, until the legal conflicts were resolved — thereby removing from him the duty to enforce interposition — he wanted desegregation delayed.

In this meeting Faubus told the school board that he was unsure as to how he might proceed. He urged, however, that the board seek a state court injunction facilitating a request for delay from Judge Miller. Of course, school officials had themselves very recently discussed with Faubus's attorney William Smith just such a course of action. At this point, however, House not only expressly opposed school officials' complicity in such a suit, but also insisted that the board would fight vigorously any attempt if it were brought by others. As Faubus departed the meeting, he told House and the board members heatedly that a suit nonetheless would be filed ordering a delay in the enforcement of the phase program. Two days later, Faubus revealed to Caldwell that he was behind the case that on August 29 resulted in the chancery court order defying the federal court, based on Faubus's testimony that violence would occur if desegregation were enforced. Faubus subsequently stated that the reason House had not cross-examined him in the *Thomason* proceedings concerning evidence pertaining to impending violence was because the lawyer knew that Blossom had been his principal source. Faubus's assertion embraced, of course, not only Blossom's previously expressed anxiety but also the secret contacts involving Judge Miller, which were consistent with Faubus's own behind-the-scenes role facilitating the *Thomason* suit. Faubus later claimed that Blossom had given him the *Thomason* complaint, which he then handed to an associate to file.

These public and private events highlight Faubus's motivations. Caldwell's report to the justice department after the chancery court proceedings conveyed what soon became the generally accepted view — that Faubus was simply a political opportunist. Initially, Faubus's request for a confidential interview perplexed justice department officials, who assumed that the southern governor in the state where the *Hoxie* case occurred knew full well that federal authorities' options were limited unless acts could be proven to have violated federal laws. Thus, Caldwell's report of Faubus's admission that he initiated the *Thomason* suit convinced federal authorities not so much that he was concerned about violence — of which he offered insufficient proof — but that he was merely using that claim to justify resisting a federal court order. Knowing about their own extensive clandestine maneuvers prior to *Thomason*, school officials also ascribed political motivation to Faubus's role in the suit; but they saw it, too, in light of his refusal to make a public statement supporting the school board as Central High desegregation loomed large. Still, they conceded privately that all Faubus sought was a delay, as he affirmed in the August 26 meeting. By contrast, since the mothers' leaguers had not considered bringing suit until one of Faubus's associates delivered the complaint to their lawyer, they and their fellow segregationists undoubtedly understood *Thomason* as successful in aligning Faubus with their states' rights stance.

On August 30, House appeared for the school board in the Little Rock federal district court. His petition sought an order restraining Thomason and others from enforcing Reed's injunction. The presiding federal judge was not Miller, who remained in Fort Smith, but Ronald N. Davies, who had arrived in Little Rock on August 26 from North Dakota to carry out a routine temporary assignment aimed at addressing a case backlog created by a judicial vacancy. LDF lawyer Wiley Branton also appeared before Davies, arguing that the chancery court lacked jurisdiction to block the enforcement of the black students' constitutional rights upheld months earlier in *Aaron v. Cooper.* Branton also, in consultation with Thurgood Marshall, who worked on the brief, filed an appeal to the U.S. Eighth Circuit Court of Appeals challenging the *Thomason* decision. Davies issued an order against anyone "interfering with and preventing the opening of integrated high schools . . . on September 3, 1957." Davies also enjoined anyone from seeking a citation placing the school board in contempt for refusing to obey the state court injunction. Asserting the superior authority of federal courts where constitutional rights were at issue, Davies held that obeying the state court injunction would "paralyze the decree of this court entered under Federal law, which is supreme under the provisions of Article 6 of the Constitution of the United States."

Faubus may have been unaware that Miller withdrew from *Aaron v. Cooper.* Upon learning about the *Thomason* decision, and aware that Davies had arrived in Little Rock on August 26, Miller did give up the case, ensuring that Davies would receive the school board petition seeking to enjoin the state court injunction. Commentators at the time and later agreed that Miller's motivations were unclear for turning over to Davies the responsibility for enforcing the Blossom plan. By contrast, Faubus publicly responded to Davies's order by claiming that Davies's arrival from North Dakota — a place foreign to southern racial mores — resulted from a conspiracy perpetrated by federal authorities. Faubus also emphasized that Davies was a Republican. Federal officials pointed out, however, that Davies arrived in Little Rock as part of a normal rotation that was necessary because of the accumulated backlog from a continuing judicial vacancy. Other commentators noted that neither House nor the NAACP requested an order as sweeping as that Davies issued. Yet, given how limited was the scope of federal jurisdiction until proven violations occurred, Davies's order probably applied only if Thomason could be shown to have engaged in illegal conduct. No one intimated that this was the case.

Another contention was that Davies's order surprised Faubus, since Miller had covertly offered to delay enforcing desegregation. This view assumes, first, that Miller would have carried through with the clandestine offer of granting the delay in a case initiated by an individual perceived to be affiliated with the segregationist extremists. Blossom admitted to Faubus, however, that Miller specifically stated that he would grant a delay only in a case brought by a "respectable" person. Among the Arkansas elite, including the school board members and Miller himself, a member of the mothers' league such as Thomason, someone publicly identified with the citizens' council, did not, as Graeme Cope noted, qualify as socially respectable. Also, this view assumes that Faubus simply ignored House's forceful statement at the private school board meeting of August 26—made in the name of his client—that the board would not be party to any effort to delay the enforcement of the Blossom plan. In light of the vigor with which House asserted this refusal, it was more likely that Faubus responded in a heated tone—insisting that a case nonetheless would be forthcoming—because he realized that he would be acting without school board complicity.

The *Thomason* suit, Judge Davies's order, and Faubus's motivations could be understood in yet another light. On the weekend of August 31 and September 1, the *Arkansas Gazette* quoted Faubus responding to a published account of Caldwell's August 28 private meeting with Faubus. Since he and Caldwell had understood that the meeting was confidential, Faubus exclaimed, the federal government action was a "betrayal," revealing "how much faith you can put in the administration." Questioned further about the meeting, Faubus condemned the federal authorities for "cramming integration down our throats," and at the same time creating political and legal demands that the states "protect ourselves while we're carrying out their orders." Faubus undoubtedly sought to overcome the impression that he remained allied with the "liberal integrationists," an intimation Georgia governor Griffin raised at the August 22 rally. But it was noteworthy, too, that Faubus defended himself also by blaming the federal government for attempting to shift the enforcement of desegregation onto state officials like himself, who faced the political consequences. Thus,

Faubus's motivations in initiating the *Thomason* suit and responding to Davies's order could be understood as his attempt to achieve a court-ordered delay in desegregation as well as to avoid any legal duty of enforcement. Indeed, school officials were asking Faubus to accept such a duty by urging him to make a public statement that he would preserve order.

Thus, during the weekend Faubus pondered his course of action. Blossom's contradictory public and private assertions, the threatening phone calls, including rumors that carloads of armed men in "caravans" were preparing to converge on Little Rock, and Thomason's statements in the chancery court suggested the possibility of violence. A subordinate's check of local pawnshops and gun stores revealed only minimal if any evidence of increased weapons sales. Even so, Faubus quietly prepared to place the Arkansas National Guard on alert. Responding to rumors of this action, Blossom and a school board member urged Winthrop Rockefeller to discourage Faubus. When Rockefeller and an associate met with Faubus, they emphasized that such defiance would precipitate a direct clash with federal authority. Faubus insisted that he feared violence was imminent unless he acted to prevent it. Nevertheless, Rockefeller said later, Faubus "appeared to be more concerned about political obligations and the future than he was with the integration of Little Rock schools." Rockefeller said further that Faubus expressed concern that if he failed to "hold the support of east Arkansas, James Johnson, Bruce Bennett . . . and Amis Guthridge would take over the state in the next election as the extremist group." Some hours later, Faubus received a telegram from Jim Johnson praising the governor's "stand for state sovereignty" in the *Thomason* case. Johnson also called upon Faubus to block integration in Little Rock just as Governor Shivers had done in Mansfield, Texas.

Faubus considered these various contingencies in light of William J. Smith's legal opinion. Smith was among the most effective lawyer-political advisers in Arkansas. His switch from opposing to supporting Faubus had been vital to the governor's political successes in winning east Arkansas support for the historic tax increase in return for promoting R. B. McCulloch's more moderate interposition measures over Jim Johnson's. When Faubus met secretly with either segregationist extremists or school officials, Smith often accompanied him. Faubus relied on Smith also to address the legal political imperatives unfolding from school officials' confidential meetings with Judge Miller, though he apparently did not deliver the petition to the segregationist lawyers who filed the *Thomason* suit. Thus, for an accurate legal evaluation of his public conduct — shaped by a penetrating grasp of the political imperatives at stake — Faubus depended upon Smith. What, then, was Smith's assessment of Faubus's claim that in order to prevent impending violence he would dispatch the National Guard to block the desegregation of Central on September 3? Reflecting a formally correct reading of state authorities' duty under police powers to suppress possible unlawful acts, Smith stated that Faubus should act only *after* enforcing the black litigants' rights resulted in disorder. Otherwise, absent strong evidence vindicating Faubus's belief that violence was imminent, the federal court would certainly declare his action to be illegal.

Ultimately, Faubus's use of Smith's advice was perhaps the best indicator of his motivations. In response to the guard's obstruction of the desegregation order, he knew, the federal court would demand from him unequivocal evidence supporting his professed concerns about impending violence. As he had shown in the *Thomason* proceedings, Faubus was unable to meet that high standard of proof. Thus, he could not have doubted that the federal court would hold that his use of the guard was unlawful, and, therefore, that enforcement of desegregation should proceed. Moreover, Faubus probably perceived that the surest political gains were to be achieved by defying and then complying with the federal court order. Why? First, because he could take political credit for following the segregationist states' rights ideology; second, by doing so he could claim the pure motive of seeking to avoid violence, but at the same time create an atmosphere in which enforcement of desegregation would engender probable if not inevitable disorder. Furthermore, the legal and symbolic moral duty of addressing such disorder would lie — clearly not with Faubus, who could assert he had done his best and been rebuffed — but with either the federal government or school officials. Finally, these legalistic and constitutional imperatives enabled Faubus to avoid the inflammatory public racism that led even many segregationist-minded Arkansans to shun extremists like Johnson, thereby casting Faubus in the familiar image of being comparatively moderate.

———

The Little Rock Crisis, September 1957

Public uncertainty pervaded Little Rock the day preceding the scheduled desegregation of Central High. Sanguine about the political imperatives impinging upon the governor yet confident that he was not, like the segregationist extremists, prone to violence and motivated by blatant racism, Bates remained cautious upon hearing a radio news announcement that Faubus would speak to Arkansas citizens that Monday evening, September 2. "Is there anything they can do," asked Jefferson Thomas, "now that they lost in court? Is there any way they can stop us from entering Central tomorrow morning?" Bates replied, "I don't think so." After carrying the primary responsibility for representing the black children in the litigation since 1956—right up to supporting the school board in seeking Davies's order reversing the chancery court injunction just days before in *Thomason*—Wiley Branton was hopeful that the Blossom plan would proceed without incident. Meanwhile, a few black students Blossom had authorized to enter Central remained unsure of whether attending segregated Horace Mann was the better option. Nevertheless, Minnijean Brown, Carlotta Walls, Gloria Ray, Elizabeth Eckford, Terrance Roberts, Thelma Mothershed, Ernest Green, Melba Pattillo, and Jefferson Thomas were certain that Central presented an extraordinary opportunity. Under Bates's guidance, these nine students were firmly committed to meeting the historic challenge that lay ahead.

As the hour for Faubus's address approached, Daisy and L. C. Bates learned that events were taking a dramatic turn. A local reporter informed them that "National Guardsmen are surrounding Central High." A hurried visit to Central confirmed the report, as did a radio newscast exclaiming that "no one is certain what this means." When Faubus finally appeared on three Little Rock television stations broadcast across Arkansas, he explained why he had dispatched the guard to Central. In his proclamation, Faubus reviewed the state's comparatively impressive progress on race relations in recent years, and reiterated his own moderation on race questions in conjunction with liberal economic policies. He insisted that until Governor Griffin spoke in Little Rock, its citizens countenanced desegregation out of a resigned respect for law. After the speech affirming Georgia's forceful maintenance of segregation, however, popular opinion in the capital changed, with a majority now doubtful that the Supreme Court *Brown* decision constitutionally bound the people of Arkansas. Moreover, Faubus declared, a majority of voters in Little Rock and across the state had endorsed the interposition measures in November 1956. The Arkansas legislature then implemented interposition in various statutes. These laws bound him as governor until the "proper authority" established their lawfulness.

Contemporary and later commentators focused upon Faubus's rationale for fearing potential violence. He had, he said, received reports of increased sales of weapons, threatening phone calls, especially those insisting that armed caravans were approaching Little Rock, and Superintendent Blossom's heated pleas for assistance. He also claimed that more blacks than whites had purchased weapons. Faubus mentioned, too, his own and Blossom's contradictory testimony given in the *Thomason* suit. Faubus blamed Blossom, the school board, and the federal courts for "forcing integration" on "the people" against their will as proclaimed through "time-honored principles of democracy" in the interposition measures passed in 1956 and 1957. Receiving less public attention were his assertions that Judge Davies's orders prevented a legal test of the interposition laws. As a result, "one of the greatest reasons for unrest and for the imminence of disorder and violence," Faubus declared, was public doubt about whether the Supreme Court desegregation decisions or the interposition laws were supreme. Until this uncertainty was resolved, state law bound him as governor. He would, therefore, preserve order by keeping black students from Central High and whites from black schools. Units of the Arkansas National Guard already were deployed around Central and Horace Mann to ensure order and, "for the time being," the schools "must be operated on the same basis as they have before."

The author of the proclamation was William J. Smith. The lawyer's expertise explained the legal dimensions of the proclamation, crafted in preparation for the inevitable challenges to be raised by LDF lawyers on behalf of the black students' constitutional rights claims, as well as those involving school board official duty. Faubus's basic argument linking fears of violence with his unproven claims that he possessed evidence demonstrating this danger paralleled closely the statements made to Caldwell in the private August 28 meeting and the *Thomason* case testimony the following day. The blame ascribed to school and federal authorities, including Judge Davies, repeated his public statements made on August 31 and September 1 that these people had unfairly forced upon state elected officials like himself responsibility that ran contrary to state law. As Arkansans had demonstrated in voting for interposition, a legitimate public question existed as to whether federal court decisions could supersede state law. The failure to test lawfully this issue of constitutional supremacy was a major reason for impending violence. This logic justified Faubus resorting to military force in the name of police powers until the legal uncertainty was resolved; it explained, too, why segregation would continue until a "proper authority" settled the question, as well as the seemingly incongruous presence of troops at both Central and Horace Mann.

The consequences of the legalistic political strategy embedded in the proclamation took hold immediately. Faubus's "words," exclaimed Daisy Bates later, "electrified Little Rock. By morning they shocked the United States. By noon the next day his message horrified the world." Indeed, not long after Faubus's image left television screens that Monday night, the school board held an emergency meeting from which it issued a public announcement "ask[ing] that no Negro students attempt to attend Central or any white high school until this dilemma is legally resolved." On September 3, following the direction of Bates and Branton, nine black students complied; several others decided they would attend Horace Mann. That morning, too, white students filed passed the guard into Central High without incident. School officials also asked Davies for guidance. Following the doctrine of "reasonableness" as defined by *Brown* II and affirmed in *Aaron v. Cooper*, Davies ordered the phase program to proceed "forthwith." Davies based his order in part on Mayor Mann's public statement that neither he nor the police were aware of evidence suggesting the sort of possible disorder Faubus claimed was imminent. Branton observed but did not participate in the proceedings. Still, he knew, the rule of *Brown* II was that constitutional rights claims were not to be denied merely because their enforcement encountered public opposition, however severe.

The following day, September 4, Faubus's proclamation precipitated a clash with the federal court. Joined by several ministers from black as well as white churches, Daisy Bates led the group of black students to Central; as a result of the governor's orders, the guard turned them away. By this point, a large crowd of whites hovered about the streets surrounding the school. Many news reporters also had arrived from across the nation. One black reporter was severely injured by white bystanders, and a white reporter was threatened with violence when someone from the crowd demanded to know if he was "a Jew." Elizabeth Eckford, however, experienced the most frightening and well-publicized incident of the morning. Because her residence did not have a phone, she did not make contact with the other black students. As she attempted to enter Central alone, the guard blocked her at several points, while people in the crowd yelled cruel racial epithets. A photographer caught a young white woman in the act, her face contorted in rage. Elizabeth reached a bus stop, where a white woman, Grace Lorch, both comforted her and appealed for sympathy from white mothers among the crowd. Finally, Elizabeth left on the bus. Overnight, the photograph of Elizabeth Eckford receiving the white girl's abuse amidst the leering crowd was transmitted around the world, arousing sympathy for the black young people's cause, denigrating the public image of Little Rock, and dramatizing the human consequences of Faubus's defiance of the federal court desegregation order.

On September 5, the school board and Branton appeared before Judge Davies. For the first time, school officials formally asked the court to delay enforcement of the Blossom plan. Branton emphasized, however, that under *Brown* II, the black students' rights should not be nullified solely because opposition arose. Davies upheld Branton's constitutional argument. On September 7, Davies formally rejected the school board request for a delay. He also asked the justice department to investigate the causes for disruption of the court order, in particular to determine whether there was any validity to Faubus's claims that violence had been or was imminent if desegregation should proceed. Confidentially, the FBI already had begun an investigation. With Davies's order, the investigation became official as numerous FBI agents engaged in hundreds of interviews and others pursued leads under disguised identities. Still, Davies indirectly revealed

Smith's effectiveness in framing the proclamation. Seeking to avoid a direct clash between state and federal enforcement authorities without unequivocal proof supporting the latter, Davies called for the FBI investigation in order to establish a factual basis for possible legal action against Faubus. Denied a delay in the desegregation order, school officials requested that federal marshals preserve order at Central, and the LDF urged protection of the black students' rights.

The unfolding confrontation between Faubus and the federal court received national and international media attention. Collectively identified as the Little Rock Nine, the black students became the public image of constitutional rights defied by state authority and threatened violence. School officials and the moderates supporting them, by contrast, described their good faith obedience to *Brown* as being sacrificed to Faubus's political ambitions. Faubus remained defiant. Responding to the federal intervention initiated by Davies, Faubus telegrammed President Eisenhower, declaring that his confrontation with the federal court involved neither integration nor segregation. Referring to his acceptance of school desegregation in northwestern Arkansas, Faubus claimed that the only true constitutional issue was whether a state governor — in the name of police powers — should prevent violence and maintain order. He then insisted that federal agents had tapped his phone and were preparing to arrest him. Eisenhower denied these accusations but also proclaimed a duty to enforce the Constitution. Faubus then noted that Little Rock aldermen had publicly supported his use of the guard. Through the good services of William J. Smith, he also offered to present "certain evidence" justifying his proclamation. Although no convincing evidence was forthcoming, the ploy heightened public expectations of the FBI findings in its ongoing investigation.

Following Davies's denial of the school board request for postponement, the lines between public and private became murkier. Eisenhower and Attorney General Brownell met in Washington, D.C., to discuss Little Rock. As long as Faubus ultimately complied with the court order, Eisenhower declared, he should be given the opportunity for an "orderly retreat." If the governor persisted in defiance, however, the administration would not "compromise" or "capitulate." The next day, an intermediary representing Faubus privately contacted the justice department asking for a meeting to address the crisis, but an exchange of views soon assured each side that an agreement was unlikely, whereupon discussion ceased. Meanwhile, Thurgood Marshall confidentially urged justice department intervention. However, Assistant U.S. Attorney Donald B. Maeguineas arrived in Little Rock from Washington, D.C., to seek privately from Branton an agreement suspending the nine students' admission to Central for a year's "cooling-off period." Little Rock U.S. Attorney Osro Cobb and unidentified "others" also confidentially urged Branton not to involve Marshall and the New York office in the case; these same people asked Branton to pursue Maeguineas's proposal.

Branton flatly rejected the covert initiatives urging him to suspend for a year the Little Rock Nine's constitutional right to attend Central. The deepening crisis led Branton to seek increased support from Marshall and the New York LDF staff. Marshall's and his colleagues' higher profile signaled, in turn, that the Little Rock NAACP was increasingly turning over control of the case to the New York headquarters of both the NAACP and the LDF. Marshall's growing role also explained federal government concern that, as Marshall reportedly told U.S. Attorney Cobb, the LDF was now "targeting" Little Rock as a test of the South's compliance with *Brown*. Since 1956, of course, the local NAACP by itself had mobilized the Little Rock black community. Although Marshall and the LDF staff had assisted Branton during this period, Branton had done the lion's share of the litigation work. Now that would change. As Branton continued to handle the increasingly complex legal tangle, Marshall's growing presence signaled the expanding influence of both national black organizations as long as Little Rock remained in the international spotlight. Moreover, federal officials' efforts to persuade Branton, essentially, to surrender to Faubus and the segregationist extremists revealed how much the Eisenhower administration endeavored to avoid involving itself in the defense of the Little Rock Nine's constitutional rights.

During the standoff, the NAACP headquarters' influence over the Little Rock branch increased. Daisy Bates was recognized as the nine students' representative by the young people themselves, their parents, the authorities, the city white and black communities, the segregationist extremists, and the media. Whites in and outside Little Rock were, however, unaware of how the Little Rock branch had on its own initiated and carried through the *Aaron v. Cooper* litigation.

Also, there was no public understanding of the distinction between the local NAACP and its New York headquarters on the one hand, and, on the other, the local LDF attorneys like Branton and the New York LDF staff headed by Marshall. Still, just as the prolonged crisis led Branton to rely more than ever on Marshall and his staff, the New York NAACP headquarters steadily asserted leadership over Bates and the local branch. Facing mounting harassment from the segregationists' boycott of white advertisers in the *State Press*, as well as from Attorney General Bennett and local tax authorities concerning the registration of membership lists and tax-exempt status, Daisy and L. C. Bates appealed to the NAACP New York headquarters for financial aid in order to keep their paper running. As the weeks of confrontation dragged on, headquarters equivocated, concerned about establishing a "bad precedent" other branches might follow when faced with trouble. Awaiting a decision on aid, the local NAACP became ever more dependent on New York.

Lee Lorch's branch membership became a growing bone of contention. Consistent with a long record of vital service to local NAACP branches in Little Rock and Nashville, Tennessee, Lorch instituted a tutorial program for the nine students in order to keep them abreast of Central High white students as the crisis dragged on. Several Central High teachers and others who were sympathetic to the nine's plight supplied the course materials upon which the tutorials were based. The tutorial program not only was vital for the students' own educational benefit as they waited to enter Central but also ensured that they were not behind white classmates amidst inevitable racial prejudices presuming white superiority. Moreover, Grace Lorch had come between Elizabeth Eckford and the looming crowd at the bus stop on September 4, assisting her escape from the traumatic experience. Nevertheless, unsubstantiated charges from U.S. House Un-American Committee investigators — resulting in acquittal in federal court — instilled an enduring image of the Lorches' radical affiliations. These intractable images jeopardized the nine students' aura of patriotic respectability, which the local as well as national NAACP cultivated in the era of anticommunism. Thus, despite the continuing support Lorch received from the local branch, the national leadership pressured him to resign.

Davies received the FBI report from U.S. Attorney Cobb on September 9. After studying the hundreds of pages of evidence — but keeping it confidential — Davies directed the justice department to file a petition for an injunction against Faubus. His order also declared that Faubus should comply at once with the desegregation decree. Davies set a hearing ten days hence to consider evidence governing Faubus's responsibility and culpability. The FBI report demonstrated that Faubus's claims of impending violence were "baseless." Davies later said he was "reluctant to believe that a governor of a State would deliberately and intentionally use troops to obstruct the orders of a Federal court." Moreover, Davies was "definitely of the view that the governor should be served with notice and afforded an opportunity to be heard before any injunction issued against him or his officers." Thus, Davies was "will[ing] to take Governor Faubus at his word that he would use the National Guard to preserve order. . . . I thought that a . . . chief executive of any state would know the difference between barring blacks from previously white schools by the use of force, and keeping the peace. The Governor apparently did not know the difference." The report also accentuated for Davies how much his presence as an outsider played into Faubus's hands, indicating that it would have been more politic to leave the unfolding confrontation to an Arkansas federal judge, either Miller or Harry J. Lemley.

The FBI report also revealed Judge Miller's contribution to the impending crisis. For the first time, Davies learned of Miller's confidential exchanges with school officials during August regarding a possible delay in enforcing the desegregation order, pending a court test of the interposition laws. "I did not have any idea of Judge Miller's involvement until reading the FBI report. I consider Judge Miller's actions, as set out in the report, if true, to be wholly inappropriate and unbecoming a federal judge," he later stated. In addition to the important problem of legal ethics Miller's clandestine conduct raised, the revelation reinforced how difficult was Davies's own situation. As a result of Miller's request to be removed from handling the *Aaron v. Cooper* order following the *Thomason* decision, Davies realized, the U.S. Eighth Circuit of Appeals chief judge, Archibald K. Gardner, had assigned Davies to Little Rock. Gardner's choice of Davies, a Republican appointee from North Dakota and a devout Catholic, created an inevitable clash with Arkansas Democratic politics, southern racial mores, and Protestant religious culture. Davies's appointment thus aided Faubus's demagoguery. Miller's actions strengthened Davies's conviction that Little Rock was being unfairly exploited. Nevertheless, the report strengthened Davies's already absolute resolve that, as long as he was the presiding judge, the momentous issues at stake in the crisis would be handled according to the strictest regard for law and the Constitution.

The press publicized Faubus accepting a summons for the September 20 hearing. In this photo opportunity and his subsequent actions, Faubus followed William J. Smith's well-considered advice. Faubus refused to withdraw the National Guard from Central. He argued that under the Supreme Court decision the standard for implementing the desegregation order was "all deliberate speed." Davies was now, however, mandating an immediate end to segregation. He declared further that Davies was ignoring states' rights by substituting his judgment for the governor's regarding potential disorder. In addition to Faubus's public criticism of Davies, Smith filed a petition stating that the governor of Arkansas challenged the federal court authority, raising doubts as to whether he would comply with a federal order. In light of the "defiance-compliance" strategy embedded in and ensuing from the September 2 proclamation, another interpretation of Faubus's public actions was that he perceived in the upcoming court hearing new opportunities for political and legal maneuvers. Over the days preceding the hearing, Faubus exploited these opportunities. In federal court, Faubus's lawyers called for Davies to withdraw from the case, claiming that the judge's call for the federal government to join the case aligned him with the federal government against the governor. The justice department filed a counterclaim demonstrating that precedent clearly supported Davies, who continued to preside.

Meanwhile, Arkansas congressmember Brooks Hays negotiated a highly publicized meeting between Faubus and Eisenhower at Newport, Rhode Island, on September 14. Based upon press reports of Faubus's apparent agreement with Eisenhower, Davies hoped that Faubus would perceive the "folly of his position, and in some manner respect the understanding" supposedly reached with Eisenhower. Like numerous other observers, however, Davies underestimated Faubus's political nerve. At the meeting with Eisenhower, Faubus did acknowledge a duty to comply with federal court orders, but nothing concrete resulted except heightened tensions and Hays mediating further private exchanges. Just two days prior to the hearing before Davies, justice department officials privately acknowledged they would not press for an injunction on September 20 if Faubus voluntarily removed the guard and allowed desegregation to proceed at Central. Faubus's position nonetheless was that he would retreat only if some way could be found that conveyed an impression that he was *not willingly* backing down. Hays suggested that Eisenhower federalize the National Guard, thus removing it from the governor's authority. Presidential adviser Sherman Adams disapproved of the idea, whereupon Faubus broke off negotiations.

Immediately before September 20, then, justice department officials' private initiatives suggested their approach to the court hearing in Little Rock. Maeguineas's and Cobb's rebuffed attempt to have Branton suspend the court desegregation order indicated that timely enforcement of the black young people's constitutional rights was not a top priority of the justice department. Alternatively, Faubus's refusal to comply with either the public agreement purportedly reached with Eisenhower in Newport or the terms considered in private negotiations convinced Brownell and his subordinates that the governor was merely a political opportunist and, therefore, quite untrustworthy. Expecting that Faubus would continue to resist federal authority even if he lost in court, Brownell ordered justice department lawyers to determine the governor's likely remaining maneuvers. They found that Faubus might comply with a court order (in which case the potential for disorder was uncertain), defy it by continuing to exclude black students, or close Central by executive order. Regardless of which course Faubus followed, the continued involvement of the justice department seemed likely. As a result, department officials recommended that an order from President Eisenhower committing U.S. military units to enforce the court order would best meet each contingency.

Recommending that Eisenhower order military intervention required the justice department to develop new legal and constitutional justifications. Prior to the Little Rock crisis, the federal government's strongest action on behalf of racial desegregation had been in Clinton, Tennessee, and Hoxie, Arkansas, where the justice department broke new ground by intervening in federal court proceedings in support of granting injunctive relief. Now, department lawyers prepared memoranda establishing legal and constitutional grounds for the president's deployment of regular military units and federalized National Guard where a state governor defied U.S. law and constitutional rights. The lawyers carefully rejected U.S. Code Section 331, which made the president's military intervention dependent on the state legislature's or governor's request. Two other provisions, Sections 332 and 333, granted the president greater discretion in order to address challenges "against the authority of the United States," or to suppress violence that interfered with the enforcement of federal law. In addition to displacing Section 331, these provisions also superseded another federal provision that prohibited the president from employing the U.S. Army as a "posse comitatus . . . for the purpose of executing" federal law. The lawyers argued that U.S. Code provisions provided an exception authorizing the president to "use such of the armed forces as he considers necessary to enforce . . . laws or to suppress . . . rebellion."

Remaining confidential, the justice department memoranda preparation coincided with the September 20 hearing. Branton and Marshall represented the nine black students; A. F. House was present on behalf of the school board. Thomas Harper, Kay Matthews, and Walter Pope were the counsel for Faubus and the National Guard commanders. The officers but not Faubus were in court. Their lawyers' brief denying federal court authority rested not only on state police power precedents and states' rights theories but also limits to federal executive power consistent with Section 331, the "posse comitatus" prohibition, and the Tenth Amendment. But instead of presenting such a case, the lawyers merely handed in the brief titled *Faubus v. United States*. Davies dismissed the submission and asked if there were "further preliminary motions." One of Faubus's lawyers then stood up. "The position of the respondent, Governor Faubus, and his military officers must be firm, unequivocal, unalterable," the lawyer declared. The governor "cannot and will not concede that the United States in this court or anywhere else can question his discretion and judgment as chief executive of a sovereign state when he acts in the performance of his constitutional duties under" Arkansas law and its constitution. The lawyers then asked to be "excused." Davies granted the request, whereupon Faubus's lawyers walked out of court before the hearing was formally under way. They soon appealed *Faubus v. United States*.

Faubus's failure to present a case left little doubt concerning the outcome of the hearing. Justice department lawyers' arguments only addressed whether a real potential for violence existed on or before September 3. The government relied upon eight witnesses, including Blossom, the police chief, and one of the Little Rock Nine; their testimony refuted Faubus's assertions that his actions were justified because violence was imminent if Central High desegregation proceeded. On this showing of evidence, Davies issued an injunction against Faubus. Even so, the federal government case did not emphasize Branton's and Marshall's fundamental constitutional argument that if Faubus resorted to police powers in the name of preventing violence, his only lawful course was to protect the constitutional rights of the black litigants by aiding the federal court in enforcing the court desegregation order.

More significantly, the government did not introduce into evidence the FBI report. Since the report demonstrated that Faubus's claims about impending violence were baseless, the federal decision not to use it was noteworthy. Indeed, after the hearing, Faubus repeatedly claimed that neither the testimony of people such as Blossom nor of the federal government itself persuasively refuted his own assertions of impending violence. The image Faubus fostered, accordingly, was that his conduct was lawful, whereas that of Judge Davies, school officials, and the federal government was suspicious. What explains the federal government choice? The question is vital, given that this action provided Faubus yet another opportunity for demagoguery. The justice department may have declined to introduce the FBI report as evidence because it revealed Judge Miller's ethically problematic involvement with school officials, which Faubus could have easily exploited. Nevertheless, the government neglected the opportunity to focus public as well as legal attention on the constitutional principle Branton and Marshall argued: under state and federal laws and constitutions, if Faubus indeed had reason to believe that disorder had been imminent, his constitutional duty was to protect the black students' constitutional rights and aid their enforcement by the federal court.

Another implicit rationale for declining to introduce the FBI report during the September 20 hearing may have involved the evolving perception of Eisenhower and the justice department concerning civil rights enforcement. The department use of the FBI evidence would have been consistent with a focus upon individual responsibility of all parties to a crisis that already had lasted for weeks. The evidence would have facilitated the sort of legal actions against individuals — especially a possible Hoxie-like injunction enjoining Little Rock segregationist rabble-rousers — school officials and the justice department itself had consistently refused to initiate. Moreover, Eisenhower's equivocation toward asserting enlarged federal jurisdiction to pursue such injunctive remedies had reinforced southern congressional success in defeating Title III in the Civil Rights Act of 1957. Eisenhower signed the weakened act on September 9, during the same period federal officials were engaged in private negotiations with Faubus. The governor's subsequent political maneuvers, especially the Newport debacle, may have strengthened Eisenhower's conviction that involvement in civil rights enforcement should occur primarily in cases of an express challenge to the president's obligation to enforce federal court orders under the separation of powers.

The views of Eisenhower and the justice department about enforcement did indeed change. Before Faubus clashed with the federal court, the justice department enforcement obligation remained within the narrow limits Caldwell had described in the private meeting with the governor on August 28. As noted above, Davies ordered the justice department to enter the case as amicus curiae (friend of the court). Now, the justice department was aligned with the plaintiffs, whereas Faubus became a codefendant with the school board. Faubus's lawyers challenged the order. On September 19, they petitioned Davies to remove himself from the case. He denied their petition. The mounting crisis thus increasingly focused public attention on federal government duty — including, ultimately, the president's — to enforce the court desegregation order. Accordingly, the justice department developed a stronger rationale for federal intervention. Prior to the September 20 hearing, justice department lawyers had prepared the memoranda establishing legal and constitutional grounds for executive military action should Eisenhower decide to employ it. As recently as July 17, 1957, Eisenhower told reporters, "I can't imagine any set of circumstances that would ever induce me to send Federal troops . . . into any area to enforce the orders of a Federal court." Faubus's defiance thus forced upon Eisenhower and the justice department the realization that the possibility so easily denied some months before was becoming ever more likely.

Reinforcing the president's preference for a stronger exercise of executive powers was the harm Faubus's defiance did to the international image of the United States. Not only did the international news media give Little Rock enormous attention during the weeks of the unfolding crisis, but it expressed sympathy for the black students and the NAACP and generally condemned Faubus, Arkansas, and the South. Throughout this period, too, the president's responsibility for enforcing civil rights received growing attention. The *Times of India* announced in a front-page story on September 6, for instance, "Armed Men Cordon off White School: Racial Desegregation in Arkansas Prevented." The next day the *East African Standard* carried a lead story titled, "Eisenhower Intervenes as School Bars Negroes." The latter reference was to the public commencement of the FBI investigation following Judge Davies's order. In addition, a September 9 letter written by John H. Morsell, executive secretary of the NAACP, replying to an Australian resident for Roy Wilkins, affirmed that "letters of protest such as yours and expressions of the kind you describe are all of great value in making it clear to people over here [in the United States] that the eyes of the world are upon them. I have no doubt that the nature of world opinion played a great part in bringing the President to his decision."

The attention the international media gave the crisis persisted. On September 13, the *Egyptian Gazette* reported, "Dr. Ralph Bunch, Negro undersecretary of the United Nations, said that violence surrounding school integration in the south 'is bound to have a harmful effect on international opinion. Photographs of jeering crowds and armed National Guardsmen stopping young boys and girls from entering schools are hardly good public relations.'" The same newspaper reported U.S. officials stating in London that "they expected Communist spokesman [*sic*] to try to gain a propaganda victory out of the violence connected with the integration in South [*sic*] schools." Such views conflated Faubus's focus upon potential violence with the psychological pain the nine black students experienced facing both the National Guard and the antagonistic white crowd on September 4. Elizabeth Eckford's frightening encounter accentuated this image. The *London Times* on September 4 expressed doubt concerning Eisenhower's stance, noting that "questions about the action taken by the state government in Arkansas brought forth from the President only a restatement of the axioms on which he has based his own 'gradual-ist' approach to the problem."

These international news reports of the Little Rock crisis coincided with massive U.S. media coverage, influencing the perceptions of Eisenhower and the justice department regarding their enforcement responsibilities. On September 9, for example, the *London Times* con-sidered Faubus's motivations, stating that the "personality and the political ambitions of Mr. Faubus are said to provide some explana-tion of his actions. There are observers who believe him to be han-kering for extremist support to elect him for a third term next year." Meanwhile, U.S. newspapers, magazines, television, and radio gave the weeks of confrontation more extended coverage than any previ-ous civil rights story since the Supreme Court *Brown* decision of 1954. Like war and national disasters, moreover, Little Rock provided many print and electronic news reporters their first major opportunity to witness directly a dramatic civil rights confrontation. Undoubtedly, a principal reason for this extended media attention was that Faubus's actions elevated the more clear-cut image of the clash between the U.S. president and the state governor over the legal technicalities and constitutional principles identified with representing the Little Rock Nine in court. Such international and domestic media scrutiny thus encouraged Eisenhower's and justice department officials' changed views toward civil rights enforcement, though the justice department memoranda supporting the use of military force were still considered confidential contingency plans by September 20.

These public and private imperatives provided the context for Davies's decision to issue the injunction against Faubus on Septem-ber 21. The third decision styled *Aaron v. Cooper* since 1956, Davies's order reflected the dramatic change Faubus's defiance had wrought. The earlier decisions upheld the Little Rock School Board token desegregation plan over the challenge from black students, the local NAACP, and LDF lawyers that it was too gradual and limited. Still, the black litigants were clearly at the center of the case. Now, the issues Faubus raised during the weeks of crisis subordinated the black litigants' rights claims to the images of the constitutional clash between federal and state authorities. Highlighting the shift, the jus-tice department and the black plaintiffs each sought an injunction against Faubus and the military commanders. Formally, the school board remained a defendant, though Faubus's actions had disrupted its "good faith" efforts to comply with repeated federal court orders, including its rejected request for a stay on September 7. Davies's decision stated succinctly the sequence of events beginning with school officials' announced desegregation plan in 1955, through the black plaintiffs' challenges and the court decisions upholding it, to the chain of defiance Faubus's proclamation initiated since September 2, impeding federal court enforcement of the black students' rights.

Davies based his order on findings of fact and conclusions of law. Most of the decision set out the facts upon which the two previous federal courts had relied to uphold the school officials' good faith efforts at desegregation, and how Faubus's actions frustrated those efforts as well as federal enforcement of the black plaintiffs' rights. These facts revealed no evidence supporting Faubus's claims that violence was imminent had the black students entered Central on September 3. Faubus and the National Guard, therefore, obstructed "this court's orders . . . contrary to the due and proper administration of justice," and, as a result of these actions, the "minor plaintiffs" and other eligible "Negro students . . . have suffered immediate and irreparable injury." Davies issued the injunction "in order to protect and preserve the judicial process . . . to maintain the due and proper administration of justice, and to protect the constitutional rights of the . . . plaintiffs and other eligible Negro students." In the "conclusions of law," Davies rejected the contention that state police powers superseded federal court jurisdiction. Although the governor possessed discretion "to determine whether an exigency requiring military state aid . . . has arisen," the "proper use of that power in this instance was to maintain" the federal court's "exercise of its jurisdiction . . . not to nullify it, to remove, and not create, obstructions to the exercise by the Negro children of their rights as judicially declared."

What would Faubus do now?

Crisis Denouement: Contested Images

Thus, during the weekend before Monday, September 23, Davies issued a temporary injunction against Faubus, his military officers, and their subordinates, making illegal any obstruction of the Little Rock desegregation plan. Three hours later Faubus ordered the National Guard withdrawn. He then departed for a conference in Georgia, declaring that his "crucifixion" would soon begin. After three weeks of crisis, Faubus intensified the anxious uncertainty in Little Rock and Washington, D.C., as well as in the state, nation, and around the world, regarding what the Little Rock Nine might encounter at Central High on Monday. Comparatively unnoticed, however, was the fact that Faubus's retreat not only avoided contempt of court proceedings but also followed repeated acknowledgments of his obligation to obey "final" federal court orders. Moreover, it was consistent with the "defiance-compliance" strategy embedded in the September 2 proclamation, which reflected the clandestine maneuvers of August. Also over the weekend, school officials asked Davies for federal marshals to support city police; it was, Davies said, a matter for U.S. Attorney Cobb to decide. Cobb, in turn, explained that he required "specific authority from the Department of Justice to seek an order from the federal judge for United States Marshals' . . . help in protecting the Negro students." But Cobb "did not get the authority from the department," perhaps because local police stated that state troopers were available upon request from city officials.

On the morning of September 23, more than one hundred city and state police officers faced a growing crowd numbering about one thousand. In compliance with the federal court order, the police attempted to enforce the Little Rock Nine's right to attend a racially desegregated Central High. The school opening bell at 8:30 A.M. galvanized the crowd into attacking four black news reporters in front of Central. At the same time, the nine entered the school through a side door. Outside the school, the crowd steadily overwhelmed the police. Confusion mounted inside Central. A white female student sent out false reports of bloodshed, and some white students protested by leaving class. Nevertheless, amidst the growing turmoil that morning the great majority of white students were noncommittal and a few even welcoming as the nine black students attended class throughout the castle-like school. The nine, in turn, were both hopeful and anxious. Even so, the basic images reported locally and regionally on the radio, as well as those captured in news photos and film for later publication and broadcast, conveyed chaotic mob action, with sporadic violence directed at police, reporters, and other individuals, white and black.

Covertly, federal agents also witnessed and filmed the disorder, ensuring identification of particular rioters should federal prosecution be initiated. As noon approached, school and police officials agreed that the nine should leave the school and go home. Thus ended the first phase of the "battle of Central High."

During the afternoon Eisenhower responded, and certain people in Little Rock pursued private contacts with presidential assistant Maxwell Rabb. From Newport, Rhode Island, the president issued a proclamation addressing the "Obstruction of Justice in the State of Arkansas." In the city of Little Rock, the proclamation stated, "certain persons . . . individually and in unlawful assemblages, combinations, and conspiracies, have willfully obstructed the enforcement of orders" of the federal district court "with respect to matters relating to enrolment and attendance at public schools, particularly at Central High School." Moreover, such defiance of "justice constitutes a denial of the equal protection of the laws secured by the Constitution of the United States, and impedes the course of justice under those laws." Under the authority conferred by the U.S. Constitution, and U.S. Code Sections 332, 333, and 334, therefore, the president "command[ed] all persons engaged in such obstruction of justice to cease and desist therefrom, and to disperse forthwith." Meanwhile, private contacts of "mutual friends" in Little Rock resulted in Mayor Mann discussing privately the state of desegregation with Rabb. Mann called for the dispatch of regular military forces as well as the president's federalization of the National Guard in order to end Faubus's control. In Little Rock only former governor Sidney McMath, U.S. Representative Hays, U.S. Attorney Cobb, *Arkansas Gazette* editor Harry Ashmore, and Superintendent Blossom knew about these contacts.

From Monday evening through the morning of September 24, tension mounted in Little Rock amidst close scrutiny from federal officials and the media. The Little Rock Nine went home to families and black neighbors who felt the ominous, abiding danger of white violence. From black neighborhoods came sporadic reports of whites driving by homes, yelling racial epithets, and throwing rocks and bottles. Daisy Bates remembered a phone call at 2:30 A.M., a man's voice declaring, "We didn't get you last night, but we will. And you better not try to put those coons in our school!" In Washington, D.C., Attorney General Brownell, supported by Solicitor General Lee Rankin

and others within the justice department, urged Eisenhower to prepare to order regular military units and federalization of the Arkansas
National Guard, based on the constitutional authority and U.S Code
provisions affirmed in the presidential proclamation. Brownell proceeded with the support of Secretary of State Dulles, who was atten-
tive to the propaganda consequences resulting from the media reports
of events unfolding in Little Rock. No decision was forthcoming on
the president's course of action, Mann learned in a call to Rabb at 5:30
A.M. Tuesday morning. At the governors' conference in Georgia,
Faubus pondered his political and legal position, and extreme segregationists like Johnson expected that the logical course of events
included further violence.

On Tuesday morning, at Mann's request, the *Arkansas Gazette* published a statement that the black students should not return that day
to Central. The nine remained at home. A taunting, jeering crowd of
whites numbering some five hundred nonetheless attempted to over-
whelm police stationed outside the school. After 8:00 A.M., Mann
made two calls to Rabb, exclaiming that the crowd had ignored the
president's proclamation and stronger action was essential. During the
second call, Rabb told Mann to draft a telegram formally asking the
president to send in federal troops, pending a decision in Washington, D.C., favoring such action. Rabb did not state that, as a contingency plan, an executive order already had been prepared a week
earlier, when Brownell in consultation with General Maxwell Taylor
of the Joint Chiefs of Staff and others agreed that only regular troops
could adequately enforce the black students' rights in the face of
violence. Brownell and Taylor reached this decision because they
doubted the loyalty of a federalized Arkansas National Guard and
considered deputization of large numbers of U.S. marshals "imprac-
tical." These actions drew upon the authority developed in memoranda justice department lawyers had prepared prior to the September
20 hearing before Judge Davies. At 9:00 A.M., Rabb discussed over the
phone with Mann the telegram; following some approved changes
Mann sent it to the president fifteen minutes later. The president
issued Executive Order 10730 at 10:22 A.M.; 101st Airborne units were
already on their way.

The executive order brought to bear the impressive force of federal authority. During the night of September 24, 1,000 troops from

the 101st Airborne "Screaming Eagle" Division began arriving at a base near Little Rock; they went to the city by truck and soon were deployed around Central High. Preparations also were made to have the nine students transported to school on Wednesday morning, escorted by paratroopers. The 10,000 members of the Arkansas National Guard now knew they were formally under President Eisenhower's direct command. Faubus rushed back from Georgia, expressing surprise at the U.S. Army presence in the Arkansas capital. Referring to U.S. Code Section 331, he asserted that federal troops could be dispatched "whenever there is an insurrection in any state against its government" only if the governor or legislature asked for such action. He did not mention, of course, U.S. Code Sections 332, 333, and 334, which justice department lawyers had provided for the president's use expressly in order to avoid Section 331. By contrast, Branton's first thought upon hearing the news of Eisenhower's order was, "Wow! What have I started. I had never felt so proud of my country . . . as I did on the day when troops moved into Little Rock to protect the right of nine black children to go to Central High School," he recalled years later. Meanwhile, members of the crowd who previously had gathered before Central prepared to do so again on Wednesday morning; newspeople did too.

Eisenhower offered reasons for the executive order in an address delivered Tuesday evening. He described Little Rock as a city "under the leadership of demagogic extremists," where "disorderly mobs have deliberately prevented the carrying out of proper orders from a federal court." Because "local authorities have not eliminated that violent opposition . . . under law, I yesterday issued a proclamation calling upon the mob to disperse." But "this morning the mob again gathered in front of Central High School . . . obviously for the purpose of again preventing the carrying out of the court's order relating to the admission of Negro children to that school." Eisenhower then explained that "whenever" the failure of "normal agencies," made it "necessary for the executive branch of the federal government to use its powers and authority to uphold federal courts, the President's responsibility is inescapable." Therefore, "I have today issued an Executive Order directing the use of troops under federal authority to aid in the execution of federal law." It was "important," Eisenhower declared, "that the reason for my action be understood by all our citizens." He then stated how the Supreme Court holding that "compulsory segregation laws are unconstitutional" in *Brown* was followed on the basis of "gradual progress" in certain "southern states," showing the "world that we are a nation in which laws, not men, are supreme." But in Little Rock, "I regret to say . . . this truth — the cornerstone of our liberties — was not observed."

Eisenhower did not stress the principles of equality established in *Brown*. Instead, he explained his motivations in terms of the constitutional duty to enforce federal court orders in the face of defiance, and the consequences — at home and abroad — resulting from the failure to do so. Following the several *Aaron v. Cooper* decisions, Eisenhower emphasized school officials' "good faith" efforts to develop and implement a limited desegregation plan. "Certain misguided persons, many of them imported into Little Rock by agitators," nonetheless "have insisted upon defying the law and have sought to bring it into disrepute. The orders of the court have thus been frustrated." All U.S. citizens' "individual rights and freedoms rest[ed] upon the certainty that the President and the Executive Branch of Government will . . . insure the carrying out of the decisions of the federal courts. . . . Mob rule cannot be allowed to override the decisions of our courts." The presence of "federal troops" did not "relieve local and state authorities of their primary duty to preserve the peace and order of the community." Even so, the "proper use of the powers of the Executive Branch to enforce the orders of a federal court is limited to extraordinary and compelling circumstances. Manifestly, such an extreme situation has been created in Little Rock." The "overwhelming majority of our people," in the "South, as elsewhere," are "united in their respect for observance of the law — even in those cases where they may disagree with that law."

Finally, Eisenhower pointedly described the cold war danger the defiance of law unleashed in Little Rock. "We face grave situations abroad because of the hatred that communism bears toward a system of government based on human rights," he said. Thus, "it would be difficult to exaggerate the harm that is being done to the prestige and influence, and indeed to the safety, of our nation and the world." Moreover, he warned, "Our enemies are gloating over this incident and using it everywhere to misrepresent our whole nation. We are portrayed as a violator of those standards of conduct which the peoples of the world united to proclaim in the Charter of the United Nations," where "they affirmed 'faith in fundamental human rights' and 'in the dignity and worth of the human person' and they did so 'without distinction as to race, sex, language, or religion.' " Finally, he said, "If resistance to the federal court orders ceases at once, the further presence of federal troops will be unnecessary." In Little Rock will prevail once again "normal habits of peace and order and a blot upon the fair name and high honor of our nation in the world will be removed." This would, in turn, "restor[e] the image of America and all its parts as one nation, indivisible, with liberty and justice for all."

The president's order projected powerful images. On Wednesday morning, September 25, a column of army vehicles rolled up to the Bates's home, where the nine students and their parents waited. When an army officer appeared at the door, Minnijean Brown said, "For the first time in my life, I feel like an American citizen." The officer said, in turn, "Mrs. Bates, we're ready for the children. We will return them to your home at three thirty o'clock." Accompanied by armed jeeps, army station wagons carried the students to Central High. Amidst paratroopers stationed around the school grounds, soldiers escorted the nine up the main stairway into the building. Meanwhile, inside the school auditorium the operation commander, Major General Edwin A. Walker, assured students that as long as the school board plan proceeded without obstruction, his troops would not interfere with the "peaceful pursuit" of education. Witnessed by an alert media outside the school, a milling crowd refused an officer's order to disperse. The crowd did not comply until it confronted an advancing unit of paratroopers with lowered, bayoneted rifles. Reporters, television camera crews, and photographers sent words and pictures across the South, the nation, and around the world. Daisy Bates later wrote, "that the nine pupils, protected by the might of the United States military, had finally entered the 'never never land.' " Returning to the Bates's home that afternoon, Ernest Green was grateful for the troops, but said, "I'm only sorry it had to be that way."

As dramatic events unfolded in Little Rock, August to September, the clash between federal and state authorities obscured the black students' constitutional rights. The growing confrontation pitted Faubus and state officials against Eisenhower's repeatedly affirmed constitutional responsibility to enforce federal court orders. The clash reflected the contentious principles established in *Brown* II, as applied in *Aaron v. Cooper.* The flexible remedies and limited desegregation those decisions sanctioned fostered the private maneuvers school officials, Judge Miller, Governor Faubus, and ultimately President Eisenhower pursued. They undertook these private initiatives in order to avoid responsibility for addressing the threatened and real racial violence segregationist extremists perpetrated in the name of states' rights and interposition. Faubus proved most adept at exploiting the unsettled parameters of federal-state constitutional obligations. Finally, Eisenhower responded with overwhelming military force. The public image such power created, however, was that its use was exceptional, arising from state officials' and outside agitators' willful defiance. Thus, formally refusing to embrace *Brown* I, Eisenhower deployed military force solely out of a constitutional duty to enforce federal court orders amidst the propaganda battle with communism. These rationales reinforced the local NAACP delegation of control to New York headquarters; they ensured, too, that the black students would secure their rights only through continued struggle.

CHAPTER 4

Cooper v. Aaron
Delay Won and Appealed, 1957–1958

From late September 1957 through spring 1958, the Little Rock Nine
achieved academic success at Central High despite relentless harassment from a group of white students. The school board asked the federal court to "suspend" the desegregation plan for two-and-one-half
years. Arkansas federal district judge Harry J. Lemley granted the delay
in June. LDF lawyers won, however, an extraordinarily expedited
review, first by the U.S. Court of Appeals and then by the Supreme
Court, which heard the case in an August special term. The Little
Rock Nine's struggle against relentless intimidation, school officials'
retreat from their own desegregation plan, and the unusual judicial
proceedings that followed occurred as Faubus adopted the extreme
segregationists' policies favoring privatization of public education in
pursuit of a third-term gubernatorial election victory. The threat of
segregationist-inspired violence hung over the city. Meanwhile, the
Eisenhower administration withdrew from Little Rock, refusing to
prosecute identified rabble-rousers, even as it faced cold war conflicts
abroad. In Congress the conservative coalition of Democrats and
Republicans pushed anti-Court legislation. The U.S. and international
media scrutinized unfolding events, heightening attention from August
25 to September 11 to the LDF, school board, and federal government
arguments in *Cooper v. Aaron*. Again, a clash over federal-state
supremacy subsumed the Little Rock Nine's constitutional rights.

[handwritten margin notes: June 1958; 6/21/5?]

The Little Rock Nine's Precarious Triumph

The nine students' historic entry into Central High on September 25,
1957, ended one struggle and began another. After the 101st Airborne
escorted the students up the stairway, the paratroopers eventually

withdrew, leaving the federalized National Guard in charge of daily patrolling the school hallways and grounds. The black students and their parents, as well as Daisy Bates, chief spokesperson and public advocate for the group, soon learned that the federalized guard usually did not intervene to stem the steady harassment fomented by certain aggressive white students, several of whom had direct connections with extreme segregationists. Well-publicized incidents periodically occurred. A few white students attempted a more conciliatory approach; but most of them remained as uninvolved as possible. Teachers and administrators generally conducted themselves professionally. Despite these ever-present tensions, the nine students seized the improved educational opportunities Central High provided. Still, on February 20, 1958, school officials decided to request from the federal court a delay in implementing the desegregation plan. They did so amidst Faubus's increasingly aggressive states' rights stance demanding privatized funding of racially segregated schools, though he did not descend to the racial crudities many segregationists readily exclaimed. Moreover, Faubus and the city segregationist leaders joined others across the South and the nation evoking images of communist conspiracy behind the "federal occupation."

The Eisenhower administration resolution of the Little Rock crisis linked desegregation to enduring images of U.S. military enforcement. In the North, Eisenhower's intervention received broad approval; across the South, however, the reverse was true. It was southern public opinion that controlled both the Little Rock Nine's and school officials' immediate fate. The Trendex organization publicized national telephone surveys on September 25. Of 1,000 respondents during the previous evening, 68.4 percent favored Eisenhower ordering U.S. Army units to Little Rock. Removing southern respondents, the positive supporters rose to 77.5 percent. In the South alone, the surveys revealed, 62.6 percent opposed Eisenhower's order; just 33.9 percent supported it and 3.5 percent had no opinion. A Gallup poll of national opinion gave Eisenhower's actions almost two-thirds support, whereas 53 percent of southerners opposed them. The president's broad support among a majority of Americans was consistent with his firmly expressed executive duty to enforce federal court orders, especially in light of the harm Arkansas officials' defiance did national security in the propaganda battle against communist enemies.

Thus, national opinion data suggested that preserving the black students' constitutional rights was a necessary condition for maintaining the transcendent principle of federal supremacy over demagogic state and local defiance. But southerners associated the Little Rock occupation with communist authoritarianism.

Local opposition amidst national support facilitated the NAACP New York headquarters' mounting influence in Little Rock. At the end of September the NAACP leadership responded to Daisy Bates's letter sent during the crisis, requesting financial aid in order to keep publishing the *Arkansas State Press*. Confronting an ongoing boycott, harassment from state "revenue boys" led by an "anti-Negro [man] from Louisiana" who had become head of the local tax office, and the "Faubus trouble," the paper faced imminent closure. The leadership agreed to "grant enough cash . . . limited to the immediate future. It is a bad precedent, and there are some delicate ethical and perhaps even legal questions involved in such a request, since Mrs. Bates is as of now a member of the [national] Board. But her paper is so obviously on the firing line that we cannot let it go under from economic pressures of our and its opponents." In addition, the continuous telephone contact between the Little Rock branch and headquarters established during the crisis continued in support of the nine after they entered Central. The regular phone calls, funded by national sources, reinforced the growing role of Clarence Laws, sent by the national office as the new field secretary. He actively assisted Daisy and L. C. Bates, Reverend Crenchaw, and other longtime members of the local executive board. National and local policy converged, committed to maintaining the nine young people's welfare as well as cooperation with the media, federal officials, and numerous visitors.

Professor Lee Lorch's affiliation with the NAACP was a casualty of the national office takeover in Little Rock. An internationally recognized mathematics professor at Philander Smith College, Lorch and his wife Grace had rendered invaluable assistance to promotion of racial justice in Little Rock since the beginning of the desegregation suit. The tutorial program Lorch established for the nine students during the crisis enabled them to do well when they finally entered Central. The Lorches' home was the object of an unsuccessful dynamite attempt, and their thirteen-year-old daughter, attending the Little Rock middle school, suffered cruel intimidation. But notwithstanding his acquittal in federal court regarding charges of communist affiliation, Lorch's identification with radicalism received publicity. Grace also came under suspicion and public attack. Concerned about preserving the NAACP image of patriotism and staunch anticommunism, Laws acted. Noting Lorch's "unauthorized" calls to city council members concerning their criticism of the NAACP, Laws wrote him a letter "to make a number of things crystal clear." He declared that desegregation in Little Rock "could be done irreparable harm by the injection of extraneous issues." Laws then stated that the "best contribution" Lorch "could make to the cause of full citizenship for Negroes in Arkansas . . . would be to terminate, in writing," his affiliation with the Little Rock NAACP branch. By summer 1958, the Lorch family had moved to Canada.

The nine students were indeed at the center of ambivalent public images. An October 4, 1957, letter signed by Eisenhower, addressed to Thelma's father, A. L. Mothershed, suggested how positively the administration viewed the students' courage and the powerful issues it symbolized. Responding to a telegram signed by Mothershed and "other parents" of the Little Rock Nine, Eisenhower noted the Supreme Court declaration of the "supreme law of our land." Under the Constitution, "my solemn oath as President . . . imposes upon me the responsibility to see that the laws of our country are faithfully executed . . . in the interest of all Americans today, as well as to preserve our free institutions of government for the sake of the Americans yet unborn." Eisenhower concluded: "I believe that America's great heart goes out to you and your children in your present ordeal. In the course of our country's progress toward equality of opportunity, you have shown dignity and courage in circumstances which would daunt citizens of lesser faith." By contrast, former Little Rock Mothers' League president Nadine Aaron, a Canadian journalist reported sometime later, "was genuinely convinced that allowing Negroes into white schools would promote widespread miscegenation . . . and she was convinced that if the federal government persisted in forcing the integration of the schools, it would lead to bloodshed."

By December 1957, the pattern of desegregation and what it cost the Little Rock Nine was clear. After the paratroopers withdrew, the federalized National Guard inaction countenanced by General Walker fostered increased white student harassment of them. Terrance

Roberts, Jefferson Thomas, Minnijean Brown, and Melba Pattillo received well-publicized attacks, including Minnijean's reaction to two boys' intimidation by dumping a bowl of chili on their heads. After further provoked incidents, Central administrators expelled Minnijean for the remainder of the school year. Assisted by NAACP headquarters and prominent black psychologist Kenneth B. Clark, Minnijean attended New Lincoln High School in New York on scholarship. Laws condemned Central officials for "a shocking and cruel miscarriage of justice." The segregationist-minded students displayed their approval, sporting badges, "One down and eight to go." Those eight students nonetheless persevered. In 1958, Gloria Ray became the first black student to win top prize in the Arkansas science fair. The class honor roll included Carlotta Walls. Ernest Green, the group's one senior, was the first black graduated from Central High, an event witnessed on May 25, 1958, by a racially integrated assembly, including Martin Luther King, Jr. Nevertheless, Laws reported, "all these harassments against the children in the school is part of a plan to show that neither whites nor the Negroes are ready for school integration."

Laws gave Roy Wilkins of the national NAACP a more comprehensive report. He ascribed the nine students' "unresolved situation" to various factors. U.S. Attorney Cobb sought authorization from the justice department to prosecute several individuals who, evidence demonstrated, had perpetrated violence. Cobb's superiors did not, however, authorize the prosecutions. A local municipal judge also dismissed charges against or suspended sentences of "mob leaders." This public environment countenancing violence exacerbated school administrators' failure to enforce a strict policy against white students harassing the "Negroes at Central." Faubus's and segregationists' "false and inflammatory utterances" about interracial contacts inside Central, behavior of troops in the school following the crisis, and conspiracies attributed to school officials and federal government authorities continually aroused tensions. In addition, according to Laws, Little Rock "so-called responsible citizens" maintained "silence" regarding the "legal and moral aspects of desegregation." Finally, Laws observed, the segregationists shared the "apparent feeling" that the "students will withdraw voluntarily if enough pressure is exerted upon them." Notwithstanding how difficult were the problems, Laws concluded, a local "ministerial group" had joined forces with the NAACP, encouraging "confidence" that "we'll be in better position" in the spring semester.

The Eisenhower administration withdrawal from Little Rock expressed mixed motivations. The poll survey data undoubtedly convinced the White House that, despite vigorous criticism from southerners generally within and outside Congress, as well as right-wing groups across the nation, most U.S. voters accepted Eisenhower's two rationales for military action in Little Rock: the duty to enforce federal court orders and the link to cold war security concerns. Indirectly, these rationales subordinated black rights claims to the issue of federal supremacy; they also presumed that federal intervention in school desegregation cases would be exceptional. The U.S. Department of State confirmed that government leaders and the media in western Europe, Asia, and much of Africa approved of the president's strong action in Little Rock on September 24, compared to his previous indecisiveness about civil rights issues. Thus, as the Soviet *Sputnik* triumph displaced Little Rock as front-page news, Eisenhower's use of the 101st Airborne seemed to have been a propaganda triumph. Indeed, state department officials informed the White House, many foreign diplomats interpreted the president's military deployment in Little Rock as an effective propaganda ploy. Such views reinforced the administration's presumption that its intervention in racial desegregation cases should be exceptional.

The justice department failure to prosecute "mob leaders" confirmed this limited view. Although the justice department rejected Cobb's efforts to initiate eight such prosecutions, one department civil rights lawyer, St. John Barrett, supported the litigation. After visiting Little Rock, he reported to his superiors that local officials were "entitled to support from the Government. Any feeling on their part or on the part of other elements in the community that they were not receiving such support could very well abate their efforts to comply with the court's order." Inaction, Barrett further suggested, "might encourage persons . . . to interfere with" court-ordered desegregation. J. Edgar Hoover, however, resisted employing the FBI in all but exceptional civil rights cases, perhaps because he was unwilling to jeopardize federal agents' informal connections with southern local police, especially regarding probes of reported communist involvement in civil rights activism. *Arkansas Gazette* editor in chief Harry Ashmore offered another view. Following the crisis, Eisenhower appointed William Rogers as attorney general after Brownell resigned. Rogers sailed through the Senate Judiciary Committee confirmation hearings, Ashmore observed, "without a single question being addressed regarding his past or future course in the Little Rock case." Was Rogers's easy confirmation, Ashmore queried, a tradeoff for the federal government retreat from Little Rock, "one of the most singular political deals in recent years?"

The rabble-rousers' impunity converged with Faubus's demagoguery. In the wake of the crisis some southern governors formed a committee to mediate between Faubus and the White House amidst mounting southern and right-wing criticism of the federal military presence in Little Rock. The committee's active members were widely recognized moderates: Luther H. Hodges of North Carolina, Theodore R. McKeldin of Maryland, Frank Clement of Tennessee, and Leroy Collins of Florida. The White House agreed to withdraw federal forces as soon as Faubus formally accepted responsibility for preserving order. Initially, a negotiated statement received each side's endorsement. As he had in the Newport episode, however, Faubus exploited the mediation effort for political gain. Prior to publication, Faubus reviewed and returned the statement to the governors; they realized he had inserted the words "by me," suggesting only that although he himself agreed not to interfere with the enforcement of federal court orders, he refused to prevent such unlawful action by "others." Governor McKeldin condemned what he believed to be Faubus's bad faith. Faubus was "no more opposed to interracial use of public school facilities," he declared, than were the committee's moderate governors. "The difference is that Governor Collins, Hodges, and Clement," as well as himself, "believe in constituted governments of law," but "Governor Faubus prefers the demagogue's dangerous and destructive appeal to the emotions of the mob."

Such criticism underestimated Faubus's political maneuvering. Although media reports focused on his aggressive claims of federal and Little Rock School Board involvement in conspiracies — including the failure to publish the FBI report — as well as the looming force of military occupation, Faubus also ascribed special meaning to the role of federal courts. In a *U.S. News & World Report* interview in June

1958, amidst his primary campaign, Faubus contradicted an earlier statement that federal law superseded state law; his interpretation of the *Thomason* case and surrounding events also contradicted the secret actions of August. When asked, however, why he had not followed established police power precedent whereby chief executives had a duty to employ force to preserve, not deny, constitutional rights when violence threatened order, Faubus's reply was expressly political. He answered the interviewer that by following such precedent the "people would have been enemies of the Guard, and enemies of mine, because we would have been forcing them to do something which they don't want to do, and which it isn't our responsibility to do. If it's a federal order . . . let the federal agents enforce it." Elsewhere in the interview, he insisted, "it isn't the duty of State authorities to enforce federal laws or federal orders. That's the duty of federal agents."

Thus, Faubus sought to shift responsibility for enforcing desegregation to federal officials. Faubus, his lawyer stated, always complied with federal court orders directed against him. Failure to do so, of course, meant contempt of court proceedings and likely criminal penalties. More significantly, however, Faubus *used* this obligation to pursue an electoral strategy. After the private negotiations in August demonstrated that he could no longer avoid the desegregation issue by asserting it to be a matter of local control, Faubus compelled federal enforcement, leading most dramatically to Eisenhower administration intervention, resulting from the violence engendered by Faubus's compliance with Davies's order published on September 21. Similarly, on April 28, 1958, in *Faubus v. United States*, the U.S. Eighth Circuit Court of Appeals affirmed the actions of Judge Davies and the U.S. Department of Justice against the governor during the crisis. Faubus's lawyers said they would appeal to the Supreme Court. Still, the court decision preceded Faubus's *U.S. News & World Report* interview asserting that federal, not state, authorities were bound to enforce federal desegregation orders. The court decision and the interview occurred, moreover, as Faubus readied a campaign platform calling for state laws permitting closure of desegregated public schools and their reopening on a "private" racially segregated basis. Should desegregation proceed from 1958 to 1959, inevitable federal court litigation would provide Faubus further opportunities to defy and comply.

This strategy had indirect bearing on the ease with which Faubus won Arkansas voters who, like southerners generally, opposed Eisenhower's dispatch of paratroopers to Little Rock. City and state moderates distinguished Faubus's justification of defiance in the name of preserving order from extreme segregationists' violent propensities. Indeed, in early November 1957, with 101st Airborne units still on duty at Central, Mary Thomason and five other segregationist candidates for city director positions were narrowly defeated in an election for a new municipal government. A seventh segregationist did win election, but the overall defeat suggested moderates' ongoing concerns about segregationists as a source of disorder. Mob leaders' escape from federal prosecution, and the federal appellate court April 28, 1958, decision upholding Davies in the *Thomason* case, aggravated such concerns. Faubus's repeated claims that he acted in the name of maintaining order solidified his support among these moderates. Faubus also won over east Arkansas, including black voters that planters controlled through paternalism and credit. East Arkansas politicos resisted extremists like Johnson and other "local outsiders" at least partially because their racist appeals jeopardized the stability of this system. Delta whites voted for Faubus, by contrast, because he tied "law and order" to R. B. McCulloch's version of interposition, including litigation testing federal court orders, not unlike the defiance-compliance strategy Faubus pursued.

Faubus also isolated Little Rock school officials. In the city, many whites embraced Reverend Pruden's Christian racism; but many other moderate Baptists were less explicit about racial differences, although they opposed disorder, in part because such images harmed evangelical Christian missionary work in poor nations confronting communism. Maintaining segregation at Hall High, however, angered most Little Rock white families living outside Pulaski Heights. Thus, Faubus attacked school officials as agents of the "Cadillac brigade" identified with the Heights elite. He did so, however, in the name of "confusion" created by federal-state law, and of course, the overriding antipathy to "federal occupation." He did not use express racist appeals. Finally, facing continued disorder resulting from Central white students harassing the black students, the school board on February 20, 1958, sought from the federal court a delay in enforcing its desegregation plan. In a *New York Post* interview, Blossom explained, school officials received aid "from no one." Faubus and the "rest of the state government fights us. The federal courts order us to integrate, but then give us no help and no protection." U.S. Attorney General Rogers "even inadvertently encourages . . . trouble[makers] when he announces that no prosecutions are planned." The justice department and the Eisenhower administration "do . . . nothing. . . . It's intolerable to expect a school board, standing alone, to fight the whole community. . . . I am an educator, not a policeman."

School officials' request for delay did not reflect a primary concern for the black students' constitutional rights. In May, Ernest Green graduated from Central. Soon thereafter, Eisenhower formally ended the U.S. military presence in Little Rock, returning the National Guard to state control. School officials now faced Faubus and the "troublemakers" alone. In March, Blossom nonetheless reported to the Arkansas Department of Education, praising Central High students' impressive academic achievement. On March 21, at a professional meeting in Grafton, Illinois, Central principal Jess W. Matthews said that despite the publicized desegregation problems, Blossom's report indicated, "We're doing our best; we're misunderstood, but we're doing a good job." In their petition to the federal court, however, school board attorneys focused on the public record of disruption that "made it difficult for teachers to teach and pupils to learn." Delaying desegregation was thus necessary in order to ensure — at some future time — the "quality of education to which all pupils, Negro and white, are entitled." The petition did not fix a date when desegregation might resume. On April 28, Judge Harry J. Lemley issued a memorandum requiring the board to stipulate such a date. Board officials also noted the discomfort they felt at being vilified by segregationists and at being shunned by respectable people. According to law, such personal issues were gratuitous to the petition.

———

Cooper v. Aaron: Delay Granted and Challenged

Judge Lemley's hearing of the school officials' petition anticipated eventual U.S. Supreme Court review. After the Little Rock federal district court temporary assignment ended, Judge Davies returned home to North Dakota. The *Arkansas Democrat* of May 4 described Lemley, by contrast, as having "roots in the South." Indeed, originally from

Virginia and educated at Washington and Lee University, Lemley and his family members became prominent in southwest Arkansas. Franklin Roosevelt appointed Lemley as federal judge for that district in 1939. Local lawyers and members of the U.S. Eighth Circuit Court of Appeals, including Chief Judge Gardner, considered him a diligent federal judge. In 1958, Lemley was seventy-four years old. He had published on the archeology of Arkansas Indian mounds and researched a history of the Confederacy. Reportedly, he once said he loved the South "almost as a religion." Lemley's affinity for southern "customs" and "mores" distinguished him from all but a few Eighth Circuit Court judges and most members of the U.S. Supreme Court. Statewide and national media predicted that if the school board won, the Supreme Court review was likely. The next regular term of the Court did not begin, however, until early October. Little Rock schools were set to open on September 2, the *U.S. News & World Report* May 30 issue indicated; should Faubus triumph in the primary election as expected, federal troops would again be necessary to maintain desegregation.

In the June 3 hearing, Legal Defense Fund lawyers challenged the school board petition. Following Lemley's April 28 memorandum, the school board filed a substitute petition requesting the delay to end in thirty months. The amended petition did not explain why the board chose two-and-one-half years. In Branton's cross-examination, lawyer and board president Wayne Upton addressed the point, declaring that by then Faubus might no longer be governor. School board attorney Richard Butler's cross-examination established also that by 1961 the various interposition laws passed since 1956 would be tested in the courts, including those Faubus currently proposed permitting closure and privatization of public schools. Technically, neither of these replies was pertinent to whether Davies's September 3, 1957, order mandating the continuance of the phase program during the unfolding crisis should be amended. Branton and Marshall argued correctly that Davies's order followed the holding in *Brown* II that "these constitutional principles cannot be allowed to yield simply because of disagreement with them." The High Court, they affirmed, included violence, intimidation, or disorder within the scope of "disagreement." Branton pointed out, too, that school officials could seek a Hoxie-like injunction in order to protect the black students' constitutional rights. The LDF lawyers also called expert witnesses who confirmed Graeme

Cope's suggestion years later that legal action could have controlled the troublemakers harassing the black students.

Judge Lemley heard contrary interpretations of *Brown* II. Though the LDF lawyers acknowledged the difficulties buffeting school officials, they insisted that under *Brown* II "defendants cannot relieve themselves of their constitutional duty to follow through on their own plan approved by this Court." Notwithstanding the flexible standard of reasonableness epitomized by the phrase "with all deliberate speed," the Supreme Court unanimously held in *Brown* II that any "surrender" to violence or disorder would "thwart the Constitution of the United States and the orders of this Court," engendering chaos and "effectively deny plaintiffs and the class they represent constitutional rights heretofore recognized and guaranteed by this Court." As Butler construed the same reasonableness standard, however, the school board "good faith" implementation of the federal court desegregation decree included ensuring a quality education to all students regardless of race. Even so, should disruption at Central High, in conjunction with powerful outside events engulfing the school board since August 1957, destroy the quality of education, a delay in desegregation was warranted at least until the internal and external harm ceased. Thus, LDF and school board lawyers admitted that *Brown* II did not allow "disagreement" as a basis for delaying implementation of a desegregation decree; they argued, however, contrary interpretations of what constituted unlawful disagreement.

Amid steady media scrutiny and Faubus's campaign, Lemley accumulated several hundred pages of testimony and more than one hundred newspaper clippings. On June 8, the *Arkansas Gazette* reported that based on this evidence, Lemley's determination of the delay turned on two questions. Would he accept the board claims that the nine months of trouble at Central significantly harmed educational quality; and what would happen after thirty months that would make desegregation more "workable" than if it proceeded on schedule in September 1958? The LDF lawyers altered the questions: would not effective law enforcement against troublemakers ensure both the black students' constitutional rights and a quality educational environment for all students regardless of race? Implicit further issues were whether Lemley would accept the school board assertion that its prosecution of troublemakers was too expensive to undertake and, anyway, was more properly left to either the federal government or the NAACP. Jay Powell, a vice principal at Central High, summed up this point. The "rabble-rousing whites that caused trouble at school during all that September rioting and demonstrating" escaped prosecution in local, state, and federal courts. "And until somebody does something legal about those people, the kids will sure not quit misbehaving against Negroes in school. Their parents will egg them on, for that matter, and probably tell school people to go to hell in the process."

Lemley's opinion was reported on June 21. Like Miller and Davies in the earlier *Aaron v. Cooper* decisions, Lemley began with a factual survey, incorporating postcrisis developments, including the Eighth Circuit Court decision on April 28 upholding Davies's orders in the *Faubus* and *Thomason* cases. Lemley presented, too, evidence gathered from school officials, including Upton and Blossom, Central vice principals Powell and Elizabeth Huckaby, Central teachers like W. P. Ivey, and servicepeople like O. W. Romaine. This evidence created an imposing image of educational quality disrupted by U.S. troops, federalized guard, student troublemakers, riotous crowds, and certain "personalities." The latter embraced Faubus, though he did not appear by name. Also conspicuously absent were Blossom's and Matthews's March public statements praising Central High students' and teachers' academic success and effectiveness. The black students' remarkable achievements, moreover, received no mention. Considering the extensive yet selective evidence, Lemley weighed defiance of "integration" against the "pattern of southern life which has existed for over three hundred years," engendering the popular "conviction" in Little Rock that the "*Brown* decisions do not truly represent the law, and that by virtue of the 1956–1957 enactments . . . integration can be lawfully avoided." Lemley also gave no weight to the LDF expert witnesses because they lacked "administrative experience in the South."

Lemley upheld school officials on each point. He accepted their judgment that respectable, informed people shared legitimate doubts about what the law was following the passage of state interposition legislation. Thus, the thirty-month delay was necessary in order to test these laws in court; over the same period, too, "changes in some of the personalities involved in the dispute" might occur. School officials also lacked "competency" to initiate criminal prosecutions. Lemley stressed that although *Brown* II did not "authoritatively define the term 'all deliberate speed' . . . it does seem to us that the term is a relative one, dependent upon varying facts and circumstances in different localities." Moreover, granting a stay of desegregation orders "will not deprive any Negro student of a good high school education" at the new all-black Horace Mann High. Lemley rejected, too, LDF lawyers' interpretation of *Brown* II that a delay would "constitute a yielding to unlawful force." Granting the school officials' petition was "merely a moratorium," or "tactical delay." The court "must" not "close its eyes and ears to the practical problem" facing the school board. "Such a judicial attitude would be most unrealistic." Accordingly, although the *Brown* decisions clearly meant that "Negro students in the Little Rock District have a constitutional right not to be excluded from any of the public schools on account of race," school officials have "convincingly shown that the time for the enjoyment of that right has not yet come."

Branton and Marshall asked Lemley to stay enforcement of his decision, pending appeal. He refused on June 23, anticipating that a review could not be completed until after the academic year was under way in Little Rock. Thus, Lemley declared, the thirty-month "tactical delay" would go into effect immediately, and the "situation at Central High School which we have found to be intolerable from an educational standpoint [at the very least] would continue from the beginning of the approaching session to the final ruling of the Supreme Court on the merits of the case." Reportedly, Lemley stated that if Branton disliked the ruling he could appeal it. "Have motion — will travel," Branton responded, flying from Little Rock to St. Louis and Washington, D.C., in order to file appeals of the stay with both the Eighth Circuit Court and the Supreme Court. The Supreme Court summer recess would begin in August. The greater difficulty, however, was that simultaneous appeals were quite rare, left solely to Supreme Court discretion. On June 30, the final day of its regular term, the nine members of the Court met in conference and decided to have the circuit court review Lemley's decision. Nevertheless, its three-paragraph per curiam order denying certiorari affirmed that the circuit court surely "will recognize the vital importance of the time element in this litigation, and that it will act upon the application for a stay or appeal in ample time to permit arrangements to be made for the next school year."

During late June the Little Rock case created ambivalent images in the print media. *Newsweek* and *Time* berated Lemley for allowing Little Rock school officials essentially to surrender to Faubus and the rabble-rousers. Expressing the general view of Arkansas newspapers, however, the *Southwest American* of Fort Smith recalled Faubus's appeals to Eisenhower and the Little Rock School Board requests to Davies for a delay. These failures they compared to the "breathing spell" granted by Lemley, "an Arkansas federal judge, who understands the customs and the thinking of Southern people." The *Arkansas Democrat* reported that U.S. Senator John Stennis of Mississippi declared the decision to be a "repudiation" of the Eisenhower administration. The outcome also pleased Little Rock school officials. Immersed in the primary campaign, Faubus took a moderate stance. He applauded Lemley and urged "Negroes" to pursue the fine educational opportunity Horace Mann offered. Accentuating conciliation, Faubus conceded that the court delay was not the "final solution," but it was a significant forward step, facilitating a return to the Arkansas tradition of "cordial" race relations. Headlines for the *New York Times* Sunday edition June 22, 1958, captured the divergent national and regional images: "U.S. Judge Lets Little Rock Halt Its Integration . . . Faubus Hails Ruling — N.A.A.C.P. Files Notice of Appeal," and "U.S. Officials See Integration Hurt — Justice Aides Considering Intervening in Appeal — Some Doubt Move."

At the end of June, the White House and Lemley each received private letters indicating similarly contentious perceptions. A New Jersey NAACP official wrote to Eisenhower stating that the "latest decision of Judge Harry J. Lemley, postponing the renewal of integration at Central High School . . . for two-and-one-half years is another attempt by the South to circumvent" the *Brown* I decision. Unless Eisenhower spoke out, the United States "will continue to be embarrassed abroad." The president's "word . . . would do much to discourage the lawless element in the South and to encourage the minorities, . . . a most patient and loyal group of American citizens," in their "struggle for equality." A manager for the U.S. Chamber of Commerce in France expressed a similar view in a letter to Lemley. "Those who welcome . . . [bad] publicity can thank you for having put Little Rock back on the front pages of the world's newspapers," he wrote. "Last fall, here in France . . . they were following it with the same interest they give to their national sports." *Sputnik* "knocked Little Rock off the pages of the world press." Now it was back. Thus, Lemley "must be very ignorant of where America is in relationship" to millions of "educated dark-skinned people throughout the world. Do you know that the opinion of the U.S.A. held by these people can be a determining factor in our struggle for existence?" In conclusion, he observed, "America's biggest liabilities are people like you, who . . . are dragging their feet in this race for survival."

Such strong public and private views increased the sense of urgency shared by the U.S. Eighth Circuit Court judges. They responded to the Supreme Court invitation for expeditious review, returning from the summer recess to hold a special session on August 4. Branton and Marshall argued for reversing Lemley's stay. When the hearing was over, the *Arkansas Democrat* reported, school board member Wayne Upton informed Branton that if the LDF won, "hell would break loose." Adding weight to the prediction was Faubus's landside victory in the recent primary election. Events in Arkansas did not prevent the court majority from reversing Lemley's decision, six to one. The court opinion, published on August 18, held that although *Brown* II recognized that certain local problems might warrant changes, even delays, to implementation of desegregation decrees, the evidence of disorder Little Rock school officials presented and Lemley cited to justify the stay "were the direct result of popular *opposition to* the presence of the nine Negro students." Thus, Branton's and Marshall's arguments prevailed regarding the meaning of "disagreements" in *Brown* II: they could not be used to nullify black students' constitutional rights. The court also acknowledged Branton's and Marshall's contention at trial "that at no time did the Board seek injunctive relief against those who opposed by unlawful acts the lawful integration plan."

Nevertheless, the Eighth Circuit Court decision did not go into effect. In principle, the majority favored proceeding with the Little Rock school desegregation plan. Indeed, Judge Marion C. Matthes's published opinion conveyed force through italics: "*We say the time has not yet come in these United States when an order of a Federal Court must be whittled away, watered down, or shamefully withdrawn in the face of violent and unlawful acts of individual citizens in opposition thereto.*" But the five judges of the court majority sympathized enough with the problems Lemley, school officials, and the people of Arkansas faced that they declined to write the opinion, delegating the difficult job to Matthes, the most junior judge. When Matthes agreed to do it, ninety-year-old Chief Judge Archibald K. Gardner said, "That's a load off my mind. But don't be too hard on Judge Lemley." Moreover, Gardner was the lone dissenter, accepting virtually all of Lemley's reasoning and result. With the Little Rock schools set to open in less than two weeks, the Eighth Circuit Court on August 21 suspended for thirty days its mandate, enabling the school board to seek Supreme Court review. But before the board attorneys filed a certiorari petition with the Court, Marshall and Branton filed a motion on August 23 in Kansas City with Justice Charles Evans Whittaker (who was assigned to the Eighth Circuit) requesting a simultaneous stay of both the thirty-day suspension and Lemley's order.

The Supreme Court August Special Term

At an American Bar Association (ABA) meeting in Los Angeles, Whittaker discussed the LDF motion with Chief Justice Earl Warren and Justices William J. Brennan and Thomas Clark. On Monday, August 25, Warren called the Court into a rare special term to begin August 28. These four returned to Washington, D.C.; vacationing in the Northwest, Justice William O. Douglas did as well. Justice John M. Harlan went to the capital from his New York summer home. Justice Harold H. Burton cut short a European trip, arriving in Washington shortly before the term started. Justices Hugo L. Black and Felix Frankfurter were already in Washington. Media reports heightened public expectations that this historic action was nearly as momentous as *Brown*. "The impending Supreme Court decision has sweeping implications. It is expected to provide the first guidance on desegregation methods and timing since the tribunal outlawed racial segregation," the Norfolk *Virginian-Pilot* front-page story declared on August 26. Perhaps for the first time ever, television cameras were allowed inside the Supreme Court building, though not in the courtroom itself.

The Court aimed to resolve the issues regarding the stay before Little Rock schools opened on September 2. Faubus increased the pressure. In a special session, the Arkansas legislature enacted the school closing and privatization measures he proposed; Faubus did not sign them, awaiting the Supreme Court decision. Meanwhile, Blossom denied three black students' transfers to segregated Hall High.

Before August 28, other developments captured public attention. As Warren, Brennan, Clark, and Whittaker departed the ABA meeting in Los Angeles, state chief justices attending their annual convention in nearby Pasadena passed a resolution censuring the Supreme Court for "usurping States' rights" through judicial activism and for rejecting "judicial self-restraint." At the ABA meeting, U.S. Attorney General Rogers responded, stating that many historic decisions that "are landmarks in the progress of our country were unpopular when rendered and evoked bitter attacks on the courts of the time." The next day Rogers defended *Brown* I, declaring that "states must enforce law" and "disorder hurts [the] U.S. at home and abroad." U.S. Solicitor General J. Lee Rankin also returned to Washington, D.C., from the ABA meeting, news reports stated, "because the Supreme Court has invited him to file a brief and take part in arguments Thursday at a special session on the Little Rock school integration." On August 26 the *Virginian-Pilot* reported that Senators Lyndon Johnson and Everett Dirksen had defeated by one vote an attempted Senate floor debate of the Smith bill, "the potent weapon of rebuke that the anti-Court coalition had wheeled up against the Supreme Court." The bill passed the House. Senate supporters included "all the orthodox Southern Democrats and almost all the orthodox Midwestern Republicans." The two senators' narrow victory thus left open the question: would "more daring attacks . . . fail?"

On the morning of August 28, more than one thousand people assembled outside the Supreme Court building. The members of the Court already were in their chambers. Having arrived from London, Justice Burton recorded in his diary that he "worked on the Little Rock case." The justices met in conference from 10:00 A.M. to 12:00 noon, discussing the special term. Thurgood Marshall arguing for the petitioners, Richard Butler representing the Little Rock School Board, and Solicitor General Rankin presenting the "cause for the United States, as *amicus curiae*, urging that the relief sought by petitioners should be granted," would present their case from 12:00 noon to 2:00 P.M. and from 2:30 to 3:30 P.M. From the end of arguments to 5 P.M. the justices would meet in conference to discuss the next stage of proceedings.

Chief Justice Warren would then announce the results. At noon, the justices took their places on the high bench. Warren was in the center seat. The other justices aligned themselves according to seniority of appointment starting with Black, the most senior, to the chief's right, then Frankfurter on his left, Douglas to the right, Burton on the left, Clark on the right, Harlan to the left, and Brennan and Whittaker at the right and left ends, respectively. This order indicated that the three most junior justices had come to the Court since the *Brown* decisions. The gavel shattered the silence in the packed courtroom. Preliminaries dispensed with, Warren called on "Mr. Marshall."

Marshall's argument raised questions primarily regarding the unusual appellate process being followed in the case. Against the publicized background of Faubus's and Arkansas public officials' defiance, Marshall declared, the federal circuit court and the Supreme Court went into "extraordinary session" in order to weigh the "constitutional rights of Negro" petitioners. These were not "rights in the abstract," but rights already affirmed by the federal courts. Judge Lemley's order delaying enforcement and the circuit court's thirty-day stay pending review raised the unusual situation in which "a procedural device of staying a mandate [would result in] actually ruling on the merits of the case." Could the Court decide affirmatively within the accepted bounds of due process of law? Harlan and Brennan questioned Marshall about a new Arkansas law delaying the schools' opening. Whittaker repeatedly pressed him on the irregularity of seeking "conjunctive" stays of both Lemley's and the circuit court orders. Clark, Frankfurter, and Whittaker focused on the "propriety" of asking the Court to decide these issues without further consideration. "We take the position," Marshall concluded, "that when you balance the rights of the kids involved, plus what this Court said in the *Brown* case, the public interest . . . of the United States, over against the School Board's position that there are some people that don't want . . . this thing to go through, then certainly, the equities involved lean toward the protection of these constitutional rights."

Butler's argument fostered more vigorous questioning. Butler defended the thirty-month delay by reference to the September 1957 crisis and its troubled aftermath, including the disorder inside Central High, Lemley's decision, the governor's defiant rhetoric, and an Arkansas law just enacted instituting a date of September 15 by which

Little Rock schools could open. Warren and Frankfurter pressed the point that should the Court refuse to address the two lower court orders staying the Little Rock desegregation plan, black and white students would attend segregated schools for two-and-one-half years. Douglas indicated that the registration requirements of the new law would result in racial segregation. But Clark asked: if the Court did not lift the stays, and, following the normal course of proceedings, decided against the school board on the merits after the school year began, could the black children then be transferred to an integrated school? Regarding these issues Butler responded affirmatively. Warren and Brennan asked how soon a formal record might be prepared, should the normal rules of review be waived for the special session. Consistent with Clark's question, Butler argued for following the established, rather than an expedited, process. The fundamental question was, he said, "Can a court of equity postpone the enforcement of the plaintiffs' constitutional rights if the immediate enforcement thereof will deprive others, many others . . . of their constitutional rights to an education in a free public school?"

Butler then addressed the issues concerning popular understanding of the obligation to obey "law." Butler conceded that "unquestionably the people in our part of the country wanted to believe that this thing [racial desegregation] could take a long time or be circumvented entirely." Nevertheless, "We are arguing for the great mass of people throughout the South who I say again . . . and again are not law defiers. They want to follow the law" but "without certain state statutes having been tested in court, do not know just exactly what the law is in a particular given circumstance." School officials nonetheless hoped that over thirty months a clear "national policy" would emerge with which "law-abiding people" could comply. "Why aren't," Frankfurter questioned, "the two [*Brown*] decisions of this Court . . . a national policy?" In different ways Warren, Brennan, Frankfurter, and Whittaker asked Butler to reconcile Arkansas public officials' defiance of *Brown* — particularly the ambiguity inherent in the "all deliberate speed" standard and the claims that it was not binding law — with school officials' request for the thirty-month delay in enforcing desegregation. "Regardless of whether or not the people of Arkansas should recognized the United States Supreme Court decisions as the law of the land," Butler insisted, "the plain fact is that they have not, and it is most difficult for them to do so, if not impossible, when the Governor of the State says that that is not the law of the land, that only Congress can really say what the law of the land is."

Butler attempted to equate Faubus's influence as a state executive with Warren's as California governor. Warren declared that he always followed the law as defined by the courts. Butler was suggesting, he said, that what a governor said about law superseded or controlled a rule the Supreme Court established. Butler denied that he held such an opinion. Still, events over the preceding year indicated that southerners generally and Arkansans in particular had been persuaded by leaders like Faubus that they, not federal courts, were to be believed regarding the issue. "I think there is no member of this Court who fails to recognize the very great problem which your School Board has," Warren said. "But can we defer a program of this kind merely because there are those elements in the community that would commit violence to prevent it from coming into effect?" Butler repeated that he was arguing for respectable law-abiding people, not for "people who form mobs . . . who are law defiers." Burton asked if Butler wanted "simply" clarification of "deliberate speed"? Butler replied that what he wanted was time for an "orderly process." Finally, Black asked, was the premise of Butler's argument that after thirty months conditions will be such that the interposition laws will have been tested in court, which will thereby provide Arkansas people with sufficient understanding as to what "deliberate speed" means? Butler agreed this was his premise.

Marshall first made a brief rebuttal, followed by Solicitor General Rankin presenting the federal government argument. Butler accepted, Marshall said, the criticisms of *Brown*, which meant that its enforcement should await endless review of state interposition laws. Although Marshall was sympathetic concerning the difficulties facing school officials, that did not justify their refusal to enforce the black students' rights now rather than later. As for the disorder in the school, Little Rock officials' own evidence revealed that they had declined to prosecute troublemakers, thereby encouraging harassment of the black students. The U.S. government, including particularly the "executive branch," Rankin said, had "great interest" in maintaining the nation's public schools through compliance with *Brown*. Notwithstanding the ambiguity inherent in *Brown* II, he asserted, "we think this Court has made it plain that there cannot be any more of this talk about what the law is." Governors and senators express differing views of the law. "This country cannot exist," Rankin declared nonetheless, "without a recognition that the Supreme Court of the United States, when it speaks on a legal matter, is the law." Making the enforcement of court orders contingent upon discovering the law's meaning, moreover, invited endless uncertainty. "And above all, no court of law in this land, state or federal, can recognize that you can ever bow to force and violence in setting aside, vacating, or modifying a decree of a court."

"The moment you do that, you give up law and order," Rankin warned. "This country cannot afford any such price. No one can, neither the Southerner, the Middlewesterner, from my country, the far West or the East." Thus, the issues of the stay depended upon maintaining the rule of law. The "error" occurred when Lemley upheld the two-and-one-half-year delay. Ending the legal status quo deprived the black students of their constitutional rights and surrendered to violence caused by "a small group of people." Despite its reversal of Lemley's order, the U.S. Eighth Circuit Court issued a thirty-day delay in order to expedite Supreme Court review. Whittaker and Frankfurter noted that such review without a certiorari petition was "unusual." Still, Rankin continued, without suggesting criticism of the Little Rock School officials, they could have preserved the black student's constitutional rights, as well as remedied disorder, had they instituted a Hoxie-like injunction. "I am confident that, as the years go by, the people of the South . . . will realize that they have a stake in each American citizen being a full citizen with full and complete rights like every other," he said. "It seems to me that we are now at the crossroads." The American "people . . . are entitled to a definitive statement from this Court whether or not force and violence, opposition to the Court's decision, are grounds" to "go back a step." The "basic question, all there really is in this case, is whether or not as" the U.S. government "we insist that there must be a rule of law."

Butler gave a short reply. Through related questions, Black and Frankfurter insisted upon Butler addressing Rankin's argument that, fundamentally, the delay school officials sought and Lemley granted reflected a surrender to "force," compounded by the fact that the school board could have preserved order and maintained the black student's constitutional rights by prosecuting the "law defiers." But-

ler replied that Rankin's arguments that the rule of law could not admit a temporary delay — including a grant of certiorari to review the
merits of school officials' claims — seemed inconsistent with Eisenhower's oft-reported statements favoring a slower process of integration. More exactly, Butler declared, school officials' position was that
in order to preserve the public school system for all races in the future,
consistent with court orders, they required a "tactical delay" in desegregation. Concerning the issue of prosecuting the troublemakers, he
said, neither the federal government nor the NAACP, with "rather
vast resources," had attempted such action. Why should school
officials be blamed for not doing so? Ultimately, hoisted on the "horns
of the dilemma," school officials merely requested more time.

After discussion in conference, Warren announced the further proceedings of the special term. The Court granted certiorari in "consideration of the merits of the Court of Appeals decision reversing the
order of Judge Lemley." The school board had until September 8 to
file its petition; by September 10, both parties were to file briefs arguing the merits. The Court invited the solicitor general to do the same.
The Court suspended the rules regarding the printing of record,
briefs, and petitions. The Court recognized, too, that Little Rock
schools were now set to open no later than September 15, indicating
that the school board had responded to the state law Butler had noted
by changing the date from September 2. At noon on September 11,
1958, the Court would hear oral arguments upon the petition for certiorari. Pending its decision on that petition, the Court deferred
action both on the "stay of the mandate of the Court of Appeals and
to stay the order of the district court of June 21, 1958."

Newspaper reports and unsolicited briefs collected in Harlan's
and Frankfurter's files suggested the justices' perceptions of national
and southern reactions to *Cooper v. Aaron*. Reflecting the national view
was a *Los Angeles Mirror-News* cartoon showing Faubus nailing boards
over Little Rock school doors, exclaiming to white young people
standing by, "We can't let education interfere with prejudice." An
Atlanta Journal cartoon, by contrast, showed a stone named "Little
Rock" held in a hand dubbed the "Supreme Court" descending on
a small agitated man titled "southern moderate," standing atop the
massive boulder named "resistance of the South." The caption read,
"Crushing what?" The members of the Court also received amicus

curiae briefs seeking review by three states' rights supporters: John Bradley Minnick and the Arlington, Virginia, chapter of the Defenders of State Sovereignty and Individual Liberties; William Burrows, a Dallas, Texas, attorney purportedly representing the "people of the South [white and black]"; and John M. Burke of Maryland arguing for the "American people" against Earl Warren and the Supreme Court. A fourth amicus brief, filed under the name of U.S. Senator J. William Fulbright of Arkansas, essentially argued the Little Rock School Board position, though focusing on the need to recognize the significance of a distinctive "Southern mind." Although the Court denied the motions for review, the briefs reflected the impression many southerners held that the *Brown* decisions were not law.

Cooper v. Aaron further tested Court standing within the federal system. On September 7, Attorney General Rogers wrote letters offering justice department assistance to Little Rock school officials, law enforcement authorities, and the new city manager by enlarging the U.S. marshal's office and making it "ready to cooperate" with them "fully" to preserve law and order "within our respective responsibilities." The department released these letters to the press and sent copies to each member of the Court. Like Solicitor General Rankin's arguments favoring *Brown* and the Court on August 28 — and Rogers's defense of both following the state chief justices' condemnation just days previously — these public letters offered more measured federal involvement in enforcing court orders compared to President Eisenhower's earlier vacillation between weak or nonsupport before the September 1957 crisis and the controversial use of military troops during and after it. The justice department action tempered Chief Justice Warren's criticism that the president's equivocation aided and abetted southern and conservative opponents of the Court in and out of Congress. Still, Butler's rebuttal argument, which embraced Eisenhower's statements condoning "going slow" in desegregation cases, suggested reasons members of the Court could feel compelled to advocate their own power in the struggle over *Brown*.

Despite the well-known unanimity in the *Brown* decisions, the Court was divided. Warren, Black, and Douglas were recognized as "activists," but Frankfurter and Harlan urged "judicial self-restraint." Burton, who during the summer of 1958 was set to retire because of complications from Parkinson's disease, and Clark tended to shift between each group. Eisenhower appointed Brennan and Whittaker in 1956 and 1957 respectively; Brennan gradually aligned himself with the activists, whereas Whittaker's position at this time generally remained fluid. Even so, the two *Brown* decisions suggested, "activism" and "restraint" were relative terms. In 1953 Warren joined a Court that since the late 1930s had been willing consistently to limit but not overturn the separate-but-equal doctrine established in *Plessy v. Ferguson* (1896), which interpreted the Fourteenth Amendment Equal Protection Clause to sanction the southern racial apartheid system. Warren was credited with winning the unanimous vote of the Court in *Brown* I, holding that in primary and secondary education the *Plessy* doctrine was "inherently unequal." At the time, however, it was little known outside the Court that Warren gained unanimity in return for accepting Frankfurter's gradual approach to enforcement in *Brown* II, epitomized by "all deliberate speed." *Cooper v. Aaron* tested whether this compromise held, despite the southern massive resistance and the appointment since 1955 of Harlan, Brennan, and Whittaker.

On September 2, Frankfurter wrote to Harlan evidencing conflicted views the Little Rock case engendered among the justices. Frankfurter reported having learned from Brennan that at lunch on August 29, Warren described the case as a "fight . . . between the Supreme Court and Faubus." Warren's "attitude towards the kind of problems that confront us are more like that of a fighting politician than that of a judicial statesman," Frankfurter wrote. For him, Chief Justice Charles Evans Hughes epitomized such a statesman in the confrontation between the Court and Franklin Roosevelt from 1936 to 1937. He also deemed Warren's perception of the case less realistic than the opinion held by southern moderates such as Richard Butler, Little Rock School Board member and lawyer Wayne Upton, "Henry [*sic*] Ashmore, the editor of the Little Rock *Gazette* [*sic*]," and "another important [but unnamed] Southerner, the publisher of the *Atlanta Journal*," whose "attitude and feelings" Frankfurter knew personally. "Of course Faubus has been guilty of trickery, but the trickery was as much against the School Board as against us," and the moderates were "not isolated phenomena in the deep South," he declared.

Black, like Clark a southerner, knew that the moderates' influence was weaker than Frankfurter believed. Though he joined in the unanimity of the *Brown* I decision, privately Black questioned the "all deliberate speed" standard in *Brown* II. The Little Rock case offered Black and his activist colleagues, then, an opportunity to reconsider that standard, especially given the moderates' failure to implement it when pitted against Faubus. Frankfurter, however, formulated the gradualist presumption underlying *Brown* II in part because he was certain that southern moderates led by lawyers could eventually defeat the proponents of resistance in the battle for southern public opinion. Through gradualism recognizing distinctive local circumstances — except outright defiance — the Court might strengthen the moderates' position. "In the procedures we adopt" and "how we express what we do," Frankfurter's letter to Harlan concluded, the Court should show that, though moderates were not to be "won to desegregation on the merits . . . they ought to be won, and I believe will be won, to the transcending issue of the Supreme Court as the authoritative organ of what the Constitution requires." Thus, he insisted, "in everything we do, and how we do it, we must serve as exemplars of understanding and wisdom and magnanimity to the Butlers and Uptons of the South, as well as the younger generation, who not only recognize the inevitability of desegregation but want to further the acceptance in action of such inevitability."

Final Arguments: Unanimity Tested within the Court

These divisions did not disappear during the unique special term. From August 28 to September 11, the justices prepared for the oral arguments in *Cooper v. Aaron* without the usual pressures from multiple cases that characterized the business of the regular full term beginning in early October. Of course, the case was the center of attention in the private conferences and more informal discussions over the following weeks concerning the Court opinion. Each justice also assigned at least one clerk responsibility for certiorari and pauper petitions to be considered after the regular term was under way. Seven of the eight associate justices had two clerks, whereas Douglas, by choice, had one. Three clerks worked for the chief justice. Most of the eighteen clerks arrived at the Court shortly before or just as the special term started. Brennan and Harlan involved their clerks in *Cooper v. Aaron;* others, such as Frankfurter, gave them comparatively little to do on the case. As the clerks carried out their respective assignments for the justices, they also usually ate and had recreation together. From this combination of highly personal individual and collective experiences — without violating the confidentiality each clerk owed his justice — they developed a shared understanding of the members of the Court, including its divisions. Thus, it became apparent that in *Cooper v. Aaron,* the justices generally agreed on the result, but how to reach it was contentious.

Other common impressions of the justices emerged among the clerks during the special term. On August 28 and September 11, they joined the justices' family members in a special section of the courtroom to one side of the bench, witnessing the oral arguments; they felt personally the historic significance of the case. Over the course of the special term, the justices and the clerks also were sensitive to past and present criticisms of the Court from Eisenhower, Congress, the states, and many judges and lawyers. Also, the justices generally were in accord regarding the unusual expedited appeal of the district and appellate court stays, but much less so concerning the extent to which the Court should address the meaning of "all deliberate speed." Only Frankfurter, however, seemed committed to singling out southern moderates, especially lawyers, as a particular target for Court deliberations or opinion making. The clerks soon learned, too, that more than his colleagues, Frankfurter was unusually active in attempting to persuade other justices to his point of view and to influence the other justices' clerks, including those who, like his own, were Harvard Law School graduates. This latter practice was indicative of Frankfurter's unintentional capacity to rile his colleagues, especially Warren, Black, Douglas, and Brennan. The clerks also realized that Frankfurter endeavored most vigorously to cajole Harlan and Whittaker.

Harlan's and Brennan's preparations for the September 11 oral arguments suggested differing perceptions. Both justices assigned clerks to address the complex procedural issues raised by the two orders staying enforcement of the Little Rock desegregation plan. Each justice wanted to uphold the circuit court six-to-one decision vacating Judge Lemley's stay; they recognized, however, that in desegregation cases the issue was conflicted, demanding a wide search for precedents in unrelated areas of law. Eventually, the two justices' clerks found precedents and developed reasoning the Court could use to enforce the circuit court's majority opinion. That clerks in both chambers working through such technical procedural issues arrived separately at the same holding suggested the consensus of the two justices regarding the result in the Little Rock case. By contrast, Brennan had another clerk draft a more expansive memorandum indicating that after some forty desegregation cases the "lower courts and school boards are obviously uncertain as to what the requirements laid down in *Brown* [II] really mean." The Little Rock case "may indicate that the time has come for a further clarification of those requirements." The "only really difficult term in" *Brown* II "at this time is 'all deliberate speed'" and the "problem" the Little Rock case "directly raises — is community hostility, whether overt or not, a . . . justifiable excuse for postponing integration."

The clerk's memorandum for Brennan favorably evaluated Little Rock school officials' arguments. Although *Brown* II included "language which . . . indicates that local hostility is not to be considered a relevant factor in formulating a plan," the memorandum stated, "community hostility must be considered a relevant factor in determining whether any particular plan meets the test of all deliberate speed. Otherwise many integration programs will be practically unworkable with consequent disruptions." The clerk then wrote, "I think the school board's argument in this case that unduly precipitate action will . . . ruin the educational system and leave scares and ill feeling that will delay successful integration far beyond the time that a more gradual program would take . . . has a great deal of merit to it." Yet "even if it is necessary to order integration of Central High School at once so as not to encourage resistance to integration, an opinion could and I believe should still state that community attitudes are relevant in the initial formulation of the plan." Though such recognition "would" practically "make it impossible to define 'all deliberate speed' with any precision . . . I doubt that the process would proceed any slower than it would . . . if hostility is not considered relevant." Ultimately, the "fact must be faced that integration in some areas will not become a reality for some time no matter what this Court says, and the less friction of the kind that took place in Little Rock that develops in the process, the . . . faster successful integration will be achieved."

This wide-ranging analysis provided Brennan useful comparisons with his own views. One of the three Supreme Court justices who had not participated in the *Brown* decisions, Brennan both favored the principle established in 1954 and doubted the wisdom of compromising it in *Brown* II. Brennan supported the first *Brown* decision while serving on the New Jersey Supreme Court; he did so despite criticism from one fellow judge and certain voters from the areas of the state that had maintained de facto racial desegregation prior to its eradication in the 1940s. On the U.S. Supreme Court, Brennan soon accepted Black's judgment that employing "all deliberate speed" had encouraged delay. These earlier and recent experiences informed his contrary assessment of the memorandum argument supporting Little Rock school officials' view that in light of the local adversity they faced, the *Brown* II standard should be read to justify delay. In addition, although Brennan was impressed with the skill and sincerity with which Butler justified the same argument by reference to the force of distinctive southern racial attitudes shared by many good people, Brennan did not believe such deeply held convictions outweighed the need for change as quickly as possible. Finally, Brennan thought *Cooper v. Aaron* was important because it presented a direct confrontation between the Supreme Court and state government, particularly the governor. The scale of defiance made the case more significant than *Cohens v. Virginia*, when Virginia defied the U.S. Supreme Court in 1821.

Meanwhile, Clark privately pondered dissenting. Sometime before the Court announced its order addressing the circuit court majority opinion following the September 11 conference, he jotted down two pages of a rough draft in longhand. "My action today in dissenting from the judgment of this Court is not to be construed in any respect whatsoever as a change of position from that taken in [*Brown*]. I adhere steadfastly to my vote there believing that every American citizen goes first class; under our Constitution there is no steerage," one of the draft pages in part read. "However, as I understand [*Brown*] integration is not to be accomplished through push button action but rather by 'deliberate speed.' The fact there are those who by 'massive resistance' attempt to deprive some of our citizens of the present enjoyment of their constitutional rights gives us no excuse to in turn strip the l[a]tter of those procedural safeguards that are the right of all other litigants," the draft page concluded. Echoing a question directed at Butler during the August 28 hearing, Clark concluded his draft: "For all practical purposes it makes no difference whether petitioners enter an integrated school on September 8 or October 6 the day we convene our next Term. But to strip from the respondent [school board] its right under the rules of the Court to the required period for appeal means much in the administration of justice. 'Equal Justice under Law' requires at least that much. I would let the case take its regular course."

By the morning conference preceding oral arguments on September 11, the justices still disagreed. As questions asked at the August 28 hearing suggested, in defense of the black students' rights, Warren, Brennan, and Black considered the meaning of "all deliberate speed" through state officials' paramount challenge to Supreme Court authority as the final expositor of the Constitution under the Supremacy Clause. Douglas concurred, though his visit to Minnesota during the special term limited his participation. By contrast, the questions Burton, Whittaker, Clark, and Harlan asked during the hearing suggested they were concerned that upholding the Supremacy Clause should not fundamentally alter the procedural guarantees emerging from federal court implementation of *Brown* II since 1955. Clark's draft dissent affirmed most vigorously the need to emphasize procedural regularity, notwithstanding "massive resistance." But the draft was no more than a brief outline. After mature consideration, Clark apparently joined those who favored making few or no changes in the *Brown* II standard. Thus, although advocates both of activism and restraint supported the final authority of the Court under the Supremacy Clause, the activists' leading concern was enforcing the black students' rights. By accepting the established construction of "all deliberate speed," the restraint proponents unintentionally made those rights contingent upon white public opinion, which, as Faubus had demonstrated, was readily manipulated.

Frankfurter again revealed his trust in southern white moderates' malleable opinion. As the author of the "all deliberate speed" standard, Frankfurter clearly sided with the other proponents of judicial restraint. Before the conference, Frankfurter also urged upon Warren the same attitude toward southern white lawyers he had expressed earlier to Harlan. In a letter Frankfurter pressed Warren to consider "the desirability of having you say, when Mr. Butler gets to his feet, that the Court takes note of the fact of the Board's vote not to open the schools until the 15th." In the September 2 letter to Harlan, Frankfurter condoned the statement in the *Washington Post* describing this vote as "courageous," given that the Arkansas legislature had passed laws, with Faubus's support, allowing elections to recall school board members who implemented desegregation plans. Frankfurter assumed that Warren's expression of sympathy would aid embattled white moderates like lawyers Butler and Upton in Little Rock and across the South. "My own view has long been that the ultimate hope for the peaceful solution of the basic problem," he wrote Warren, "largely depends on winning the support of lawyers of the South for the overriding issue of obedience to the Court's decision. Therefore I think we should encourage every manifestation of fine conduct by a lawyer like Butler."

In a thirty-minute conference before noon on September 11, the justices discussed the proceedings. The Court did not accept the idea Warren received from Frankfurter. After some disagreement over whether to admit all the unsolicited amicus briefs, including Senator Fulbright's, the vote was nine to zero against. "This was done," Burton recorded in his diary, "to get unanimity — the vote was eight to one to grant all — but nine to zero to deny all." From noon to 4:00 P.M., the order of presentation was Butler, Marshall, Butler (rebuttal), Rankin, Marshall, and Butler (rebuttal). Previously, Rankin informed the Court that his argument required no new brief, as the one submitted for the August 28 hearing was sufficient. Butler and Marshall based their arguments on new briefs. From 4:00 to 4:30 P.M., the justices would meet in conference to decide whether to uphold the circuit court reversal of Lemley's order staying enforcement of the Little Rock desegregation program for two-and-one-half years. The following day the Court would announce its decision. As had been the case on August 28, a full courtroom witnessed the afternoon arguments amidst national and international news coverage. In Little Rock, Faubus awaited the outcome; upon it depended whether he would enforce the school closing and privatization laws. In nearby Virginia, leaders prepared to pursue the same sort of resistance.

Warren called on Butler to begin. Although the Court denied the motion to accept the Fulbright brief, when arguments were under way, Butler read from a copy, urging the Court to recognize how much a distinctive "southern mind" influenced racial perceptions. These attitudes

were in fact impressionable, Butler suggested, open to persuasion.
Extremists and demagogues like Faubus might dominate such thinking
for some time. Moreover, as long as these forces held sway, it was unrealistic to expect school officials to prosecute troublemakers. Not only
were school board resources too meager to attempt such litigation —
especially compared to the supposedly superior means possessed by the
other side — but as educators they simply were ill-equipped to mount
law enforcement actions. Ultimately, the Little Rock majority of
respectable people would return to the moderate ways prevailing when
the school board began its desegregation plan in good faith. Indeed,
after the contrary state laws could be reviewed and presumably overturned, the good people of Little Rock would accept the obligation to
follow the Supreme Court *Brown* decision. With time the influence of
extremists and demagogues would abate. The question was, then, did
the standard of "all deliberate speed" in *Brown* II allow time to bring
about this change, or did it require the rights of the black litigants to
prevail immediately, despite the possible destruction of education for
some two thousand other students?

The questions the justices directed at Butler suggested they were
not persuaded. Warren asked if "the real issue before this Court is not
just whether the school board is frustrating the rights of these children,
but whether the acts of any agency of the State of Arkansas are preventing them from exercising their constitutional rights, and whether
. . . if it did frustrate the rights of these children is a violation of the
Constitution, isn't that the issue that we have before us?" Harlan
observed that the requested delay "presupposes that the leadership in
your State will take some affirmative action" to desegregate, and, "if
federal courts themselves are going to take a step to delay integration,
why wouldn't it give more hope to the opposition?" Emphasizing that
regarding federal supremacy there was "not any question about what
the Constitution says," Black asked whether the school board was not
effectively asserting that "if any State by its Governor and all the great
majority of public officials charged with enforcement of the law, and
most of the people, are opposed to carrying out the court's decree, the
matter should be delayed in that State. It comes down to that does it
not?" Brennan asked: "Just how was this Court in a position to . . .
approve a delay sought on the ground that the responsible State

officials, rather than be on the side of enforcement of these constitutional rights, have taken actions to frustrate their enforcement?"

Marshall's and Rankin's arguments resonated with these questions, though Frankfurter and Clark offered Butler some respite. Clark asked if school officials had prepared for the resumption of desegregation in 1961. Butler suggested "tentative" preparations; however, the "first thing is for the Court to grant" the postponement. Echoing the views expressed in letters to Harlan and Warren, Frankfurter asked Butler if "the mass of people in Arkansas are law abiding, are not mobsters, they do not like desegregation, but they may be won to respect for the Constitution as announced by the organ charged with the duty of declaring it and therefore adjusting themselves to it, although they may not like it?" This surely was his own view, Butler replied; it was, he believed, also the "feeling of the school board as an organization." Marshall and Rankin, however, kept the focus on lawlessness. "The one single issue in this case . . . is . . . whether or not a federal district court can delay an integration plan . . . already in progress, solely because of violence, and threats of violence," Marshall said. "I am not worried about the Negro children. . . . I worry about the white children . . . who are told, as young people, that the way to get your rights is to violate the law and defy the lawful authorities." As for the federal government, Rankin declared, "We think that this case involves the question of the maintenance of law and order, not only in this community and the State of Arkansas, but throughout the country."

At the close of arguments on September 11, the Court met in conference for thirty minutes. In his diary Burton wrote that the Court agreed unanimously to affirm the Eighth Circuit Court decision, thereby overturning Lemley's thirty-month stay. The Court would announce the decision "to affirm" the following day and then "hand down [the] opinion later (by October 6). Frankfurter and Harlan to draft the order of tomorrow. Brennan to draft opinion for Court." Thus, during the weeks after September 12, the South, the nation, and the Supreme Court itself confronted the consequences of an order requiring desegregation to proceed immediately. As the public awaited the full opinion of the Court, however, it became clear that Faubus intended to implement the school closing laws. As a practical matter, the opening of Little Rock schools was "suspended" until Faubus called, and Little Rock citizens voted in, a special election to open or close the schools. Faubus, in turn, would not act to enforce the inevitable outcome of that vote until the Supreme Court announced its full opinion in *Cooper v. Aaron*, which most likely would come near the end of September. Once more, intractable confrontation engulfed the black students' constitutional rights.

CHAPTER 5

The *Cooper v. Aaron* Opinions
Unanimity and Division, 1958

The two *Cooper v. Aaron* opinions of the Supreme Court held ambiguous meaning. Contemporary and later commentators emphasized the forceful Court affirmation of its own authority in the most important racial desegregation decision since *Brown*. Nevertheless, Faubus and the segregationists closed and privatized the schools the Supreme Court ordered desegregated, again blocking the black students' rights. Thus, in Arkansas and elsewhere, defiance prevailed over self-asserted Court power. This chapter reconsiders causation and consequence through the opinion-making process of the Court from September 12–29, along with Frankfurter's subsequent concurring opinion. When Justice Brennan attempted to draft an opinion limiting the discretion *Brown* II permitted, a consensus emerged within the Court favoring instead an expansive assertion of judicial supremacy. Responding especially to Justices Harlan's and Frankfurter's proposals, Brennan reaffirmed the flexible "all deliberate speed" standard and a unique expression of unanimity, but maintained broad judicial supremacy amidst contradictory public reactions in the North and South. Frankfurter's controversial separate opinion presented a subtle defense of *Brown* II. Reflecting a hidden story, Frankfurter's decision to issue the concurring opinion coincided with congressional defeat of major anti-Court legislation and the more favorable approach of the Eisenhower administration toward the Court during cold war battles.

Justice Brennan and the Vicissitudes of Judicial Supremacy

With the Court order of September 12, confrontation thus began anew. In its morning conference on that date, the Court approved with few alterations the three-paragraph per curiam opinion Frankfurter and Harlan drafted; at noon the justices assembled on the bench and Warren read it before a full courtroom. The issues having been "fully deliberated upon" in briefs and the oral arguments of August 28 and September 11, the Court decided "unanimously" to uphold the U.S. Eighth Circuit Court of Appeals judgment of August 18, 1958. "In view of the imminent commencement of the new school year at the Central High School of Little Rock, Arkansas, we deem it important to make prompt announcement of our judgment affirming the Court of Appeals. The expression of the views supporting our judgment will be prepared and announced in due course." The per curiam opinion overturned Lemley's order granting the thirty-month delay on June 21, as well as the court of appeals one-month stay of its own order on August 21. The Court held that Miller's original *Aaron v. Cooper* opinion of August 28, 1956, and Davies's order on September 3, 1957, "enforcing the School Board's plan for desegregation in compliance with" *Brown* I and II, must "be reinstated." Finally, Warren declared, the "judgment of this Court shall be effective immediately, and shall be communicated forthwith" to the federal district court in Arkansas. Soon thereafter Faubus signed the laws authorizing him to close schools and to hold a special election if federal courts and/or troops enforced school desegregation.

Warren's choice of a justice to draft the full opinion of the Court in *Cooper v. Aaron* suggested concerns about unanimity. Court internal rules left the selection of opinion writers to the chief justice, unless he was dissenting, in which case the most senior justice in the majority made the assignment. Also, the chief often wrote leading or controversial opinions, as Warren had done in *Brown;* sometimes, however, intangible factors might result in the chief's choice of another justice in such instances. In the Little Rock case, Court private conference deliberations during its special term, as well as the per curiam opinion, emphasized the unanimity established in *Brown.* Even so, in his diary entry of September 12, Burton implied that his impending retirement might have an indirect bearing on the public perception of unanimity in the most important desegregation case since *Brown.* "Neither the C.J. nor I have heard anything about the announcement of my retirement by Oct. 13 or the [president's] selection of my successor. We are anxious that the Little Rock opinion come down by Oct. 6." This personal remark probably involved concern that Eisenhower's announcement of Burton's retirement because of Parkinson's disease might expose the confirmation process to public controversy because of the Little Rock case. In addition, Burton had participated in *Brown*; replacing him would thus raise the question whether the Court could maintain unanimity in *Cooper v. Aaron*, especially given Eisenhower's appointment of three new justices since 1955.

authorship of opinion

These factors possibly influenced Warren's reasoning in choosing the opinion writer in *Cooper v. Aaron*. Probably, Warren declined to write the opinion himself because he personified to southern and conservative critics of the Court the evils of judicial activism. Thus, his authorship of the opinion would overshadow the legitimacy the Court sought in maintaining unanimity. Burton's physical condition prevented him from drafting the controversial opinion in the weeks before his retirement; similarly, Whittaker's dogged determination to research and ponder cases could take an unusual amount of time. Douglas's periodic absence during the special term ensured that Warren did not choose him. By contrast, during the 1957 term Clark had to be dissuaded from filing a dissent in the Alabama NAACP membership registration case, one like that involving Daisy Bates and the Little Rock branch. Although not a school segregation case, his colleagues convinced Clark not to dissent by appealing to the need for unanimity in race cases generally. Given Warren's overriding commitment to preserving unanimity, Clark's evident willingness to consider a dissent (privately repeated without effect in the Little Rock case itself) removed him from consideration as the author of the opinion in *Cooper v. Aaron*.

This process of elimination left those justices who most diverged upon the issue of "all deliberate speed." The *U.S. News & World Report* story about the oral arguments on September 11 and the per curiam opinion delivered the following day reflected public perception that the Little Rock case raised new issues. "Now you have the Federal Government pitted against the States of the South in a test of power. That's the meaning of the Supreme Court's ruling in the Little Rock case. The Court says: Integrate now; no more delay, even though there's violence," the introduction to the September 19 story read. "Yet, in Little Rock, in Virginia, throughout the South, there is no sign of surrender. Every resource at the command of Southern States is being mustered to resist. Prospect: closed schools instead of mixed schools." For Warren, this public impression undoubtedly accentuated Frankfurter's and Black's contention over delayed desegregation inherent in the "all deliberate speed" standard. Admittedly, this disagreement was confined within the Court. It nonetheless reflected the well-known polarization between activism and restraint each justice personified, which in turn effectively disqualified them as Warren's choice. Warren also considered Harlan too close to Frankfurter. Brennan, by contrast, was becoming Warren's confidant; moreover, he possessed an unusual capacity, previously displayed as a state high court judge, to achieve consensus when writing difficult opinions. Warren thus selected Brennan.

Brennan circulated the first draft of an opinion on September 17. Like Davies's and Lemley's reported decisions, Brennan stated the evolving facts of the Little Rock case. The question arising from the order granting a thirty-month delay was "whether the desegregation process in the Little Rock schools, actually commenced according to an approved plan, may be arrested because the orderly carrying out of the plan has been made difficult by actual and continually threatened mob violence and disorder occurring in a situation of stiffened hostility toward desegregation encouraged" by state authorities. He began with the "fundamental proposition" established in *Brown* that "racial segregation" in state public schools "is a denial of the equal protection of the laws guaranteed by the Fourteenth Amendment." Since school officials argued that the Arkansas authorities' actions "spread doubt and confusion as to the significance of this decision under our federal system, it may be well to recall some elementary constitutional propositions which are no longer open to question," starting with Chief Justice John Marshall's affirmation in *Marbury v. Madison* (1803) that the Constitution is supreme U.S. law. From Marshall's "basic principle that the federal judiciary is supreme in the exposition of the Constitution," Brennan concluded, "the interpretation of the Constitution enunciated by this Court in the *Brown* case is the supreme law of the land, and is made by Art. VI of the Constitution of binding effect on the States."

Upon these basic principles Brennan established the duties state agents owed black students under *Brown*. To buttress his case he cited the Article VI affirmation of federal supremacy, "any Thing in the

Constitution or Laws of any State to the Contrary notwithstanding," and historic Supreme Court decisions, *United States v. Peters* (1809), *Ableman v. Booth* (1859), and *Sterling v. Constantin* (1932) holding that state officials were "solemnly bound not to war against the Constitution." Accordingly, a century and a half of "our constitutional history must" overcome any "doubt and confusion" concerning federal supremacy. It demonstrated, too, that the "constitutional rights of schoolchildren not to be discriminated against on grounds of race or color declared by this Court in the *Brown* case can neither be nullified openly and directly by state legislators or state executive or judicial officers, nor nullified indirectly by them through evasive schemes for segregation 'whether accomplished ingeniously or ingenuously' [*Smith v. Texas*]." Moreover, *Brown* confirmed, all public schoolchildren possessed "a constitutional right not to be discriminated against by reason of race or color," and this "constitutional right is personal and present." As a result, "responsible school authorities" not only had an "immediate duty" to make a "prompt start" in desegregation plans, as had Little Rock school officials, but in accord with "all deliberate speed," they were permitted no "delay in any guise to avoid discharge of the constitutional duty to desegregate."

Brennan thus tied the language of federal supremacy to an interpretation of "all deliberate speed." In construing this standard, Brennan stated, "a prompt commitment to initiate and complete desegregation at specific times is a necessary requirement for compliance with the constitutional principles expressed in *Brown*." The desegregation plans school boards and federal courts approved, then, should stipulate and comply with a specified timetable, facilitating rather than discouraging immediate desegregation. Little Rock school officials undoubtedly were sincere in arguing that a "prompt start" made in "good faith" should embrace the need for delaying desegregation when private and state action beyond their control caused disruption harming educational standards. However, like the Eighth Circuit Court *Cooper v. Aaron* opinion, Brennan declared, "It is the duty of the educational authorities to maintain standards in a way consistent with the preservation of constitutional rights, not by foregoing the enforcement of those rights." If serious difficulties encumbered school officials' implementation of their plan, the school board "should also invoke the assistance of the courts to remove any obstacles to a peaceful and orderly carrying out of the plan."

On this latter point Brennan cited the Hoxie precedent. In case "state and local officials cannot or will not control the situation, it becomes the ultimate duty of federal power, ordinarily exercised by the Executive Department, to enforce the decrees of federal courts."

Finally, despite other southern school board failures to desegregate, Little Rock authorities must enforce the constitutional rights owed black students. Congressional action may be "warranted" in order "to secur[e] the constitutional rights of the schoolchildren by individual lawsuits against each school board" under the Fourteenth Amendment. "But the fact that uniform enforcement of the relevant constitutional rights and duties has not been effectuated does not alter the existence or the compelling nature of those rights and duties," Brennan said. Ultimately, "in a conflict between the Constitution and state recalcitrance, the Constitution must and will prevail. It may be expected that the full force of federal power will be used, if necessary, to achieve this end. Failing this, in Chief Justice Marshall's words, 'the Constitution becomes a solemn mockery.' " Thus, notwithstanding school officials' "subjective sincerity" in asserting that agitated local circumstances justified delaying enforcement of their desegregation plan, they and the federal courts "must meet the test of compliance that we have outlined here," which, Brennan concluded, "reiterated" the "principles we have enunciated in the *Brown* case." Thus, "only through such scrutiny can the present constitutional rights of these children receive the full vindication by judicial power of the United States to which they are entitled." Accordingly, in the September 12 per curiam opinion "we made our judgment effective immediately."

During the two weeks that followed, Brennan responded to input from colleagues. Preparing for a September 19 conference, Harlan noted the suggestions Brennan had received. Warren urged streamlining the section about the facts of the Little Rock case and giving more attention to the cases defining the limits of federal judicial power. Frankfurter suggested printing the whole September 12 per curiam opinion in a footnote and called for a "compact" opinion; more substantively, he queried whether the Little Rock plan had an end date and urged focusing upon the federal court rather than the school officials' administrative discretion. Targeting Brennan's effort to incorporate deadlines into the *Brown* II standard, Burton said that "all deliberate speed" should not extend to including in desegregation plans an "end date." He also noted that issues involving the Fourteenth Amendment were "already at rest." Black wanted the reference to public schools "broaden[ed]" to cover all schools supported by public funds, in order to "anticipate state-supported private schools." Unlike Burton and Frankfurter, Black "wants an 'end date' for any plan." Generally, he was "standing up for [the] decision," with modest changes. "Some," apparently including Clark, preferred "no ref[erence] to Congress." Clark, too, was "against" Brennan's treatment of the Fourteenth Amendment, including the scope of "state action"; he also wanted the "number of children involved" in the Little Rock plan "put in the opening statement."

Brennan revised his draft, incorporating formal and informal commentary. By September 25, he produced a fourth, substantially final draft; following minor changes in two further drafts, the Court announced its final opinion on September 29. Thus, from September 19–29, eight justices met in conference several times to discuss Brennan's revisions; in Minnesota, Douglas remained involved through mail and telegram. As Brennan's revisions progressed, Burton recorded in his diary having periodic lunches with different groups of justices, including Warren and Whittaker. Brennan worked steadily with one clerk and his secretary to accommodate the changes received informally over lunch and formally in letters, handwritten comments in the margins of each printed draft, and from the conferences. Many revisions stipulated more precise wording, such as Burton's substitution in the first draft, mentioned "at luncheon today" and restated in a September 18 letter: the "validity of the Fourteenth Amendment, in turn, is itself so completely established that it is not . . . open to question." On the first draft Clark wrote, "Leave out about Congress," and, like Black's comment in the September 19 conference, "After admonishing State cannot evade by ingenuity, etc., [opinion] should be enlarged to include any scheme supported by public funds though tagged *private*." Suggesting the pace of the revisions, Burton's September 23 letter read, "I shall be glad to join your opinion as circulated September 22."

Although Brennan generally acquiesced to many changes, on several substantive points he presented counterarguments. Brennan's preconference memorandum readily accepted Warren's call for a more compressed rendition of the facts, perhaps confined to a footnote,

Frankfurter's restatement of the per curiam decision in a footnote, Burton's revision of Fourteenth Amendment language in order "to meet the argument widely made in the South that the Amendment was not validly adopted," and Black's suggested revision to use the "quotes" from Chief Justices Marshall, Roger Taney, and Charles Evans Hughes in *Peters, Ableman,* and *Sterling v. Constantin,* respectively, "to greater effect." Brennan also embraced Black's revision, "after admonishing the states they cannot evade the Constitution by 'schemes ingenious or ingenuous,' a sentence should be added to the effect that the obligation applies to every school system maintained from the public purse." Brennan added, moreover, "that leasing alone would be state action," and thus be prohibited from discrimination under the Fourteenth Amendment. Regarding the treatment of the "questions of prompt and reasonable start and with all deliberate speed," however, Frankfurter's suggestions targeted Brennan's statement that "every school board must formulate a plan which provides specific dates both for the initiation and completion of the desegregation process. Felix questions whether the principles should be stated in such rigid terms."

Brennan urged limiting the lassitude *Brown* II permitted. Frankfurter, however, "would emphasize the obligations to start a process and let the matter of completion alone be developed in local communities as best suited individual local needs and problems," Brennan said. He questioned, too, Brennan's attempts to distinguish delay from legitimate "administrative problems" in the application of the "all deliberate speed" standard. "I recognize a contradiction," Brennan said, "in the thought that the rights of the children are personal and present and the notion that their recognition may be delayed for some children so long as the start is made to enforce them for other children." Nevertheless, responding to the draft opinion, Burton and Harlan eliminated the language framing this "thought," including the end date for desegregation plans. Like Frankfurter, then, these two justices disapproved of Brennan's effort to incorporate more specified terms into "all deliberate speed." Brennan noted that Burton "has suggested some language which would emphasize a commitment to initial steps toward desegregation," reflected in Little Rock officials' "good faith" start, "but interpose a caveat that the steps taken are by no means restricted to any one pattern or timetable and that the approval of the Little Rock plan neither precludes its amendment nor indicates that elsewhere under other circumstances some different plan would not equally well meet the requirements of the [*Brown*] case." Thus, only Black expressly favored Brennan on this point.

Although his treatment of "all deliberate speed" was contentious, Brennan's memorandum suggested an emerging consensus regarding federal supremacy. He addressed the Little Rock School Board argument that a "good faith" start to desegregation, followed by enormous resistance, "entitled" it to "postponement." Despite "limitations upon its effectiveness in face of the attitudes of other state officials," the school board remained bound by its "obligation . . . as an arm of the State both in its role as litigant and apart from this role," including the "various remedies it should attempt to employ in effecting its plan," such as a Hoxie-type injunction. Brennan also noted the "roles of the executive and the Congress if federal power must be asserted to enforce the decrees of federal courts." The draft language asserted the "imperative nature of the Board's constitutional duty notwithstanding other school districts having done nothing." Finally, Brennan embraced Black's and Frankfurter's "suggest[ion] that this is the kind of an opinion which should close with two or three sentences highlighting for the public the true nature of the issues at stake." Brennan's memorandum thus reflected his colleagues' growing agreement regarding federal supremacy, including the noteworthy assertion that Court interpretation of the Constitution in cases such as *Brown* had the same legitimacy as the Constitution itself.

———

Justice Harlan and the Limits of Unanimity

Justice Harlan prepared an alternative draft opinion. Headed J.M.H.-Draft-9/19/58, the twenty-five page, double-spaced typescript was titled No. 1— *Cooper v. Aaron*. He may have given only Frankfurter and Clark a complete copy, but its contents became sufficiently known among the justices that in the September 23 conference, Warren and others referred to the "JMH draft." Unlike Brennan's, Harlan's discussion of "all deliberate speed" omitted reference to a possible timetable, including end dates. Harlan's language, by contrast, "made plain that delay in any guise to avoid discharge of the constitutional duty to desegregate could not be recognized, and that only a prompt start, unremittingly pursued, to eliminate racial segregation from the public schools at the earliest practicable date could constitute good faith compliance." He also removed *Smith v. Texas*, which Brennan cited for the proposition that the Supremacy Clause prohibited either "ingenious or ingenuous" state action to circumvent *Brown*. Harlan also deleted *Marbury v. Madison*, thereby eliminating Brennan's use of the precedent establishing judicial review to buttress the equation of Court decisions with the Constitution itself. Instead, he wrote, the "constitutional oath required by" the Supremacy Clause, "of every person holding state or federal executive, legislative or judicial office embraces of course both acts of Congress and the judgments of this Court, which under our federal system has the final responsibility for constitutional adjudication."

The most conspicuous change related the Little Rock case to the Court unanimity established in *Brown*. That "basic decision," Harlan's typescript concluded, "was unanimously reached by a Court, composed of Justices of diversified geographical and other backgrounds, only after the cases had been briefed and twice argued by lawyers of the highest skill and reputation, and the issues had been under deliberation for . . . [many] months." These words rebutted conservative states' rights arguments publicized throughout the nation, and presented in briefs the Court had rejected during the special term, claiming that the *Brown* decisions violated fundamental constitutional principles. Under Warren, the symbolic rejoinder of the Court to such claims rested on unanimity; *Cooper v. Aaron* provided a new opportunity to restate that principle most forcefully. "Since the first [*Brown*] opinion three new Justices have come to the Court," Harlan wrote. "They are at one with the Justices still on the Court who participated in the original decision as to the inescapability of that decision, believing that whatever history may be offered in justification of racial segregation, such discrimination in the public school systems of the States can no longer be squared with the commands of the Fourteenth Amendment that no State shall 'deny any person . . . the equal protection of the laws.'" Harlan closed, stating, "These are the reasons for our unanimous affirmance of the judgment of the Court of Appeals" in *Cooper v. Aaron*.

Aware of the divergence between Harlan and Brennan regarding "unanimity," Frankfurter introduced an unusual proposal. Burton's letter indicated that he joined Brennan's second "recirculated" draft of September 22, which had not addressed the changes proposed by Harlan's typescript. Also on September 22, in a longhand note headed No. 1— *Cooper v. Aaron*, on stationery from the Radisson Hotel in Minneapolis, Douglas wrote Brennan, "Please tell the Brethren for me that I think the opinion in this case should follow the customary format — 'Mr. Justice Brennan delivered the opinion of the Court' — and not carry each of our names, as someone suggested." Unknown to Douglas, Harlan noted privately and Frankfurter proposed to the Court this idea. According to Warren's memoir, the Court accepted the "joint opinion" idea, though the chief justice did not recall that it had ever been done before. Located within the chronology established by Burton's and Douglas's separate letters, it is reasonable to conclude that Frankfurter offered this unusual suggestion in order to ameliorate the disagreement between Brennan and Harlan. Along with the other justices, Frankfurter had received Brennan's revised draft. Only Frankfurter and Clark had seen Harlan's full typescript headed 9/19, which began: "The opinion of the Court, in which (naming each Justice) join, was announced by the Chief Justice." Thus, Frankfurter and Harlan may have sought to reinforce unanimity, notwithstanding the Harlan-Brennan disagreement.

By the September 23 conference, Brennan disputed Harlan's key points. He conceded that most of Harlan's "suggested changes" were "largely entirely verbal," not altering the "substance except in two respects." First, Harlan's removal of the *Smith v. Texas* "idea" that the Supremacy Clause "inhibits a State from circumventing [*Brown*] by any method ingenious or ingenuous" took out "a vital statement very essential to the point we are making. Secondly," Brennan challenged Harlan's "omit[ted] reference" to *Marbury v. Madison* "and the detailed discussion in my draft of the Court's responsibility for the exposition of the law of the Constitution. That too I think is a very essential part of what I believe our opinion should contain." Ultimately, Harlan's "suggestions" removed Brennan's formulation of the "principle of equal justice under law and the inescapability of the [*Brown*] decisions for a Court having responsibility for expounding the law of the Constitution." Instead, Harlan's language "would substitute an emphasis upon the adherence of three new members of the Court to the [*Brown*] principles. I feel any such reference to the three new members would be a grave mistake." The suggested change "lends support to the notion that the Constitution has only the meaning that can command a majority of the Court as that majority may change with shifting membership. . . . I think it would be fatal in this fight to provide ammunition from the mouth of this Court in support of it."

This contention provided the context for the September 23 conference and the revisions shaping the final opinion. Warren asked directly only why the "Harlan draft" left out Chief Justice Taney's quote affirming the framers' "anxiety" to maintain the Constitution despite state defiance or "evasion." Supporting as it did Warren's basic formulation of the Little Rock case as a clash between state authorities (especially Faubus) and the Supreme Court, the comment reinforced Brennan's propositions. Brennan's own conference presentation essentially repeated the points developed in his rejoinder to Harlan. He also noted that Douglas was "opposed to 'joint' opinion." He remained silent regarding Harlan's reconstruction of the "all deliberate speed" analysis, probably because he knew that only Black went along with his attempt to limit federal court discretion over desegregation plans. Generally satisfied on this point, Frankfurter questioned primarily the use of "immediate desegregation." Responding to Warren's earlier statement that the detailed presentation of the litigation seemed "dry," Brennan tried restating it as an appendix. Black alone expressly supported that approach. Otherwise, Black favored Brennan's draft, including citation of *Smith v. Texas* (which he wrote), and the concluding pages "better than JMH draft." Except for minor word changes, Burton also "liked" Brennan's third draft (which dropped the appendix) "better than JMH — more 'readable' for the public."

From September 24–25, Brennan's drafts approached a final opinion. On the third draft, in addition to relatively minor word changes, Brennan incorporated Harlan's proposal to remove from the appendix the detailed reconstruction of the litigation and include it in the opinion. He also added Harlan's citation of *Buchanan v. Warely* (1917) for the words, "important as is the preservation of public peace, this aim cannot be accomplished by laws or ordinances which deny rights created or protected by the Federal Constitution." At another place, where Harlan wrote, "Terrible! [HLB — says this was his suggestion!]," Brennan also omitted from the discussion of the Supremacy Clause the sentence: "The Constitution does not specifically declare how the meaning of that Constitution is to be finally and authoritatively determined." Suggesting that Harlan's own changes had reached a limit, he wrote at the end of draft three: "Overall this draft shows on the face a patchwork job," and "all Justices [accept] 'joining formula.'" Even so, on the fourth draft, Brennan's basic approach prevailed on the Supremacy Clause and also on the proposition that the Little Rock School Board lawyer and the LDF had argued that state agents could evade *Brown* by neither "ingenious" nor "ingenuous" actions.

In the September 26 conference, the justices finalized the opinion Warren would read in the courtroom three days later on Monday morning. Initially, Brennan attempted to develop a broad opinion limiting the discretion inherent in the "all deliberate speed" standard and demarcating the shared enforcement responsibilities of federal and state authorities as well as rejecting the Little Rock school officials' arguments that state and private interference with their desegregation plan justified a thirty-month delay. As the intense drafting process advanced from September 17–26, Harlan, Burton, Frankfurter, and, less so, Clark succeeded in narrowing the opinion, essentially maintaining the open-ended "all deliberate speed" standard and stressing federal judicial supremacy instead of a shared judicial, congressional, and executive enforcement role. Most significantly, Brennan formulated a forceful and innovative articulation of federal judicial supremacy, linking the Supremacy Clause, judicial review, and historic state challenges to both in order to establish the principle that Court interpretation of the Constitution in cases such as *Brown* had the same binding legitimacy on state authorities and private citizens as the Constitution itself. Brennan also successfully incorporated Black's language targeting privatized public school funding intended to preserve racial segregation. Clark, too, concurred in Black's idea. Though not formally before the Court, the Little Rock school officials' lawyer had suggested the point as a recent example of Faubus's defiance.

Brennan thus reshaped the opinion along the lines of strongest agreement among the justices. Although he personally agreed with Black that the "all deliberate speed" standard effectively invited the delay and defiance Little Rock and Faubus epitomized, the rest of the Court could not separate the standard from a shared overriding commitment to maintaining unanimity. Similarly, Warren occasionally expressed dissatisfaction over Eisenhower's lack of support for the Court and *Brown*; the justices also were conscious of southern Democratic and conservative Republican congressional attacks on the Court, unified by opposition to judicial activism. Brennan's initial drafts asserting shared federal enforcement authority reflected these pressures. Attorney General Rogers's defense of the Court and *Brown* and the bipartisan defeat of the Smith bill just days before the special term began, as well as Rankin's eloquent oral arguments on behalf of the Court and *Brown* during the term, undoubtedly reinforced the input Brennan received from his colleagues that the focus should be upon the obligation imposed by oath upon federal and state authorities alike to obey the Constitution. All these officials also owed the same duty to the Court interpretation of the Constitution in *Brown*. Rogers's and Rankin's statements suggested that the Eisenhower administration accepted this duty. Even so, Faubus's and southern public officials' ongoing defiance justified the Court consensus that its decision should emphasize federal judicial supremacy.

The opinion Warren read on Monday, September 29, thus reflected a noteworthy change regarding unanimity. In *Brown*, the Court relied upon unanimity to convey solidarity in the face of anticipated southern defiance. Arising from the globally reported September 1957 Little Rock crisis, *Cooper v. Aaron* posed the most conspicuous test yet of the unanimity principle's persuasive authority. Brennan's narrowing of the draft opinions evidenced a consensus among a majority of his colleagues that a strong, precise reaffirmation of unanimity was necessary, especially given the appointment of three new justices since 1955 and Burton's impending retirement. Thus, despite Brennan's and Douglas's initial objection, the Court accepted Harlan's and Frankfurter's "joining formula," thereby supporting both a unique expression of the unanimity principle and Brennan's expansive interpretation of the Supremacy Clause. Accordingly, the opinion Warren read before a full courtroom on September 29 did not suggest the full range of contentious issues arising from *Brown* II and the "all deliberate speed" standard, Eisenhower's equivocal approach to enforcement, or congressional measures targeting judicial activism. Instead, the opinion communicated to an international audience a unanimous reaffirmation of the *Brown* decision through the most forceful declaration ever of Court power.

The sense of drama prevailing when Warren convened the special term was repeated one more time. At noon on September 29, eight justices took their seats on the bench; remaining in the West, only Douglas was absent. Turning to and naming each justice present, Warren declared that all nine members of the Court had authored the opinion. Warren began with its first paragraph drafted by Black. The case "involves questions of the highest importance to the maintenance of our federal system of government. It squarely presents a claim that there is no duty on state officials to obey federal court orders resting on this Court's deliberate and considered interpretation of the United States Constitution," particularly the "actions" of the Arkansas governor, legislature, and "other agencies . . . upon the premise that they are not bound by our holding in [*Brown*] that the Fourteenth Amendment forbids states to use governmental powers to bar children from attending schools which are helped to run by public management, funds, or other public property." The Court was "urged to permit continued suspension of the Little Rock School Board's plan to do away with segregated public schools until state laws and efforts to upset and nullify our holding in [*Brown*] have been further challenged and tested in the courts. We have concluded that these contentions call for clear answers here and now."

Warren read the full opinion in forty-five minutes; nationwide response was contradictory. Those present in the courtroom and future readers of the opinion in the *U.S. Reports* readily grasped its core principle: the Supreme Court interpretation of the Constitution imposed a duty upon all government officials to obey. Thus, Warren affirmed "the basic principle that the federal judiciary is supreme in the exposition of the law of the Constitution and that principle [is] a permanent and indispensable feature of our constitutional system." This principle upheld in *Brown* was the fundamental law overturning segregation. Warren's voice rose, concluding that the principles established in *Brown* "are indispensable for the protection of the freedoms guaranteed by our fundamental charter for all of us. Our constitutional ideal of equal justice under law is thus made a living truth." He then said, "The Special Term is now adjourned," whereupon the eight justices arose from their seats and filed out to their respective chambers. Suggesting the press reception outside the South, the *New York*

Times reported upon the opinion's "clear and simple language, under-
standable even to the most fanatic segregationists." Fanatic or not,
segregationists in Arkansas, Virginia, and across the South remained
defiant. Indeed, Faubus and his followers in Little Rock closed and
privatized the public schools; segregationists also prepared slates of
candidates for the local, statewide, and federal November elections.

more accommodstion

———

Justice Frankfurter's Concurring Opinion

The contradictory public response to the opinion was matched within
the Court. Despite the overriding commitment to unanimity reflected
in the Court consensus favoring the "joining formula," at the September 26 conference in which Brennan presented the final revisions
of *Cooper v. Aaron*, Frankfurter announced he would write a separate
concurring opinion. "The Conference could not dissuade him from
writing separately," Burton's diary recorded, "but he agreed not to file
his separate opinion until a week or so after the Court opinion is
filed." When Warren delivered the final opinion there was no mention of Frankfurter's intent, though Burton's diary indicated the justices again attempted but failed to dissuade him from the idea. Years
later, Warren's memoir acknowledged that Frankfurter's insistence
upon filing the concurring opinion "caused quite a sensation on the
Court." Historians of the Supreme Court eventually revealed that
Frankfurter's action created consternation. Warren, Black, and Brennan were angry, and Harlan, joined by Clark, searched for some
accommodation. Warren asked Black and others to urge Frankfurter
not to pursue the separate opinion, but he remained resolute. Black
and Brennan then drafted their own "separate opinion" affirming that
"they stand by" the Court's "opinion as delivered" on September 29;
they insisted further that Frankfurter's concurrence "must not be
accepted as any dilution or interpretation of the views expressed in
the Court's joint opinion."

Frankfurter's separate opinion thus revealed how circumscribed the
unanimous "joining formula" in *Cooper v. Aaron* was. On a printed
copy of the concurrence Frankfurter circulated on October 3, Harlan
scribbled, "This opinion was the subject of a Special Conf[erence]
called by the C.J. (at the instant of W. J. B.) on October 6, 1958."

Throughout he marked "C.J." where Warren apparently questioned Frankfurter's language. Finally, he wrote, "C.J. says this is the worst thing in the opinion," referring to the last paragraph, which began, "Lincoln's appeal to 'the better angels of our nature' failed to avert a fratricidal war," and concluded, "But the compassionate wisdom of Lincoln's First and Second Inaugurals bequeathed to the Union, cemented with blood, a moral heritage which, when drawn upon in times of stress and strife, is sure to find specific ways and means to surmount difficulties that may appear insurmountable." Measured against the value of unanimity, such lofty sentiments aroused objections from Warren, Black, and Brennan. The latter two justices withdrew their own "concurrence," however, after Harlan circulated a statement to which Clark acquiesced, questioning Frankfurter's "wisdom" in issuing the concurrence, but leaving the matter to his "good judgment." Harlan "dissented" from Black's and Brennan's "separate opinion, believing that it is always a mistake to make a mountain out of a molehill." Harlan's half-serious effort thus quieted the dispute and Frankfurter got his way.

Accordingly, both the jointly signed unanimous opinion and Frankfurter's concurrence were reported as *Cooper v. Aaron*. The two opinions were essentially consistent, except that Frankfurter's prose was characteristically condescending and verbose. Frankfurter both "unreservedly participate[d] with my brethren in our joint opinion," and "deem[ed] it appropriate to deal individually with the great issue at stake." In Little Rock, federal litigation over the compliance standards of *Brown* II affirmed that "by working together, by sharing in a common effort, men of different minds and tempers, even if they do not reach agreement, acquire understanding and thereby tolerance of their differences." Neither the violence arising from state authorities' efforts to block the Little Rock Nine's admittance to a racially desegregated school, school officials' "undoubted good faith efforts" to the contrary notwithstanding, nor federal "action or nonaction" mitigated the "illegality" of the "interferences with the constitutional right of Negro children qualified to enter the Central High School," Frankfurter declared. The "tragic aspect of this disruptive tactic was that the power of the State was used not to sustain law but as an instrument to thwart law," thereby "disabling" the "Little Rock School Board from peacefully carrying out the Board's and the State's constitutional duty." Admittedly,

Arkansas was "not a formal party in these proceedings" subject to an enforceable decree, but "it is legally and morally before the Court."

Like the majority opinion, Frankfurter's concurrence targeted the claim that disorder justified delaying enforcement of the desegregation order. "No explanation that may be offered in support of such a request can obscure the inescapable meaning that law should bow to force," he said. "To yield to such a claim would be to enthrone official lawlessness, and lawlessness if not checked is the precursor of anarchy." Frankfurter compared the claim to the "few tragic" struggles between North and South, impelling the question whether "disorder under the aegis of a state has moral superiority over the law of the Constitution? For those in authority thus to defy the law of the land is profoundly subversive not only of our constitutional system, but of . . . a democratic society." Citing case law decided by a Court including his friends Justices Oliver Wendell Holmes and Louis Brandeis, public statements by John Adams and Andrew Jackson, and former Harvard colleague Roscoe Pound, Frankfurter then affirmed the Court decisions as equally authoritative to the U.S. Constitution, because "our kind of society cannot endure if the controlling authority of the Law as derived from the Constitution is not to be the tribunal specially charged with the duty of ascertaining and declaring what is 'the supreme Law of the Land.' " The shared supremacy of the Court decisions and the Constitution was especially binding where such decisions resulted not from a divided Court, but were "the unanimous conclusion of a long-matured deliberative process."

Frankfurter's conclusion, however, subtly deviated from the majority opinion. Although the bulk of Frankfurter's concurrence basically endorsed Brennan's construction of the Supremacy Clause, the final portion employed that construction to reinforce the initial federal court decisions in 1956 and 1957 upholding the Little Rock desegregation plan under the *Brown* II "all deliberate speed" standard. Addressing the segregationist assertion that *Brown* was not law and therefore subordinate to racial mores implemented through Jim Crow and interposition, Frankfurter said that the "Constitution is not the formulation of the merely personal views of the members of this Court, nor can its authority be reduced to the claim that state officials are its controlling interpreters." Frankfurter then suggested an essential precept of *Brown* II: by exercising their discretion properly, the federal courts could promote displacement of "local customs, however hardened by time. . . . Habits and feelings they engender may be counteracted and moderated. Experience attests that such local habits and feelings will yield, gradually though this be, to law and education." Neither fomenting "violence and defiance employed and encouraged by those upon whom the duty of law observance should have the strongest claim — nor by submitting to it under whatever guise employed" would, of course, overcome such constitutional supremacy.

Frankfurter's final paragraphs explicitly linked the Little Rock case to preserving the "all deliberate speed" standard. "Only the constructive use of time will achieve what an advanced civilization demands and the Constitution confirms," he said. The Court holding in *Brown* "that color alone cannot bar a child from a public school . . . has recognized the diversity of circumstances in local school situations." Indeed, in Little Rock, there was clear "progress . . . made in respecting the constitutional rights of the Negro children, according to the graduated plan sanctioned by the two lower courts." Should the Court affirm, however, the Little Rock school officials' request for a delay, the progress those two federal courts upheld "would have to be retraced, perhaps with even greater difficulty because of deference to forcible resistance." Thus, was it not reasonable to conclude that the Court sanction of "a suspension of the Board's nonsegregation plan, would be but the beginning of a series of delays calculated to nullify this Court's adamant decisions in the *Brown* case that the Constitution precludes compulsory segregation based on color in state-supported schools?"

Answering this question, he returned to the theme of federal supremacy. Enforcement of school desegregation plans "in cities with Negro populations of large proportions" presented the "lesson" that the "responsibility of those who exercise power in a democratic government is not to reflect inflamed public feeling but to help form its understanding . . . especially . . . when they are confronted with a problem like a racially discriminating public school system." Many times throughout U.S. history, "compliance with the decisions of this Court, as the constitutional organ of the supreme Law of the Land . . . depended on active support by state and local authorities. It presupposes such support. To withhold it, and indeed to use political power to try to paralyze the supreme Law, precludes the maintenance of our federal system as we have known and cherished it for one hundred and seventy years." Finally, although like the majority opinion Frankfurter's ended with ringing phrases, his concurrence appealed to the force of North-South struggle and reconciliation Lincoln proclaimed in the first and second inaugurals. According to Harlan, this was the same language Warren found most objectionable even as Black and Brennan failed to overcome Frankfurter's adamant insistence on publishing the separate opinion.

Why was Frankfurter determined to publish the concurring opinion? The question suggested Frankfurter's declining influence upon the Court regarding unanimity in school desegregation cases. As Burton's September 26 diary comments intimated, Frankfurter's announcement that he would file a separate opinion engendered opposition among his colleagues. By September 29, Black, Brennan, and Warren were angry, a view Douglas apparently shared as he returned from the West to begin the Court term in early October. Harlan, Clark, Burton, and Whittaker sufficiently doubted Frankfurter's idea that they persisted in trying to dissuade him, though confronted with Black's and Brennan's threatened second concurrence and Harlan's rejoinder, everyone's opposition dissipated. Nevertheless, Frankfurter could not help but grasp that the separate opinion further aggravated the growing dissension between himself and Warren, Black, Douglas, and Brennan. By contrast, during the disputed *Brown* decisions in 1954–1955, Frankfurter gained support within the Court for the "all deliberate speed" standard by endorsing the constitutional legitimacy unanimity symbolized. Moreover, as recently as June 1958, he helped to persuade Clark not to dissent by appealing to the value of unanimity in the Alabama NAACP registration case. Now, just three months later, he seemed to be rejecting that same advice.

Soon after its publication in early October, Frankfurter privately justified his separate opinion. In a letter to his friend C. C. Burlingham dated November 12, Frankfurter queried, "Why did I write and publish the concurring opinion?" He answered his own question, asserting "anybody reading the two opinions [majority and concurring] would find the answer." Then Frankfurter said, "my opinion, by its content and its atmosphere, was directed" at "a particular audience . . . an audience which I was in a particularly qualified position to address in view of my rather extensive association, by virtue of my twenty-five years at the Harvard Law School, with a good many Southern lawyers and law professors." Elaborating upon this point, he repeated the "conviction" expressed to Harlan in his letter of September 2 and to Warren on September 11 "that it is to the legal profession of the South on which our greatest reliance must be placed for a gradual thawing of the ice, not because they may not dislike termination of segregation," but most significantly "because the lawyers of the South will gradually realize that there is a transcending issue, namely, respect for law as determined so impressively by a unanimous Court in construing the Constitution of the United States."

Although Warren, like later commentators, accepted Frankfurter's justification for the separate opinion, such a rationale had unintended consequences. Frankfurter, Warren's memoir stated, had "many friends in the Southern states" whom "he intended to reach . . . by writing and circulating a concurring opinion of his own." Warren noted, too, the "sensation" this announcement caused among the justices, without revealing the heated reaction from Black and Brennan, as well as Harlan's ameliorative response. Nevertheless, if, as Frankfurter confirmed in the Burlingham letter and elsewhere, southern moderate lawyers' consciousness was to be raised by grasping the Court's unanimous pronouncement equating the *Brown* decision with the Constitution's supremacy, how could he believe that the separate opinion did not deny the very unanimity and judicial supremacy it proclaimed? The question suggested in turn the contrary reading Brennan gave to Harlan's effort to demonstrate the Court's continuing unanimous support for *Brown* by emphasizing the arrival of three new justices between 1955 and 1958. Such an assertion, Brennan warned, reinforced the claims of the Court's enemies that its decisions reflected solely the will of the justices and were not, therefore, binding law. This disagreement fostered the unique "joining formula" in *Cooper v. Aaron*. Another unintentional result was that Brennan's drafting process facilitated Frankfurter's decision to issue his separate opinion.

The *Cooper v. Aaron* Opinions: A Hidden Story

The opinion-drafting process in *Cooper v. Aaron* converged with public and hidden stories. On September 12, following the Supreme

Court per curiam order upholding the Eighth Circuit Court overturning of Lemley's authorized suspension of desegregation in Little Rock, Faubus signed the laws the legislature had enacted earlier calling a special election to vote upon whether the city should close and privatize the schools. On September 27, Little Rock voters endorsed closure and privatization rather than integration of the entire school system. Framed in terms of such extreme choices, Faubus's triumph and ongoing southern resistance were inevitable. In addition, LDF lawyers confronted Judge Miller's resistance. Meanwhile, from September 12–26, Brennan and his colleagues narrowed the initial scope of Brennan's drafts, finally announcing the Court opinion on September 29. As it grappled with several cold war confrontations, the Eisenhower administration expressed more support than previously for the Supreme Court desegregation decisions. Thus, Brennan's opinion drafting proceeded amidst Faubus's and others' ongoing defiance as well as a new legitimacy the Court received from Eisenhower. Keeping the matter to himself, Frankfurter conceived of the separate opinion in order to reassert the unanimity the Court gave the "all deliberate speed" standard in *Brown* II. Frankfurter's use of judicial supremacy to reaffirm unanimity, however, undermined both.

Brennan's early opinion drafts reflected this shifting context. As previously discussed, prior to the September 23 conference, Brennan's drafts included passing references to the school privatization-closure legislation Arkansas had enacted. During the drafting process, Black successfully defended including these references in the final opinion. Although critics later claimed the legislation was not properly before the Court, Butler's briefs and arguments mentioned it, albeit cryptically, during the August 28 and September 11 hearings. By contrast, his colleagues did not accept Brennan's suggestion that Congress, as well as the executive branch, shared with the Court a duty to address the southern states' defiance. Clark's marginal note on one draft urging omission of significant references to Congress reflected most justices' unwillingness to even hint at the struggle over anti-Court legislative proposals introduced by Senators William Jenner, John Marshall Butler, and others. Brennan may have removed the references to executive authority in part because Eisenhower administration support for the Court was improving. Prior to the Little Rock crisis, Eisenhower's stance toward *Brown* and the Court was problematic. But in the days preceding and coinciding with the special term, Attorney General Rogers publicly defended the Court and the *Brown* decisions amidst criticism from the state chief justices. Solicitor General Rankin vigorously repeated this defense in his brief and oral arguments during the two hearings of the special term.

Days before Warren convened the August special term, Eisenhower himself offered a more favorable view of the Court and *Brown*. Questioned about his "personal feeling on the principle of school integration" in an August 20 news conference, Eisenhower responded, "I have always declined to do that for the simple reason that here was something that the Supreme Court says . . . is the instruction of the Constitution. That is, they say this is the meaning of the Constitution." Eisenhower went on to say, "I have an oath; I expect to carry it out. And the mere fact that I could disagree very violently with a decision, and would so express myself, then my duty would be much more difficult to carry out I think." He admitted, too, suggesting a "slower" approach. Still, these words were more positive compared to Eisenhower's problematic public statements following *Brown* I. Indeed, on August 20, Faubus suggested that Eisenhower was saying it was "my duty as Governor to use the military to enforce integration in any school district in this State." Nevertheless, he said, "my position of last fall is unchanged." Eisenhower indirectly offered a rejoinder in a September 5 news conference. The president denied having said he "wishes the Supreme Court had never handed down its [*Brown*] decision," claiming that the August 20 statement correctly expressed his feelings on the matter. Eisenhower also said that closing schools "would be a very terrible outcome" of desegregation, resulting in "a whole basketful of litigation."

Members of the Court probably did not know how much cold war imperatives influenced Eisenhower's shifting public position toward the desegregation issue. At the same time the domestic and international news media covered Court handling of the Little Rock case during the special term, Eisenhower dispatched Marines to Lebanon and faced opposition from a new nationalist government in Iraq. A September 5 *U.S. News & World Report* story queried: "If Small War Comes — Is U.S. Ready?" Just days before, the Hong Kong *South China Morning Post* questioned Eisenhower's previous lack of moral support for *Brown* and the Court and his dependence instead on the

constitutional obligation to enforce the law. "Adroit though this was
. . . other presidents . . . held that their duty was also to be moral leaders. They did not wait for public opinion to push them along any
one path. . . . Moralist though Eisenhower is, he still shrinks from
leadership." International media coverage of the Court special term
sometimes appeared on front pages, other times further back. The
propaganda appeal of justifying presidential action in terms of such
constitutional abstractions as "federalism," rather than moral justice,
nonetheless was apparent. Eisenhower administration public relations
imagery thus linked the president's constitutional obligation to enforce
the federal judiciary racial desegregation orders to his exercise of constitutional powers resisting communism on distant cold war battle-
fields such as Lebanon or Iraq.

These media images suggested ties between Eisenhower administration cold war propaganda and the desegregation issue. The international press publicized the full range of civil rights cases and
confrontations, including a September 15 *South China Morning Post*
story about Martin Luther King, Jr.'s protest and arrest. Most reports
nonetheless focused on the federal court and presidential constitutional enforcement obligations versus state defiance. Such reports
popularized the values of shared power and checks and balances enabling state and federal authorities and the Supreme Court to accept
or avoid the constitutional duty to enforce desegregation. Eisenhower's explanation of his desegregation stance in terms of such duty
rather than moral obligation was consistent, then, with a September
10 *South China Morning Post* story commenting favorably on U.S.
political science professor Donald Flaherty's assertion that the Little
Rock case revealed the "U.S. system of government" at work. Even
so, "there was always the possibility of strife between the national government and one or more of the state governments under the federal
system." Flaherty also expressed the opinion that "complete integration would be accomplished gradually. If this could be done peacefully . . . then the federal system of government would have achieved
something of major importance." The statement regarding "gradualism" repeated Eisenhower's own publicized preference for a "slower"
pace of integration.

This public context revealed the unintended consequences resulting from Brennan narrowing the scope of his opinion drafts. His re-

circulated draft on September 22 dropped any significant reference to the shared federal executive, congressional, and judicial constitutional duty to implement racial desegregation despite state defiance. Instead, the emerging consensus opinion emphasized the principle that Supreme Court decisions such as *Brown* construing constitutional provisions possessed the same force as the Constitution itself. Brennan's initial language asserting shared constitutional obligation was consistent with Solicitor General Rankin's brief and oral argument in the August 28 and September 11 hearings, which in turn reflected the administration's reportedly more favorable views toward the Court and *Brown* that Attorney General Rogers and Eisenhower expressed in the days immediately preceding the special term. By removing Brennan's initial references to a shared constitutional obligation among the three branches of the federal government, the justices emphasized Court supremacy in order to refute Faubus's and the segregationists' contrary constitutional claims. At the same time, this affirmation of judicial supremacy reinforced Eisenhower's public statements embracing his constitutional duty to enforce Supreme Court decisions; it was consistent, too, with the administration's use of "federalism" as a cold war propaganda device.

Maintaining the unanimity principle, Brennan further narrowed the scope of the opinion regarding the "all deliberate speed" standard. Brennan's initial drafts attempted to limit the discretion inherent in *Brown* II by suggesting that school desegregation plans should impose timetables, including stipulated beginning and end dates. Since only Black supported the proposition, Brennan removed it. Amidst this discussion it became clear that Harlan, Frankfurter, Burton, and probably Clark perceived a connection between Brennan's effort to tighten up the "all deliberate speed" standard and the principle of unanimity the Court had evolved legitimating *Brown* and its other race decisions. Harlan introduced what his colleagues termed an alternative draft opinion in part to preserve the flexible "all deliberate speed" standard, which Frankfurter, of course, also supported. In addition, Harlan proposed alternative language in order to reinforce the unanimity principle, which, in conjunction with the publicity attending the Little Rock case and the special term, received attention because of the appointment of three new justices since *Brown* II. Despite Brennan's and Douglas's initial resistance, the Court adopted this language as well as Harlan's unique "joining formula," though Frankfurter rather than Harlan actually introduced the latter idea to the justices. After September 19, moreover, the justices could have been more anxious about unanimity upon learning, confidentially, that the Eisenhower administration would soon announce Burton's retirement.

These disputes over the "all deliberate speed" standard and unanimity preceded Frankfurter's decision to issue his separate opinion. At the September 26 conference, the members of the Court first learned that Frankfurter intended to file a separate opinion. Not until the Black-Brennan-Harlan exchanges ended resistance within the Court did Frankfurter finally file the separate opinion on October 6. Historians' study of the justices' private papers confirmed that to a greater or lesser extent the justices resisted Frankfurter's separate opinion because of concerns about unanimity. Historians also confirmed that Frankfurter apparently believed issuing the concurring opinion was nonetheless warranted because it would inspire the various moderate southern lawyers he knew to carry on their desegregation struggle against defiant state authorities such as Faubus. Moreover, historians discovered, prior to the beginning of the August special term, Frankfurter prepared two memoranda on the Little Rock case, one of which he circulated among the members of the Court on August 27. Revised and somewhat expanded, this latter memorandum became Frankfurter's concurring opinion. Locating these two memoranda within Frankfurter's attempt to influence the Court prior to and during Brennan's opinion drafting in *Cooper v. Aaron* revealed, however, a hidden story.

Frankfurter's two Little Rock memoranda were consistent with a proposal he offered the Court the preceding September. By summer 1957, southern Democratic and conservative Republican U.S. senators pushed hearings for the Jenner-Butler bill, seeking to strip away Court jurisdiction in controversial national security cases. Employing the same political maneuvers used to defeat the anti-Court Smith bill in August 1958, Senator Lyndon Johnson won a vote narrowly defeating the Jenner-Butler bill forty-nine to forty-one in February of the same year. Not since Franklin Roosevelt's Court-packing plan in 1937 had the Supreme Court experienced such a threatening political attack. During the 1957–1958 term, Frankfurter attempted to convince his colleagues that a more measured approach to decision making would result in less politically explosive opinions. On September 30, 1957, he circulated a memorandum suggesting, among other things, "in doubtful, difficult, important cases, would it not on appropriate occasion be desirable that the case be assigned to a Justice for a full report on the issues without taking a vote?" His fellow justices apparently construed Frankfurter's whole memorandum to mean that he believed the Court was intentionally massing significant opinions until the end of term, resulting in hasty decision making. Frankfurter felt such heat from his colleagues that on October 7 he circulated a "memorandum in order to dissipate a wrong impression that I have evidently created."

Frankfurter's Little Rock memoranda conformed to the proposal rebuffed in late 1957. "In a very few cases do we postpone a vote after argument for further study. As illustrated by the course of deliberation in the *Segregation Cases* [*Brown* I and II], resort to such a maturing process, designed for reflection that can only come from an unhurrying atmosphere, emphatically vindicates itself," the 1957 memorandum noted. On June 30, 1958, the Supreme Court issued the per curiam order in *Cooper v. Aaron* precipitating the Eighth Circuit Court special session of early August, followed by Chief Justice Warren calling the Supreme Court special term on August 25. Frankfurter's clerk, who drafted this per curiam order, later wrote that, "I had a hand in FF's concurring opinion [*Cooper v. Aaron*]. Since I left Washington on August 1, we must have worked on a draft of the opinion before that date." Actually, the drafts of this memorandum entitled "Facts Pertinent to No. 1 Misc., *Aaron v. Cooper* prior to Proceedings before Judge Lemley" conform to the clerk's recollection. This five-page double-spaced printed narrative traces the origins and evolution of the litigation preceding and during the Little Rock crisis to September 20–21, 1957, when judge Ronald N. Davies issued the injunction against Faubus's use of the National Guard to exclude the nine black students from Central High. Initialed "F.F.," the copy ended citing a petition in *United States v. Faubus* for certiorari to the Supreme Court dated July 24, 1958.

Within the Court, Frankfurter circulated a second memorandum on Little Rock dated August 27, 1958. Essentially, the memorandum comported with the process Frankfurter proposed and the Court rejected in September–October 1957. Frankfurter kept private the "facts" memorandum. Its focus on federal court administration of the Little Rock litigation up to Davies's September 21, 1957, reported opinion nonetheless informed this second memorandum's broader emphasis upon the issues arising from the appeal of Lemley's order culminating in the historic Court special hearing on August 28. Before August 27, Frankfurter prepared a handwritten and then typed draft of the memorandum, to which one of his new clerks added modest edits. The handwritten draft title was simply "Little Rock," but the printed version addressed to the "Brethren" read "Memorandum by Mr. Justice Frankfurter on Little Rock." The note accompanying the memorandum explained, "I have prepared the enclosed memorandum for my own information. It may not be without help or interest to you." Meanwhile, the Senate had narrowly defeated the Jenner-Butler bill in February 1958 as well as the Smith bill days before Warren convened the special term. Thus, this opposition converged with the trial and appeal of the most significant school desegregation case since *Brown*, a case in which Faubus and other southern state leaders justified defiance by contending that the *Brown* decisions — including the "all deliberate speed" standard — did not bind them.

Why would Frankfurter follow a process his colleagues had rejected? Perhaps because the Little Rock case tested whether the Court would maintain the more measured decision making the *Brown* decisions epitomized, which, after all, had resulted in Frankfurter successfully tying unanimity to the "all deliberate speed" standard. Frankfurter's two Little Rock memoranda shaped the details of the litigation to vindicate the wisdom of *Brown* II. Frankfurter circulated the August 27 memorandum after the Court digested the appellate briefs from the black students and the LDF, the federal government and Solicitor General Rankin, and Butler for Little Rock school officials. Styled a memorandum from Mr. Justice Frankfurter to his brethren, it presented a consistent argument for reading the issues in the Little Rock case as a test of complying with the "all deliberate speed" standard. Many of Frankfurter's handwritten comments on the August 27 draft included virtually the same language that appeared in the concurring opinion published on October 6. Thus, although Frankfurter expanded upon the memorandum in the following weeks, this initial draft and later additions presented, as noted above, a coherent rational for reading the issues raised and decided in *Cooper v. Aaron* as logically consistent with *Brown* II. Most modifications were minor, such as replacing specific references to Louisville, Kentucky, and Baltimore, Maryland, with the "lesson to be drawn from . . . ending enforced racial desegregation in public schools with Negro populations of large proportions."

Frankfurter's most significant additions to the revised memorandum appeared in response to Brennan's effort to curb the "flexibility" *Brown* II sanctioned. Frankfurter and Clark apparently received Harlan's "alternative" draft opinion on September 19. Harlan's draft included the unique "joining formula" and a rejection of Brennan's attempt to limit the discretion *Brown* II permitted through "all deliberate speed." Brennan delivered his fullest formulation of this limitation in his draft opinion circulated among all the justices on September 22. On the very same day, Frankfurter prepared for his personal use a revised and expanded version of the August 27 memorandum; for the first time, the heading read — "Mr. Justice Frankfurter, concurring. While unreservedly participating with my brethren in our joint opinion, I deem it appropriate to deal individually with the great issue here at stake." These were the same lines appearing in the published concurring opinion. The revised memorandum also included the handwritten note, "Sept. 22/58 as received by FF," and the inserted words "our joint" preceding "opinion." Thus, the juxtaposition of these dated drafts strongly suggest that Frankfurter decided to issue the expanded August 27 memorandum as a concurring opinion in response to Brennan's attempt to circumscribe the "all deliberate speed" standard, a position identified with Justice Black, Frankfurter's leading activist opponent on the Court.

Frankfurter's decision to issue the separate opinion highlighted his perceptions of unanimity linked to "southern lawyers." As Brennan's draft opinions revealed, and notwithstanding Clark's inchoate consideration of dissent, the justices agreed that *Cooper v. Aaron* should affirm the unanimity principle identified with *Brown*. Nevertheless, Brennan's reformulation of the "all deliberate speed" formula aroused dissension among the justices before their September 23 conference. Harlan, Burton, Clark, and Frankfurter successfully preserved the more flexible remedial standard of *Brown* II. The contentiousness was sufficiently strong, however, that, despite Brennan's objections, the Court accepted Harlan's reference to the unanimous support the three new justices gave *Brown*, as well as the unique "joining formula" Douglas resisted. The contention over *Brown* II and unanimity undoubtedly accentuated for Frankfurter his own failure to win Court support for Warren offering encouraging words to Butler when the special term final oral arguments began on September 11. In a letter on that date to Warren justifying the request, Frankfurter admitted Faubus's "trickery" but also said, "My own view has long been that the ultimate hope for the peaceful solution of the basic [desegregation] problem largely depends on winning the support of the lawyers of the South for the overriding issue of obedience to the Court's decision. Therefore I think we should encourage every manifestation of fine conduct by a lawyer like Butler."

Early desegregation in Arkansas seemed to vindicate Frankfurter's conviction that, despite defiance, aroused lawyers would fight to win compliance with *Brown* II. Frankfurter's "Facts Pertinent to . . . Proceedings before Judge Lemley " memorandum emphasized that up to and through the September 1957 crisis, Little Rock school officials represented by Butler and others developed and implemented their desegregation plan in compliance with *Brown* II. Frankfurter's August 27 memorandum rejected Lemley's affirmation of school officials' request for a delay in part because it departed from those standards the federal courts had previously affirmed. These memoranda, in turn, reflected Frankfurter's understanding that moderate lawyers such as Butler were not alone in struggling to maintain the *Brown* II standards. Harvard Law School graduate Robert Leflar taught at the University of Arkansas School of Law in Fayetteville. Leflar was recognized as a moderate on school desegregation and states' rights–interposition during the desegregation of Fayetteville schools in 1956. According to Leflar, Frankfurter maintained correspondence with unnamed Harvard Law School graduates in Little Rock whom he believed to be moderates. Frankfurter also felt he had special understanding of Arkansas racial moderation because early in his career he had benefited from association with former U.S. senator and sometime American Bar Association president U. M. Rose, founder of the leading law firm in Little Rock.

These connections probably influenced Frankfurter's pursuit of the separate opinion even after the Court rejected Brennan's limitation of *Brown* II. From September 23–26, Brennan incorporated into the opinion drafts not his own and Black's, but his colleagues' construction of the "all deliberate speed" standard. To the extent, then, that Brennan's draft of September 22 triggered Frankfurter's decision to transform the August 27 memorandum into a concurring opinion, that rationale soon dissipated. Yet events in Little Rock confirmed that Faubus and his supporters were as defiant as ever. A *Washington Post* headline on September 24 declared, "Faubus Plan Put up to Court." The LDF filed a case before Judge Miller challenging the constitutionality of the legislation authorizing privatization and closure of city public schools. Following problematic procedures, however, Miller stalled the suit. Thus, amidst Brennan's last drafts, Frankfurter reasonably might have concluded that the beleaguered moderate lawyers in Little Rock and elsewhere could benefit from the direct encouragement he had already formulated in the August 27 memorandum-turned–concurring opinion. Consistent with this interpretation, as Burton's diary confirmed, Frankfurter informed the Court of his decision to issue the separate opinion on September 26, at the same conference where it approved Brennan's final draft of *Cooper v. Aaron*.

The parallel opinion-drafting process Brennan and Frankfurter pursued, within a conflicted public context, led to unintended outcomes. The Court did not accept Brennan's attempt to craft an opinion suggesting that the president, Congress, and the judiciary possessed shared authority in responding to the southern states' defiance of *Brown*. Ultimately, the Court affirmed the constitutional supremacy of its desegregation decisions sustained by the unique expression of unanimity, all nine justices signing *Cooper v. Aaron*. Although Brennan did not achieve the more comprehensive mandate, Eisenhower employed Court judicial supremacy to justify his more positive defense of school desegregation, not because racial equality was a moral imperative, but because of his own constitutional duty to enforce the law in conjunction with cold war propaganda necessity. Moreover, Brennan could not limit southern federal judges' and school officials' discretion in implementing *Brown* II. Within the Court the contentiousness arising from Brennan's efforts nonetheless led Frankfurter to expand his personal Little Rock memoranda into a separate opinion defending the "all deliberate speed" standard. Amidst the justices' rejection of Brennan's proposal and Faubus's continuing defiance, Frankfurter finally decided to issue the separate opinion in support of embattled moderate lawyers in Arkansas and across the South. For the first time since 1950 in a de-segregation decision, however, the Court failed to maintain unanimity.

The break in unanimity was ironic. In the Little Rock case, the justices resolved the contentiousness over *Brown* II out of deference to unanimity, which they believed conferred legitimacy fostering compliance with school desegregation. R. B. McCulloch, author of Faubus's original interposition program, addressed the "all deliberate speed" standard in a letter to Judge Lemley on September 5, 1958, declaring, "What we want is plenty of elasticity. What I *don't* want is for the Supreme Court to fix a definite deadline for the completion of integration in all the schools." Such sentiments vindicated Black's and Brennan's conviction that "all deliberate speed" encouraged delay. Yet, Frankfurter believed, defending the standard in the separate opinion aided southern moderate lawyers, including Harvard Law School graduates. Coincidently, McCulloch was educated at Harvard Law School. Fred N. Fishman, New York city attorney, Harvard Law School graduate, and the justice's former law clerk, noted in an October 10 letter to Frankfurter that the intimation in the concurring opinion that it was a "unanimous conclusion of a long-matured deliberative process" ignored that "there may well be times when certain elements in the country would want to take advantage of a division in the Court for purposes of evasion, and I wonder whether it is advisable to have in the opinion a statement which might be twisted by such elements to their own ends."

The extraordinary appellate process and the two opinions in *Cooper v. Aaron* did not prevent continued defiance in Arkansas and the South. The Court announcement of its decision on September 29 precipitated further defiance from Faubus and his supporters in Little Rock over the course of 1958 to 1959; it also failed to stem continuing resistance across the South for years to come. These immediate and long-term outcomes, contemporary and later commentators observed, contrasted sharply with forceful affirmation of Supreme Court authority to pronounce the meaning of the Constitution, holding that its interpretations in *Brown* and *Cooper* were as lawfully binding as the constitutional text itself. A viewpoint emphasizing the gap between Court articulation of judicial supremacy and defiance of that same principle, however, neglected the extent to which the *Cooper* decision restricted Faubus's and his counterparts' channels of lawful maneuver. From 1958 to 1959 in Little Rock and the civil rights movement struggle thereafter, the next chapter argues, civil rights activists combined nonviolent resistance with the judicial supremacy principle, ultimately defeating Jim Crow. Even so, the Supreme Court decision-making process in *Cooper* revealed a succession of choices narrowing Brennan's and Frankfurter's conflicting views of *Brown* II to the judicial supremacy principle *Cooper v. Aaron* affirmed. Brennan's opinion drafts looked more to the future, whereas Frankfurter's concurring opinion remained bound by the past.

CHAPTER 6

Protean Precedent since 1958

The impact of the Supreme Court *Cooper* decision gradually became apparent. From 1958 to 1959, Faubus and the segregationists initially blocked enforcement of the Court order that desegregation should proceed without further delay. Nevertheless, viewed from the perspective of the black students' rights claims defended by the NAACP Legal Defense Fund (LDF), the *Cooper* decision was a catalyst, narrowing the maneuvering room of Faubus, his supporters, and Little Rock white moderates until defiance was no longer politically tenable and compliance was the only constitutional and legal option. Token desegregation nonetheless prevailed, allowing only a few black students at Central and Hall High Schools. By the mid-1960s, civil rights leaders incorporated federal litigation — much like the Little Rock NAACP had done to mobilize black community support around the *Cooper* litigation — into the strategy of nonviolent protest, winning over the national media and northern public opinion, as well as politically isolating the South and its "massive resistance" campaign. From the 1960s to the 1980s, the images and actualities of racial struggle changed. Northern and western racial unrest soon overshadowed civil rights movement victories, transforming civil rights issues into new clashes over federal coercion. During the same period, judicial activism enforced ambivalent outcomes. Ultimately, the judicial supremacy proclaimed in *Cooper v. Aaron* achieved a compromised ideal of equal justice.

Implementing *Cooper v. Aaron* in Little Rock, 1958–1959

The Court *Cooper v. Aaron* decision became law in Little Rock on September 29, but only nominally. On that date, after rather extraordinary procedures, a hastily called two-judge federal court of appeals meeting in Omaha, Nebraska, relayed the decision to the city federal attorney. On the same day the Little Rock School Board signed an agreement leasing the public schools to the private school corporation. The court of appeals order implementing the Supreme Court decision overruled this move, and on November 10 it directly ordered the school board to carry out its integration plan. But the schools remained closed. The LDF lawsuit challenging the private school corporation was in progress, but no decision was expected for months. Reasoning that they had done all they could for more than a year to comply with the law, five of the six members of the school board and Superintendent Blossom resigned on November 12. As had been the case since the Little Rock NAACP first initiated suit from 1955 to 1956, defiance and compliance with the principles of *Brown* from white leaders and the public reaction to litigation culminated in two historic moments, the September 1957 Little Rock crisis and the Supreme Court special term in August 1958. The *Cooper* decision defined the constitutional terms of compliance, finally overcoming Faubus's and the segregationists' defiance of, and white moderates' equivocation toward, black students' rights.

Two days before the final decision on September 29, the people of Little Rock voted 19,470 to 7,561 to close city public high schools. Accordingly, Faubus closed the schools on the day the Court ordered desegregation to proceed. On September 23 Judge Miller had already denied the school board petition for instructions regarding the closure and privatization of city schools. The next day, LDF lawyers challenged the constitutionality of the private school corporation. In a significant departure from its earlier pattern of reluctance to initiate independent action, the U.S. Department of Justice became an amicus party to the LDF suit. Judge Miller declined to prevent the transfer of public educational facilities to the private corporation because, he said, such action required consideration by a special three-judge tribunal.

The Supreme Court *Cooper* decision no doubt seemed irrelevant to Little Rock young people unable to attend the public high schools. The families of the Little Rock Nine especially suffered. Like all students, the nine pursued alternatives — attending schools in other Arkansas districts or out of state or enrolling in University of Arkansas correspondence courses. Unlike whites, however, the parents of the nine encountered harassment, including loss of jobs. For whites, the response was divided. Although teachers and staff remained employed at closed public schools, some segregation supporters enrolled their children in the public-funded private institutions. Indirectly, the school closing exacerbated social class tensions between upscale and less-affluent whites, aggravated by the original school board refusal to desegregate Hall High in Pulaski Heights, which in turn enabled Faubus and segregationists to claim discrimination against Central High white parents and students. Future Arkansas Supreme Court Justice Robert L. Brown recalled this experience. A sophomore in 1956–1957, he attended Central High. "During the year of the Little Rock Nine," he later wrote, "I attended Hall, the new all-white high school in Little Rock. Hall had been built in the affluent part of the city. There were no black students enrolled that year as there were in Central. This, in itself, was a significant bone of contention with some Central High parents." His senior year of closed schools, Brown was among the "Lost Class of '59."

Yet, the school closing enhanced national and local black activist solidarity. Little Rock middle-class blacks, some of whom had voted for Faubus in his Democratic primary victory of summer 1958, ceased supporting him because the school closing made desegregation an issue of moral principle. The nine students' courage and academic accomplishment despite relentless harassment the preceding year also engendered enduring pride and support among blacks within and outside Little Rock. The national NAACP gradually embraced Daisy Bates's leadership in the struggle. In early 1958, the NAACP selected the nine, but not Bates, as recipients of its prestigious Spingarn Medal. Bates was excluded because some NAACP leaders considered her too militant. After the nine refused to accept the award unless Bates was included, however, she received the honor with them. Martin Luther King, Jr.'s presence at Ernest Green's graduation from Central in May 1958 suggested, moreover, that Bates's activism placed her squarely within the growing nonviolent civil rights movement. In addition, Arkansas authorities' use of tax policies to harass Bates and the local NAACP contributed to the amicable split in 1957 between the national NAACP and the Legal Defense Fund, which until then had been the organization's legal arm. Thus, the work of Thurgood Marshall, Wiley Branton, and other LDF lawyers in *Cooper v. Aaron* and the school closing litigation was one of their first significant cases within the newly independent organization.

Meanwhile, segregationist Dale Alford won a surprise victory over Brooks Hays in the race for Congress. Hays had served his congressional district for eight terms. He had attempted, unsuccessfully, to mediate between Faubus and Eisenhower early in the crisis. Alford, an eye specialist with strong segregationist convictions, was a member of the Little Rock School Board. Two weeks before the November 4 congressional election, he initiated a write-in campaign to get his name on the ballot. Insisting on the value of segregation and the threat of communism, Alford won. Hays's defeat indicated the level of prosegregationist sentiment engulfing Little Rock.

By mid-November it seemed that the Supreme Court had indeed "made nothing happen" to bring about desegregation. Governor Faubus's clout in Little Rock and across the state seemed as strong as ever. The governor's supporters prepared new legislation that would make possible the packing of local school boards and the attainment of other segregationist goals; the measures would be introduced in the forthcoming regular February and March session of the Arkansas assembly. Complicating matters further was the status of the school board. Following the resignation of the five members, only Alford technically retained a seat, but his congressional victory meant that he too must leave the board. Thus, in the heat of the school closing crisis, Little Rock citizens would have to vote on filling the vacant positions. In addition, LDF efforts at getting *Cooper* enforced were stalled in Judge Miller's court, which contributed further to the stalemate.

December 6 was the date set for school board elections, and they became yet another contest over desegregation. Prior to the elections, the Little Rock Chamber of Commerce persuaded five prominent business and professional leaders to run. A significant factor influencing the chamber action was the pernicious impact the crisis had had on city business. The candidates did not publicly acknowledge the assistance of the Women's Emergency Committee, which had worked diligently against the school closing referendum; but privately the five moderates accepted the aid and support of the organization. In line with the position of the chamber of commerce, the moderates campaigned on the need to open the schools on a basis consistent with the minimum plan of integration that had been affirmed by the federal courts. The segregationists also nominated a slate, but their position was weakened when a split developed among members of the Capital Citizens' Council, the most vocal segregationist group. This split resulted in two rival sets of segregationist candidates running, and as a consequence three moderates and three segregationists were elected.

A new round of legal maneuvering began in early 1959. On January 6, Thurgood Marshall and Wiley Branton, along with the justice department, requested from Judge Miller an order that would desegregate city schools immediately. The judge refused, asking instead that the school board provide what amounted to a new desegregation plan. The board declined and requested that Miller permit it to open the schools on a segregated basis. The justice department responded by urging Miller to consider initiating contempt proceedings if the school board did not move to open desegregated high schools. The judge turned down the board appeal; he also expressed disapproval of the department request. The LDF and the justice department did not appeal Miller's decision, but instead filed a new suit testing the constitutionality of the school closing laws. Marshall decided to file this new litigation rather than appeal the original case because, he told a department lawyer, "it was obvious" that Judge Miller would not hand down a favorable decision. A three-judge federal tribunal was mandated to hear the new case, but it would not convene until the spring.

Meanwhile, the election of three moderates to the school board nudged Little Rock business leaders toward taking a firmer public stand on desegregation. In February 1959 officials of the chamber of commerce took a formal poll of its members by mail, asking for responses to two questions: (1) "Do you favor Little Rock's continuing with closed public schools?" and (2) "Do you now favor the reopening of Little Rock's public high schools on a controlled minimum plan of integration acceptable to the Federal Courts?" The responses to the first question were: yes, 230; no, 632; not voting, 285. The responses to the second question were: yes, 819; no, 245; not voting, 83. Encouraged, the chamber board of directors issued a formal resolution on March 23 stating that it was a matter of practical necessity to follow the Supreme Court decision in *Brown*. By implication, this view applied to *Cooper v. Aaron* as well.

The resolution represented a concise statement of the constitutional-legal justification for integration asserted by moderates since 1954:

"The decision of the Supreme Court of the United States, however much we dislike it, is the declared law and is binding upon us. We think that the decision was erroneous and that it was a reversal of established law upon an unprecedented basis of psychology and sociology." However, the statement continued, "We must in honesty recognize that, because the Supreme Court is the Court of last resort in the country, what it has said must stand until there is a correcting constitutional amendment or until the Court corrects its own error." The resolution also stressed two other principles. Little Rock schools should be opened "using a pupil placement system acceptable to the school board and the Federal courts." As noted above, pupil placement laws gave school boards great discretion in the placement of students in local school districts so long as race was not the basis for transfers. The resolution also urged the school board to make sure that the contracts of "all teachers" would be "promptly renewed, in order that we do not lose our valuable and loyal staff."

The latter statement was a response to rumors that segregationists sought to prevent the renewal of certain teachers' contracts. These rumors had been given credence by the introduction in the Arkansas legislature of bills to give the governor authority to appoint additional members to the Little Rock School Board. On February 9, 1959, Governor Faubus had told reporters that he favored not rehiring the principal and two vice principals at Central because of their actions during the crisis in fall 1957. The next day, one of the segregationist members of the board, who claimed to speak for his two colleagues, said that some teachers should not be reemployed because of "their views on integration and segregation." As it turned out, a filibuster defeated this bill.

Events now began moving toward a climax. In late March the Arkansas legislature passed a new set of segregationist bills concerning such matters as prohibitions on hiring NAACP members, tuition grants, and blood bank labels registering racial distinctions. By spring 1959, Governor Faubus's legal policies regarding integration were little different from those espoused by Jim Johnson and Amis Guthridge. In late April and early May, the Arkansas Supreme Court upheld two of the segregation measures. In one suit, Little Rock school district taxpayers challenged the use of public funds to support private schools; in another, they questioned the constitutionality of the school closing act itself. The Arkansas supreme tribunal upheld lower court decisions that declared the two measures constitutional. Only in regard to the school closing act was the majority position questioned: in dissent, Justice E. F. McFaddin argued that "the Arkansas Legislature cannot, under the guise of police power, enact legislation contrary to the Arkansas Constitution." On May 4, the segregationist provisions finally came to trial in the federal tribunal; after hearing arguments, a three-judge court announced that it would issue its decision in mid-June. By this time Little Rock young people had not attended high school for nearly a whole academic year, and despite the continued support given Faubus, there were growing indications that many parents could no longer tolerate such a disruption.

As local citizens waited for final action by the federal court, segregationist demands for the removal of more than forty teachers became the focal point in the prolonged conflict. According to state law and school board administrative procedures, decisions on renewal of teachers' contracts were made in the spring. A vote against renewing a contract amounted to dismissal. The school board met on May 5, with a large number of observers present from moderate and segregationist groups. Contract renewal was not formally on the board agenda, but it became at once the central point of discussion. The board was split three to three on a motion not to renew the contract of Superintendent Terrell Powell. After repeated votes on other reappointments, the board remained deadlocked. After various parliamentary maneuvers, the three moderates walked out.

During the three weeks following the walkout, events in Little Rock moved swiftly. The departure of the moderates left the board without a quorum and thus legally unable to adopt binding decisions. Even so, the segregationists voted not to renew the contracts of forty-four employees of the school district. The stated reasons for most of the dismissals involved the employees' alleged views favoring desegregation. It was readily apparent, however, that the action was aimed also at rewarding the segregationists' political supporters. Opposition coalesced quickly around Stop This Outrageous Purge (STOP), an organization formed to defend the dismissed employees and to remove the segregationist members of the board. With the support of the chamber of commerce and the Women's Emergency Committee, identified with Adolphine Fletcher Terry, a member of one of the most distinguished families in Little Rock, the organization campaigned to recall the segregationists. The segregationists' supporters formed a counterorganization called the Committee to Retain Our Segregated Schools (CROSS), the purpose of which was to remove the three moderates. In a recall election on May 25, the moderates retained their positions and the segregationists were removed. The vote on each board member was quite close. Making the moderate victory possible was the traditional pattern of black and high-income white wards voting together. The election broke the power of the governor and his supporters over the Little Rock schools.

On June 18, the federal court decided that the state laws closing the schools and establishing the private school corporation were unconstitutional. The three-judge court overruled the Arkansas Supreme Court decisions and enjoined school officials from actions that might "delay or frustrate the execution of the approved plan for the gradual integration of the schools of Little Rock." After private discussion with the justice department, the new school board president, Everett Tucker, Jr., and his fellow moderates decided independently to open city schools on a desegregated basis.

Again, Governor Faubus raised the possibility of a special legislative term to intervene, but this time nothing came of it. To the governor's surprise, the board opened the schools in August, a month early. City police maintained order without difficulty and without federal assistance. The new school board had learned from the experience of its predecessor. When Little Rock high schools opened in August 1959, a few blacks were registered in Hall High School as well as Central. This diffused the social class tensions that had contributed to the segregationists' strength. Furthermore, the board publicly challenged Governor Faubus to present any plan that could constitutionally provide for segregated schools. Faubus responded with only veiled hints. Given the June federal court holding, no plan was forthcoming, and this and other decisions undercut the claims of the governor and segregationists that interposition made possible some legal basis for resistance to *Brown*. Unlike its predecessor, the new school board also benefited from popular endorsement and from the outspoken support of many private business and civic organizations. Finally, a privately funded white segregated high school opened in Little Rock, which gave parents an alternative to integration.

The end of confrontation in Little Rock fostered reflection upon the immediate impact of *Cooper v. Aaron*. Initial commentators such as Anthony Lewis and J. W. Peltason affirmed that the forceful decision of the Supreme Court narrowed the options available to Faubus, the segregationists, and Little Rock school officials. Later observers, however, subordinated the Court decision to what seemed to be the more spontaneous mobilization of white moderates and black voters in the school board election of 1959, which finally overcame Faubus's defiance. Nevertheless, it is unlikely that the moderates would have acted when they did had not the Supreme Court finally closed the channels of political maneuver sanctified by appeals to constitutional symbols of states' rights and interposition. Moreover, contrary to Justice Frankfurter's conviction that local federal judges would facilitate popular support for desegregation in the spirit of "all deliberate speed," Judge Miller equivocated throughout the confrontation. The moderates prevailed by appealing to Supreme Court assertion of final authority in *Brown* I, which ultimately achieved force in *Cooper v. Aaron*. Inferentially, Justice Brennan's conviction affirmed in the early drafts of the *Cooper* opinion received vindication in that the judicial command of immediacy brought compliance with the principles of *Brown* I sooner than the authorization of gradualism and delay permitted in *Brown* II.

Thus, *Cooper v. Aaron* was the catalyst for overcoming defiance. After Warren announced the decision, Faubus privatized the public schools, whereupon the new segregationist-controlled school board arbitrarily dismissed many dedicated teachers. Only then did civic leaders organize the STOP campaign, which triumphed through the combined votes of blacks and moderate whites. Several weeks later, the lower federal courts enforced the judicial supremacy affirmed in *Cooper*, declaring unconstitutional the school closing–privatization laws. When Little Rock schools opened on August 12, the school board finally extended desegregation beyond Central High to include Hall High. One thousand segregationists rallied at the state capital and two hundred others marched peacefully before police outside Central, where Jefferson Thomas and Elizabeth Eckford walked together into the school. At Hall High city police officers watched quietly as Estella Thompson, Elsie Robinson, and Effie Jones became the first blacks to attend that school. Elizabeth Eckford departed after learning she already had enough credits to graduate. Carlotta Walls waited to enter Central until she completed summer school in Chicago. Employing the pupil assignment procedures, school officials denied Thelma Mothershed and Melba Pattillo admission to Central; expelled from the school the preceding year, Minnijean Brown stayed in New York. Gloria Ray and Terrance Roberts also had left Little Rock; Ernest Green was attending Michigan State University.

This characterization of the *Cooper* decision emphasizes the black students' eventual triumph over white defiance. The Little Rock NAACP reversed its initial support for the phase program and initiated the federal lawsuit in 1955–1956 only after it became clear that Superintendent Virgil Blossom intended the barest minimum of desegregation at Central High. Although the federal courts upheld the Blossom plan as consistent with *Brown* II, extreme segregationists, Faubus, and white moderates reacted as if the Little Rock Nine's admittance to Central threatened the police powers upon which rested the southern racial apartheid way of life, precipitating the momentous September 1957 crisis. The resulting media images — accentuated by Elizabeth Eckford's traumatic experience and the arrival of the 101st Airborne — aroused national and international attention, galvanizing equivocal support and opposition in Congress and from the Eisenhower administration. The crisis proceeded along a tumultuous course of litigation. The Little Rock Nine's academic success despite relentless harassment did not prevent school officials' retreat from their own plan. The trial, appeal, and decision of *Cooper v. Aaron* enabled the Supreme Court for the first time to affirm *Brown* on the basis of the judicial supremacy underpinning U.S. constitutional democracy. The historic Court decision thus ended the options for defiance by prescribing *Brown*'s and its own constitutional supremacy, finally enforcing the black students' equal rights.

The Little Rock Case, Federal Court Litigation, and the Civil Rights Movement

During the decade following the Little Rock crisis and *Cooper v. Aaron*, the U.S. experience with racial justice was tumultuous. In New Orleans, Louisiana; Oxford, Mississippi; Tuscaloosa, Birmingham, and Selma, Alabama; and elsewhere local and state leaders and their fellow southerners remained defiant. The campaign against public school desegregation paralleled confrontations over public accommodations and voting rights that resulted in bloodshed on country back roads and main streets, most notoriously in rural Mississippi and Birmingham and Selma, Alabama. With skill and courage, supporters of nonviolence identified with Martin Luther King, Jr. aroused national and world public opinion against the aggressive conduct of southern government authorities, coinciding with terrorist tactics perpetrated by groups like the Ku Klux Klan. As a result of the civil rights movement — in conjunction with the ongoing struggle for public school desegregation generally litigated by the LDF — Congress enacted the revolutionary Civil Rights Act of 1964 and the Voting Rights Act of 1965, overturning Jim Crow and establishing the basis for continuing federal intervention in state and local affairs in defense of constitutional rights. Racial injustice persisted, however, suggesting that the Little Rock case presaged the ambivalent civil rights movement heritage of hope and continuing struggle.

The LDF systematically challenged the constitutional and legal claims underpinning "southern massive resistance" and ultimately won. King and other civil rights activists incorporated this judicial action into a broader nonviolent protest campaign to gain enduring victories over institutionalized racial injustice. At the same time, states' rights and surrogate racist images resonating among southerners enabled Faubus, George Wallace, and many others to shift to federal authorities not only legal and political responsibility and accountability — but also blame — for implementing desegregation policies. To a greater or lesser extent these leaders repeated the defiance-compliance strategy Faubus pioneered in Little Rock. Sometimes public officials overplayed their hand, such as Bull Conner's deployment of fire hoses and police dogs in Birmingham from May 2–7, 1963, against peacefully demonstrating African American children, or Dallas County sheriff Jim Clark's attack upon peaceful marchers at the Edmund Pettus Bridge in Selma on "Bloody Sunday," March 7, 1965. In such instances, the leader's error was not only the brutality itself, but that he carried it out before media that transmitted the images across the United States and around the world. These public images merged, moreover, with the bombers' killing of four little black girls in Sunday school on September 15, 1963, at the Sixteenth Street Baptist Church in Birmingham.

Federal litigation, King perceived, was integral to the nonviolence campaign; state court litigation, however, worked against it. Thus, in his 1963 "Letter from a Birmingham Jail," King said, "I can urge men to obey the 1954 decision of the Supreme Court because it is morally right, and I can urge them to disobey segregation ordinances because they are morally wrong." Furthermore, King said, "as federal courts have consistently affirmed . . . it is immoral to urge an individual to withdraw his efforts to gain his constitutional rights because the quest precipitates violence. Society must protect the robbed and punish the robber." During the Montgomery bus boycott, King noted the practical distinction between federal and state judicial action. "Our local [Alabama] judges, it seems, succumb to whims and caprices of local custom in deciding cases like ours. In the federal courts, a judge is appointed and doesn't have to worry about being reelected. God grant them the moral courage and integrity to interpret the Constitution in its true meaning." Although he was disappointed in Judge Frank Johnson's initial order against the Selma march, King shaped his protest strategy around the ultimately prescient hope that the federal judge would eventually order the voting rights marchers to proceed under federal protection. It was reported at the time that King described Judge Johnson as "a man of great honor, [who] gave true meaning to the word justice."

Thus, King criticized the "legalism" southern white leaders employed to further massive resistance, but he increasingly incorporated LDF litigation into nonviolent protests. African Americans "must not get involved in legalism [and] needless fights in lower [state] courts." This was "exactly what the white man wants the Negro to do. Then he can draw out the fights. . . . Our job now is implementation [of the full constitutional spirit and substance of the *Brown* decision]. . . . We must move on to mass action . . . in every community in the South, keeping in mind that civil disobedience to local laws is civil obedience to national laws," he said. Prominent leaders of the NAACP in New York clearly disagreed with King during the late 1950s; following *Cooper v. Aaron*, however, the LDF and the civil rights protesters cooperated, especially after local officials in Albany, Georgia, outmaneuvered King in 1961, employing tactics reminiscent of Faubus's manipulation of police powers in Little Rock. "Because of Dr. King's initial belief that the federal government was sure to intervene," wrote former LDF lawyer Michael Meltsner, "little effort was put into attempts to challenge the machinations of Albany city fathers by pressuring them in court. It was a mistake that King and his southern allies would largely succeed in avoiding thereafter, and this solidified his future relationship with the LDF."

By the early 1960s, it was clear that Supreme Court sanction of delayed public school desegregation "with all deliberate speed," as Justices Brennan and Black expressed during the opinion writing of *Cooper v. Aaron* in September 1958, fostered southern white violence-prone "massive resistance." George Wallace replaced Faubus as the symbol of states' rights defiance. Meltsner's LDF-centered account documents how often King and his followers combined nonviolent protest and judicial vindication of constitutional rights claims the LDF won from a few federal judges like Alabama's Frank Johnson, federal appellate courts, and the Supreme Court. Admittedly, the Student Non-violent Coordinating Committee (SNCC) was impatient with such reliance on federal judicial action, though its members, too, expected LDF aid when they found themselves in southern jails. Even so, a civil rights protest/litigation "synergy" shaped the outcome in Birmingham, Selma, and elsewhere, somewhat like the litigation the local NAACP pursued that mobilized the Little Rock black community. Of course, civil rights movement victories occurred on a grander scale, including finally overcoming southern Democratic and conservative Republican opposition in Congress to pass the Civil Rights Act of 1964 and the Voting Rights Act of 1965.

Civil rights activists also affirmed their patriotism, especially following Eisenhower's more positive assessment of *Brown* and Supreme Court supremacy to gain cold war propaganda advantage during the appeal of *Cooper* and the August 1958 special term. Within the South, of course, McCarthyism fueled criticism that civil rights activists were dupes or even agents of the communist conspiracy. Leaders such as Marshall and King countered such assaults by linking their litigation campaign or passive resistance to the advocacy of an American democratic faith that espoused the equality of the Declaration of Independence and the constitutional sanction of minority rights. In a public address before Chicago business leaders prior to the march on

Washington in 1963, King said, "I believe that one of the weaknesses of communism" is Lenin's advocacy of deception and aggression. "And this is where nonviolence breaks with communism or any other system that would argue that the end justifies the means, for in the long run the end is pre-existent in the means, and the means represents the ideal in the making and the end in process." Similarly, Marshall stated, "At the present time all eyes are focused on democracy in the United States and it seems the fate of democracy depends on the United States. The true test of democracy is the equality of rights and privileges granted all citizens, which is measured by the protection given minority groups."

This rhetoric aligned African Americans with the dominant northern liberal consensus, and it politically isolated the southern segregation system as aiding the communists' anti-American propaganda. Clearly, Marshall and King realized, anticommunist appeals would positively influence presidents fighting the cold war propaganda battle who identified the nation's democratic resistance to communism with postwar anticolonialism. During the time of the Little Rock confrontation, King told supporters privately that colonialism and racial segregation were essentially the same form of oppression. Comparing the U.S. civil rights struggle to African independence movements, he said further: "The oppressor never voluntarily gives freedom to the oppressed. . . . Privileged classes never give up their privileges without strong resistance. . . . Freedom comes only through persistent revolt, through persistent agitation, through persistently rising up against the system of evil." On another public occasion he told Kenyan leader Tom Mboya: "I am absolutely convinced that there is no basic difference between colonialism and segregation. They are both based on contempt for life, and a tragic doctrine of white supremacy. So our struggles are not only similar; they are in a real sense one."

The reality and symbolic imagery of struggle associated with Little Rock also helped to consolidate northern elite opinion in favor of black community resistance. During the confrontation in the fall of 1957, Hannah Arendt wrote a short essay entitled "Reflections on Little Rock," which *Dissent* published in 1959. Arendt's arguments about the relations and distinctions among public, social, and private spheres led her to oppose federally enforced school desegregation. Arendt believed that her own German-Jewish experience and that of southern blacks were, for analytical purposes, complementary; as a result she misunderstood the distinctively American racial and institutional character of the civil rights struggle that Little Rock epitomized. What Arendt failed to grasp, Ralph Ellison wrote, was that a black person in the American South had to "face the terror and contain his fear and anger precisely because he is a Negro American." The coalescing of support for the Little Rock Nine among northern white liberals, as well as southern and northern blacks, was consistent with Ellison's rather than Arendt's views, thereby strengthening African American self-consciousness in support of ongoing nonviolent protests fought through mass political activism and the federal courts. The practical amelioration of institutional and societal discrimination may have been continually contested, but it began to open the way to attaining the ideal of equal justice.

Meanwhile, the triumph of Supreme Court supremacy in *Cooper v. Aaron* divided white Protestant opinion, at least in Arkansas. Soon after the Little Rock crisis erupted, informed contemporaries observed that white Protestant churches there were not united concerning the racial conflict. A small percentage designated as progressives contributed to the 20 percent of Arkansas whites who, in a 1956 survey, favored desegregation. A larger minority espoused a biblical interpretation justifying racial segregation. The religious view that came to be shared by the majority of Arkansas white Protestants accepted desegregation out of deference to legal-constitutional supremacy eventually proclaimed in the *Cooper* decision, which included the cold war imperative. Shortly after the 101st Airborne arrived to quell the white mob, an editorial in the moderate *Arkansas Baptist* stated: "Jesus would not be a part of any crowd committing acts of violence in resistance to duly constituted law and order. He taught His disciples to be law abiding and to respect those in authority." A subsequent editorial warned readers that the disorder supported by Baptists advocating extreme segregationist views threatened both the immediate religious and larger cold war reach of church missionary efforts: "The cause of missions and of democracy [in the struggle against communism] have suffered inestimably from the 'Little Rock' incident."

These conflicted Arkansas religious beliefs paralleled the larger split between northern and southern public opinion, reflecting divergent perceptions of constitutional legitimacy. Following Eisenhower's dispatch of the 101st Airborne to Little Rock, surveys of public opinion revealed a sharp regional divide between northerners overwhelmingly favoring Eisenhower's action and southerners opposed to it by a similarly large margin. Increasingly among northerners, abstractions of federalism and constitutional supremacy merged with northern and western media presentations of a stereotypical South identified with the gothic violence of *The Birth of a Nation*, the impoverished desperation of Depression-era *Tobacco Road*, the deplorable romantic racism of *Gone with the Wind*, and the principled sheriff of *The Andy Griffith Show*. These mixed images presented African Americans either as dignified and courageous or as dependent victims, and most white southerners as uneducated. Into the 1960s, print and television journalists transmitted these stereotypes in their reports of civil rights struggles. Among southern whites, however, the result of this media-constructed imagery was not shame but anger, resentment, and a feeling of impugned respectability agitated by leaders like George Wallace in order to defy federal law in the name of states' rights and police power appeals symbolizing the "southern way of life" threatened by racial miscegenation.

By the mid-1960s, stereotypical popular images and constitutional symbolism consolidated black unity and northern opinion and politically isolated the South. The Little Rock NAACP desegregation litigation culminating in *Cooper v. Aaron* facilitated media images favoring the black community struggle against states' rights claims, claims that too often appeared to be little more than transparent rationales for violence. Thus the successful mobilization of Little Rock blacks in the name of equal justice enforced under the Constitution confirmed what civil rights leader Julian Bond said about the movement generally. It was, he said, "a great testament to the Constitution's strength. Although . . . that code of law had . . . been bent and twisted to deny black Americans their rights, it also provided the basic tool used by the movement to win justice." Like the Little Rock NAACP, Bond and other civil rights activists "knew that segregation was wrong on the basis of the nation's highest law. People were willing . . . to fight through the legal system for change, because the Constitution was their ultimate shield." Indeed, among the most significant outcomes of the Supreme Court *Cooper v. Aaron* decision was the image of federal supremacy, which civil rights activists, the northern media, and presidential administrations alike could deploy in the name of cold war patriotism against southern defiance.

The Images and Actualities of Changing Racial Struggle

From the 1960s forward, public images of racial struggle changed. At the point the civil rights movement overcame the southern suppression of the black franchise through the enactment of the Voting Rights Act of 1965, the Los Angeles Watts race riots erupted in August of the same year. Racial unrest recurred in northern and western cities for years to come. During the same period that the Supreme Court overturned the standard of "all deliberate speed" with orders requiring public school desegregation "now," enforcement more than ever depended upon federal bureaucratic construction of Title VI of the Civil Rights Act of 1964. These enforcement efforts gained further strength when the Supreme Court authorized busing in *Swann v. Charlotte-Mecklenburg Board of Education* (1971). Increasingly, after that decision, civil rights struggle in the South, busing, and northern urban racial unrest blurred into public images associating federal enforcement with coercion, which conservative Republicans and southern Democrats exploited for political advantage. Moreover, this transformation of federal civil rights enforcement into images of coercive big government accelerated the profound demographic movement of white middle-class property holders from the cities to the suburbs known as *white flight*. The politicized public imagery of federal coercion also shaped the controversial national implementation of affirmative action and the rise of black voting in the South.

Arkansas suggested national trends. The Montgomery bus boycott of 1955–1956 and the Little Rock crisis the following year influenced passage of the Civil Rights Act of 1957. The dramatic resolution of *Cooper v. Aaron* in the August special term of the Supreme Court followed by the school closing clash in Little Rock from 1958 to 1959 contributed to the Eisenhower administration proposing and Congress passing the Civil Rights Act of 1960. After Little Rock schools underwent successful desegregation in 1959, Faubus abandoned the extreme segregationists' program of defiance. He remained governor until

1966, employing repeated rhetorical attacks on the federal government. During the same period, however, he became the "best ever" economic liberal in Arkansas history who also maintained black voter support by fairly administering economic opportunity and returning to his initial support for desegregation of public schools and public accommodations, doing so on the basis of local electoral control even as he railed against federal coercion. Meanwhile, in the *Clark* litigation beginning in 1966, black parents sued in federal court arguing that the pupil assignment laws were being used to maintain token integration. By the late 1970s, when Bill Clinton was first elected Arkansas governor on a moderate economic and racial justice platform, Little Rock race relations were enmeshed in controversies over busing, affirmative action, and white flight, as was the case throughout the United States.

Historian Daniel J. Boorstin articulated the distinction between actual events and their media images that proved so vital to civil rights movement triumphs. In *The Image: A Guide to Pseudo-Events in America* (1961), Boorstin explored the formation and consequences of a growing postwar mass market for cheap graphically reproduced images — especially through television, by the 1950s an indispensable commodity for U.S. consumers. "The central paradox — that the rise of images and of our power over the world blurs rather than sharpens the outlines of reality — permeates one after another area of our life," Boorstin wrote. Indeed, there was "hardly a corner of our daily behavior where the multiplication of images, the products and by-products of the Graphic Revolution, have not befogged the simplest old everyday distinctions." As an example, Boorstin noted how media events were constructed regarding the "school integration disorders in New Orleans" during the final months of 1960. Mayor de Lesseps S. Morrison requested from print and television journalists a "three-day moratorium" on reports of the struggle. Claiming that media coverage harmed the good name of New Orleans as well as its tourism, Morrison also asserted, Boorstin stated, that "people were given an impression of prevailing violence, when, he said, only one-tenth of 1 percent of the population had been involved in demonstrations. But he also pointed out that the mere presence of telecasting facilities was breeding disorder."

Although Boorstin's characterization clearly underestimated the scope of actual violence in the civil rights struggle, he was correct concerning the larger-than-life impact it produced. Even so, during the early days of organizing the Southern Christian Leadership Conference (SCLC) from 1957 to 1959, King grasped the significance of Little Rock for nonviolent black protest. Although northern whites were receptive to Eisenhower's shifting position toward *Brown* and the Supreme Court, King stated that "much of the tension in the South and many of the reverses we are now facing could have been avoided if President Eisenhower had taken a strong, positive stand on the question of civil rights and the Supreme Court's decision as soon as it was rendered." Suggesting the later strategy of arousing public opinion against the violence identified with George Wallace and other southern leaders, King in 1959 publicly identified Faubus's impact on national and global public opinion: "His irresponsible actions brought the issue to the forefront of the conscience of the nation," and unlike Eisenhower's vacillation, "allowed people to see the futility of attempting to close the public schools." Inferentially, this statement vindicated *Cooper v. Aaron*, coming as it did during late summer 1959.

Civil rights activists perceived the need for mobilizing black community solidarity in the confrontations the media covered. King's understanding of the power of media images was consistent with black civil rights activist Pauli Murray's assessment of Daisy Bates's stand with the Little Rock Nine. The Little Rock NAACP litigation was an early form of protest that eventually won over middle-class blacks to the rights claims asserted against Faubus and the segregationists. Thus, Bates "represents the tough-minded tactical leadership in this struggle," Murray wrote, "as Martin Luther King represents the moral and spiritual leadership." J. L. Chestnut, Jr., a black NAACP LDF lawyer from Selma, expressed a similar view about representing in court poor Alabama African Americans from its rural Black Belt. The example of black lawyers "walking around the courthouse without fear had to mitigate against the utter hopelessness that so engulfed black life," Chestnut later wrote. "It also gave a presence to the NAACP Legal Defense Fund. It let black people know: You don't have to take *every* damn thing. Even down there in those fields, isolated, apparently at the mercy of white landowners, there is someone else you can call on and, damn it, they will come [italics in original]." As one of the LDF lawyers representing King and the other protesters in the Selma voting rights struggle, Chestnut spoke from experience.

Federal litigation sometimes promoted contradictory images of civil rights protests and southern defiance. The Ku Klux Klan's and others' bloody assault on the Freedom Riders in Alabama produced, as Raymond Arsenault's *Freedom Riders 1961 and the Struggle for Racial Justice* (2006) shows, the court order from Judge Frank Johnson that helped to mobilize federal-state cooperation to preserve order. Johnson responded to further defiance, however, with an even broader court order threatening all parties with imprisonment if resistance continued. Mississippi then became the center of protest, which did not end until the buses carrying the Freedom Riders reached New Orleans. The Freedom Riders' progress achieved media images benefiting their cause and hurting the South. From bus windows white and black protestors held out signs with such messages as: "Take a Stand with the Law of the Land," "Freedom Now," "Enforce the Constitution 13th, 14th, 15th Amendments," "Freedom's Wheels Are Rolling," and "The Law of the Land Is Our Demand." By contrast, U.S. Nazi Party storm troopers drove a van along the same route to New Orleans displaying slogans exclaiming: "We Do Hate Race Mixing" and "Lincoln Rockwell's HATE BUS." Amidst such clashing messages, especially given the spring 1961 cold war environment, the Freedom Riders' obedience to Frank Johnson's order reinforced a public impression of the moral and constitutional high ground against violence-prone destroyers of true American freedom.

Yet just when nonviolence seemed victorious in the South by the mid-1960s, racial violence erupted in northern and western cities. The U.S. government responded to this new conflict with policies that further enlarged federal responsibility for individual opportunity. Throughout the nation, however, the use of the new authority sparked controversy involving affirmative action, busing, and reverse discrimination. By the mid-1980s the office of the president was committed to limiting federal involvement in these and other desegregation issues. But to what extent did this commitment represent a fundamental revision of the policy of the preceding twenty years?

Well into the 1960s, the federal government approach to desegregation sanctioned tokenism. The decade following *Brown* found only 2.3 percent of black school-age children attending schools with whites in the South. Despite the persistence of southern massive resistance, and in marked contrast to eloquent public statements espousing activism, the Kennedy administration hesitated until the violence-scarred summer of 1963 to advocate strong civil rights legislation. During the controversy over the desegregation of the University of Mississippi, the U.S. attorney general's office, like its counterpart in the Little Rock crisis, surreptitiously negotiated with the state governor to work out a politically expedient solution, though the effort failed as it had with Faubus. The Kennedy administration also secretly negotiated with Wallace preceding his orchestrated withdrawal in the "schoolhouse door" of the University of Alabama in Tuscaloosa. This same commitment to compromise shaped the provisions governing public school desegregation in the Civil Rights Act of 1964. Although it outlawed discrimination, southerners triumphed in that the final version of Title VI of the act (the public education section) specifically rejected measures that would have permitted the use of coercive practices such as busing to achieve racial balance.

The implementation of Title VI depended upon the formulation of administrative guidelines by the office of the chief executive. Congressional debate showed that sponsors of the law assumed that standards governing enforcement would closely follow judicial precedent. But the officers of the Department of Health, Education, and Welfare (HEW), whose administration of federal grant programs depended upon amiable relations with state and local authorities, wanted the terms of compliance to depend primarily upon the good faith of local officials. The Civil Rights Commission and other supporters of the civil rights movement within the Johnson administration, however, urged a broader and more vigorous policy. The justice department wanted to follow the approach set out in the congressional debates. This view ultimately prevailed. HEW assigned the responsibility for drafting specific guidelines to the Office of Education. An ad hoc group of law professor consultants hammered out general standards based on judicial principles. By means of an unconventional procedure, the professors' handiwork acquired official status as "general guidelines," establishing the terms of federal government enforcement of Title VI in the South.

From the mid-1960s on, the federal government desegregation policy followed a twisting course. The Johnson administration used the general guidelines and litigation to achieve increased school desegregation. In 1968, HEW began monitoring compliance with the guidelines not only in the South but in the North and West as well. If a community failed to develop a desegregation plan, it faced cutoff of federal funding. In the last year of Johnson's term, HEW initiated twenty-eight such reviews. But the dictates of the Republican southern strategy, George Wallace's dramatic rise, the explosive issue of busing, and the developing conflict over desegregation in urban schools in the North led Richard M. Nixon to change this policy. Espousing law, order, and judicial self-restraint, President Nixon used constitutional symbolism and appeals to the rule of law to deflect public opinion away from the ideal of equal educational opportunity. Action followed rhetoric: HEW community reviews dropped to sixteen in 1969 and declined steadily thereafter until 1977, when there were none.

An emphasis upon constitutional abstraction and legalism remained central to the Nixon administration desegregation policy. The president's politicization of Supreme Court nominations was in part a response to public questioning of judicial activism that had begun with the constitutional revolution in *Brown*. Ironically, the advocacy of judicial self-restraint obscured the extent to which that doctrine compelled obedience to precedent, which meant of course *Brown*. When Nixon Supreme Court appointees joined unanimous or near unanimous majorities in sustaining compulsory techniques such as busing to achieve desegregation, the ambivalence inherent in the president's strategy became apparent. But administration reaction to this development again stressed appeals to constitutional symbolism, for it supported a constitutional amendment to outlaw busing. Moreover, the federal government became more dilatory in its initiation of desegregation litigation. In at least two instances, government enforcement of civil rights measures was so reluctant that it became necessary for federal courts to intervene to compel action. Thus, under President Nixon, law and order meant preserving rather than overturning the status quo.

Ironically, to support their demand for change, even critics accepted the White House emphasis upon constitutional and legal values. The Center for National Policy Review, quoted in Richard Kluger's *Simple Justice* (1976), reported there was "little question that the Nixon Administration's negative policy declarations have impaired [desegregation] enforcement action." Consequently, "minority citizens face continued disappointment of their legitimate expectations that the federal government will protect their children's rights." What was the solution? A "Congress prepared to exercise its oversight responsibilities to assure that its laws are obeyed by the executive branch . . . new political leadership committed to the rule of law and ready to appeal to the people's aspirations rather than their fears . . . [and] federal officials determined to be faithful to their oaths of office." The opposition rejected the Nixon desegregation policy; yet its call for a better one depended upon the same public rationale used by the party in power: constitutional symbolism and the rule of law. This argument suggested that a change in the party controlling the presidency would be enough to realize the promise of *Brown*.

Even though the Carter and Reagan administrations pursued distinct approaches to desegregation, the impact of their policies was similar. To be sure, the Carter White House was more vigorous than its successor; after 1976, HEW and the justice department again stepped up enforcement of the general guidelines. By contrast, four years later the Reagan administration renewed support for the antibusing amendment and the government began curtailing compliance proceedings. Yet, at least from the perspective of Reagan's landslide reelection in 1984, federal government implementation of *Brown* was generally consistent with the gradualism that had characterized the course of desegregation since the beginning. Desegregation policy was defined by legal and political exigencies rather than by an overriding commitment to equal justice. Consequently, leading scholar David L. Kirp observed that desegregation in the 1980s was characterized by no "single national standard, authoritatively set and effectively implemented, but rather a bewildering diversity of arrangements, ad hoc in nature, varying enormously both in content and in implementation." Even so, he said, "some communities have undertaken to balance their schools racially; others have retained neighborhood schools while improving the quality of instruction in predominantly black schools; still others have done nothing at all." Neither segregation nor integration but a compromised ideal of equal justice prevailed.

Divergent Outcomes of Judicial Activism

The federal courts, especially the Supreme Court, clearly performed a central role in the U.S. desegregation experience. Often the judiciary was so conspicuous — as in *Brown* and *Cooper* — it seemed to stand alone. After U.S. civil rights legislation ended massive resistance, the courts, despite mounting public concern about busing and white flight, remained in the forefront of the desegregation struggle. But appearances could be deceiving. Some federal judges clearly were courageous and their self-restraint was not exactly pronounced. Yet often, the federal judiciary role was neither as independent nor as bold as surface images suggested. Supreme Court acquiescence to limited and token desegregation under the "all deliberate speed" formula lasted until the mid-1960s. Overall, the Supreme Court delegated to lower federal court judges the responsibility for translating the *Brown* principle into concrete policy. The Court left standing a number of lower court decisions that called for only the barest minimum of desegregation, though in a few instances the justices sanctioned court of appeals decisions that required more effective measures. Finally, Justice Hugo L. Black for the Court in *Griffin v. County School Board* (1964) exclaimed, "The time for mere 'deliberate speed' has run out." But even though this formative era of desegregation decision making ended, its imprint remained after the passage of the Civil Rights Act of 1964.

Until the 1970s, Supreme Court sanction of southern pupil assignment laws ensured token desegregation. Little Rock school officials employed such laws when they allowed just a few students to enter Central and Hall High Schools in 1959, finally ending two years of confrontation. Daniel J. Meador's 1959 *Virginia Law Review* article suggested how important the Supreme Court's affirmation of pupil assignment laws was in *Shuttlesworth v. Birmingham Board of Education* (1958). "While not so dramatic as the running Little Rock tragedy, with its federal troops, international publicity, and special session of the Court," Meador wrote, "this case in many ways seems the most significant event since *Brown*." He declared the decision "a real victory for moderation. . . . Surely the judges know that an assignment law will retard widespread, indiscriminate mixing of races, which some people interpret 'desegregation' to mean. Who could doubt," he continued, that "the judiciary understands that desegregation under those laws will come slowly . . . . And the judges undoubtedly realize it was the hope of the state legislators that the assignment statutes would do just these things and perhaps more." The supporters of meaningful integration were more precise; under such laws, the Civil Rights Commission declared, there would be "little or no actual desegregation."

The limited approach of the judiciary shaped congressional drafting of Title VI of the Civil Rights Act of 1964. The provision became law in part because its supporters convinced southerners that its original enforcement provisions would not permit government action beyond that sanctioned by judicial precedent. For the southern representatives, the standard that should control the meaning of the act was the one pronounced in *Bell v. School City of Gary, Indiana* (1963). In this case, the federal court held, "Desegregation does not mean that there must be intermingling of the races in all school districts. It means only that they may not be prevented from intermingling or going to school together because of race or color." Moreover, school assignment by neighborhood was permissible even where "the resulting effect is to have a racial imbalance in certain schools where the district is populated almost entirely by Negroes or Whites." On this point, proponents of Title VI were explicit. Senator Hubert Humphrey, one of the provision's chief sponsors, exclaimed that the *Gary* case was "clear that while the Constitution prohibits segregation, it does not require integration." In fact, he continued, busing as "an act to effect the integration of schools . . . would be a violation because it would be . . . transporting children because of race. The bill does not attempt to integrate the schools, but it does attempt to eliminate segregation in the school systems."

Title VI also required the president and Congress to take an active role in desegregation policy making. The president had considerable discretion over the standards that would govern enforcement of the law. Civil rights activists in the administration who espoused true integration urged a broad interpretation that would enable the fulfillment of the *Brown* promise of equal justice. But when the Johnson administration accepted the justice department view that judicial precedent should shape the enforcement guidelines, it implicitly embraced the position advocated by southerners during the congressional debates. The guidelines the Office of Education subsequently issued reinforced this dependency upon federal case law.

The federal judiciary desegregation decisions entered a new stage after the U.S. government began enforcing the Title VI guidelines. After 1964, elected and administrative federal officials shared with federal judges the responsibility for implementing the desegregation principles. A "national effort, bringing together Congress, the executive, and the Judiciary may be able to make meaningful the right of Negro children to equal educational opportunities," observed the U.S. Fifth Circuit Court in *United States v. Jefferson County Board of Education* (1966). "*The courts acting alone have failed* [italics in original]." Consequently, by *Green v. County School Board* (1968), the Supreme Court began requiring that desegregation programs must "promise realistically to work . . . *now.*" But not until 1971 did the Court uphold the strongest assertion of federal power since the Little Rock case in *Swann v. Charlotte-Mecklenburg Board of Education.* This decision established particular criteria — including limited busing if necessary — to measure whether a desegregation plan in fact "worked."

This federal effort claimed mixed success in the South. By the mid-1970s, approximately 46 percent of the black young people in the states of the Old Confederacy attended schools with whites. At the same time, however, white flight and private schools fostered an ad hoc, uneven pattern of integration that was often just one step beyond the token policy sanctioned under "all deliberate speed." Although the Johnson and Nixon administrations pursued opposing policies regarding HEW community reviews, both relied primarily upon the judiciary to achieve desegregation. Even the Republican dilatory enforcement policy did not preclude a construction of HEW guidelines in the *Swann* case that circumvented congressional intent regarding the propriety of busing. Moreover, the public uproar over busing obscured the degree to which, after 1964, federal authorities pursued a middle course. *United States v. Jefferson County Board of Education* (1966) established the basic approach of the government and the courts to the enforcement of Title VI guidelines. The U.S. Fifth Circuit Court held that the law did not require a "maximum of racial mixing or racial balance" that accurately reflected "the racial composition of the community or school population." Nor did it require that "each and every child attend racially balanced" schools. The court emphasized, however, that adequate "redress for school segregation calls for much more than allowing a few Negro children to attend white schools."

In the North and West, public school desegregation aroused new tensions. Lower federal courts had dealt with school desegregation outside the South; the first major Supreme Court case to address these issues was *Keyes v. Denver School District No. 1* (1973). In *Keyes,* the

Denver School Board funded new school construction and established attendance zones with the express goal of maintaining racial segregation. Unlike the South, where segregation had been mandated by state statute, Colorado law provided no basis for the school board actions. *Brown* overturned de jure segregation of the sort imposed by southern state law, but it was unclear whether a locally formulated board policy was also invalid. The Court focused upon the school board intent, deciding that since its purpose was to achieve segregation, the board actions were unconstitutional. The Court, however, did not stop there. Justice William J. Brennan for the majority also held that racially motivated policies in one portion of a school system required districtwide desegregation. Brennan's decision brought into play the *Swann* precedent and opened the way to the use of busing to desegregate the entire city school system. After some local resistance, the Court order brought desegregation to Denver, though by the 1980s the movement of white families to the suburbs mitigated the long-term outcome.

The desegregation struggle in *Milliken v. Bradley* (1974) further defined the parameters of school desegregation outside the South. Under a plan approved by the federal district court, fifty-three suburban school systems that were nearly all white would integrate with the Detroit systems, which were approximately three-quarters black. To implement the plan it was necessary to bus about 800,000 students. Moreover, busing would not occur *within* a single district as in the Denver case, but would instead involve independent and separate systems. The interdistrict nature of the plan was significant because in *Keyes* the Court held that intent determined whether an act was unconstitutional. No one contended that the suburban schools were overwhelmingly white due to an officially sanctioned policy of segregation; they were included in the plan simply because there were too few whites in Detroit to make meaningful desegregation possible. But the Supreme Court overturned the lower court. For a five-to-four majority, Chief Justice Warren Burger held that without a showing of proof that Detroit's racial imbalance involved race-conscious intent, which resulted in policies extending across district boundaries, the Court could not permit an interdistrict remedy. Even though the Court could have corrected a gross racial imbalance by extending the Denver precedent to the *Milliken* case, it chose instead to preserve the status quo.

After 1974, Court desegregation decisions shifted within these limits. The Court did not interfere when extensive popular resistance reminiscent of Little Rock compelled the federal district judge to impose a systemwide desegregation plan in Boston. At the same time, however, the justices overturned a federal judge's activist attempt to maintain meaningful integration in the schools of Pasadena. In this case the Supreme Court rejected a plan that mandated annual alteration to ensure a particular racial balance and prohibited any school from having black students in the majority. But three years later the Court returned to its Denver precedent in two Ohio cases. In the twentieth century, Ohio state law had not sanctioned racial segregation; yet the Court found that because of "intentional discrimination" school boards in Columbus and Dayton had maintained dual school systems. This failure to carry out an "affirmative duty" to desegregate placed the school officials in violation of the Constitution.

After more than a decade of litigation involving desegregation in Indianapolis, the Court again upheld an exception to *Milliken v. Bradley*. The Detroit opinion recognized that interdistrict busing was permissible where the intent to segregate was proven to have applied across district boundaries. Clearly, intentional segregation existed in the Indianapolis school district, but there was no contention that the suburban schools were predominantly white because of race-conscious policies. When the schools were left out of a metropolitan reorganization consolidating the city and its suburbs, however, the intent test applied, and in 1981 the Supreme Court left standing a lower court interdistrict plan. Ironically, in this case the federal tribunals used *Milliken* to sustain a result more in keeping with the Denver and Ohio precedents. But more broadly, Indianapolis demonstrated that the Court could use "intent" to sustain divergent results. Thus, even though during the 1970s and 1980s the Court sanctioned integration in principle, public resistance kept equal justice an elusive ideal.

The struggle for equal educational opportunity is rarely considered, as Daniel Meador suggested in 1959, a triumph of moderation. Critics of integration attacked coercive federal authority, such as mandating busing to achieve integration. Conversely, some integrationists argued that ever greater federal power was necessary to overcome opposition to equal educational opportunity. Others assumed that racism was so fundamental to U.S. culture that white resistance to meaningful desegregation was inevitable. Consequently, the integrationists' emphasis upon interracial mixing not only represented an unattainable goal but also encouraged the dissipation of valuable resources that could be used to upgrade black educational opportunity. A moderate group stressed the need to work patiently through politics and the courts. In this way, it was hoped, the modest yet — compared to Jim Crow — meaningful gains achieved since *Brown* might eventually open the way to attaining the ideal of equal justice.

Still, the enduring legacy of Little Rock and *Cooper v. Aaron* may well be an ongoing interplay of politics, constitutional symbolism, and judicial processes resulting in compromise. The Civil Rights Act of 1964 clearly increased educational opportunity; although measured against the promise of *Brown* I, politics and bureaucratic administration circumscribed its enforcement. The role of the federal judiciary was ambivalent. The Supreme Court blunted the activist thrust of the 1954 *Brown* decision through the standard of "all deliberate speed." Although *Cooper v. Aaron* held that outright defiance was never lawful, continued Court authorization of "all deliberate speed" until the mid-1960s permitted southern leaders' massive resistance against the civil rights movement nonviolent protests, which, in turn, fostered violence perpetrated by certain southern officials as well as terrorist groups like the Ku Klux Klan. Moreover, because of concessions to southerners regarding the specific language of the Civil Rights Act, meaningful integration was not the principle that guided the implementation of Title VI. The Johnson administration and the federal courts initially circumvented the original meaning of the law through the formulation of administrative guidelines. But the impact of these measures depended upon continued cooperation between the federal government and judiciary. As successive presidential administrations pursued inconsistent policies, the Supreme Court fashioned doctrines that sanctioned divergent results.

Thus, activist federal authority like that enforced in Little Rock and *Cooper v. Aaron* was necessary for progress, but such progress was ambiguous. A liberal construction of Title VI sanctioned the use of such measures as busing to enforce local compliance. What formerly had been a recognized distinction between desegregation and integration blurred, and integration became synonymous with federal compulsion. One response to this perceived coercive authority was sporadic disorder, but white flight and the private school movement were more pervasive and important forms of resistance. Even though Democratic administrations were more progressive than Republican ones, conflicting pressures did not undercut the attainment of at least mixed success, particularly in the South and in places such as Denver and Indianapolis. Moreover, progress — circumscribed though it was — neither resulted from giving in to nor retreating before resistance, but meeting it through struggle sustained by unswerving dedication. Even this moderate progress was, however, fragile. If the federal government retreated from a commitment to equal justice as it had in the past, the ideal would be forever elusive.

Epilogue

As of the millennium, three disparate incidents suggested the enduring lessons of the Little Rock confrontation and *Cooper v. Aaron*. The February 2000 *Organization of American Historians (OAH) Newsletter* reported Elizabeth Eckford's and Hazel Massery's October 1999 presentations to an audience of several hundred people at Indiana University in Bloomington. The story recounted Eckford's harrowing experience on September 4, 1957, walking alone into the aggressive crowd of whites resisting her entrance into Central High. Massery identified herself as the young white woman, Hazel Bryant, angrily yelling at Eckford's back in the famous photograph taken by Ira Wilmer Counts. Appearing together, the two explained how over the years since the terrible incident they achieved reconciliation. The newsletter account placed their inspiring attainment of mutual respect and true friendship within the conflicted history of U.S. desegregation. Several months after this story appeared, the Supreme Court decided the *Morrison* case, overturning the Violence Against Women Act (VAWA) as contrary to the Commerce Clause of the U.S. Constitution. In December 2000, the Court handed down *Bush v. Gore*; its reversal of a Florida Supreme Court decision gave George W. Bush disputed electoral votes over Albert Gore, who had received approximately 200,000 more votes in the national election. Opinions in these two cases cited the *Cooper* precedent; the case results, however, did not reflect the conciliatory message of the newsletter.

Measured against ongoing problems of racial inequality in the United States, the newsletter story about Eckford's and Massery's appearance was hopeful, yet guarded. Entitled "Reexamining Central High: American Memory and Social Reality," the story conveyed well Eckford's courage as well as Massery's apology to Eckford in 1963. Since 1997, the fortieth anniversary of the Little Rock crisis, Eckford and Massery were "devoted . . . to promoting racial understanding through traveling . . . and speaking to schools, community groups, and other organizations about their roles during Central High's desegregation." The story acknowledged that the two women's transformed "images . . . from symbols of conflict, fear, anger, and courage to that of reconciliation, friendship, and openness" was hopeful, like the medal the U.S. Congress bestowed in 1998 recognizing the Little Rock Nine's "selfless heroism" when confronted with the "bitter stinging pains of racial bigotry." It contrasted these promising images with the harsh social and economic inequality in which so many African Americans live. "While celebrating the progress that has been made, historians should be mindful of the complex economic and social problems that keep racial inequalities stubbornly entrenched," the article concluded, noting the forthcoming fiftieth anniversary of the *Brown* decision in 2004.

Although the newsletter placed Eckford's and Massery's inspiring message within an important historical context, the story also reflected subtle erasure. Except for a passing reference to *Brown*, the constitutional and legal conflicts arising from the Little Rock NAACP decision to challenge the school board desegregation plan — which ultimately compelled the fateful September 4, 1957, encounter between the two women — received no mention. Indeed, the National Guard blocked Eckford from Central High, the story suggests, solely because Faubus ordered it, ignoring the contested legal imperatives and constitutional symbolism Little Rock moderates and extreme segregationists, the governor, the local NAACP, and even the black students themselves employed to justify their conflicting rights claims preceding, during, and after the crisis, culminating in *Cooper v. Aaron* and the token desegregation of two Little Rock high schools in 1959. Moreover, presenting *Brown* as a disappointing milestone measured against the massive social and economic inequality engulfing African Americans at the millennium, the story was silent concerning the dynamic relationship of the decision to the civil rights movement victory over the southern Jim Crow system, which had legitimated racism and terror. Essentially, the story reflected a wariness of litigation-driven reform prevailing since the 1990s among Americans and historians alike, including the belief that, compared to democratic mass action, *Brown* was insignificant.

In Little Rock the response to *Brown* demonstrated, this book has argued, that judicial authority fostered public acceptance of racial desegregation. But the chief consequence was a confrontation over the scope, character, and legitimacy of federal power that obscured the ideal of equal educational opportunity and narrowed the reach of the constitutional rule established in *Brown* I and reaffirmed in *Cooper v. Aaron.* Even so, a comprehensive 1997 report analyzing community attitudes toward the Little Rock School District (LRSD) demonstrated that claims of constitutional rights held meaning most immediately in the ongoing controversial federal remedy of busing. The survey data gave a clear picture of Little Rock public opinion in the mid-1990s. Among white households, 56 percent supported "sending my child to a racially integrated school"; African American households approved of that statement by a margin of 68 percent.

But interracial approval of desegregation in principle disintegrated when considered in terms of particular outcomes. The only specific desegregation program a white majority supported was magnet schools, which 52 percent of whites characterized as effective. African Americans, by contrast, were divided in their response to this question: "Has desegregation had a positive, negative, or no effect on the quality of education in the LRSD?" Thirty-three percent perceived a positive effect, 22 percent a negative effect, 24 percent no effect, and 22 percent were not sure. White opinion was more clear cut: 18 percent replied that desegregation had a positive effect, 14 percent saw no effect, and 18 percent were undecided. The proportion of whites, however, who perceived a negative effect was 50 percent.

Regarding busing as a constitutionally sanctioned tool for bringing about compliance with federal court desegregation orders, the difference between the group responses was still more pronounced. Sixty-eight percent of whites held that cross-town busing was not effective, and only 16 percent stated that it was effective. By contrast, 43 percent of African American households considered the remedy effective. On questions that asked whites and African Americans whether creating *one-race* neighborhood elementary, junior high, and high schools was acceptable, whites approved of such an outcome by an average 73 percent; African Americans disapproved of such a result by 39 percent and favored it by 40 percent.

This divided public opinion reflected the enormous challenges facing the LRSD. Security measures were needed to address discipline and safety concerns. Yet state law that sanctioned an incongruity between the school district boundary and the city limits contributed to potential bankruptcy. Ultimately, however, these issues were symptomatic of a fundamental reality: white flight. A return of between five and eight thousand white students to city public schools would alleviate the financial woes of the school system and likely bring unitary status, a level of racial integration permitting an end to federal judicial supervision. After forty years, the report urged whites to understand the alienation African Americans felt as a result of their history of discrimination; African Americans in turn, it pointed out, needed to have faith that their children would continue to receive material resources from the white taxpaying majority if federal court intervention ended.

This contrast between Little Rock public education in 1997 and the newsletter interpretation of the historic confrontation forty years earlier acquires additional meaning in light of two Supreme Court cases announced in 2000. The story's silence regarding legal imperatives and constitutional symbolism shaping events and outcomes in Little Rock paralleled the Court majority citation of *Cooper v. Aaron* in *United States v. Morrison*. Following legislative findings demonstrating that rape had profound consequences affecting the economic welfare of both the victims and the states where such violence occurred, Congress based VAWA on the Commerce Clause. From 1937 to 1995, the Supreme Court declined to substitute its will for that of Congress, upholding virtually all exercises of the commerce power. In 1995, however, a new five-to-four conservative majority in *United States v. Lopez* struck down congressional reliance upon the Commerce Clause when Congress made firearm possession in or near a school a federal criminal offense. The *Morrison* decision extended this rejection of congressional use of the commerce power. In order to justify the new substitution of its will for that of Congress, the majority cited *Cooper v. Aaron* language declaring that a "permanent and indispensable feature of our constitutional system" is that "the federal judiciary is supreme in the exposition of the Constitution."

The majority citation of *Cooper v. Aaron* in order to impose new limits on the commerce power potentially embraced Title II of the Civil Rights Act of 1964. That provision outlawed discrimination in public accommodations such as restaurants, theaters, and hotels. It arose from the civil rights movement sit-ins and, most directly, the shocking media images resulting from Bull Conner's use of police dogs and fire hoses in Birmingham against black children's peaceful protests in 1963. Rejecting decades of contrary precedents, congressional findings from 1963 to 1964 established connections between economic factors such as interstate travel and food sales that justified basing Title II on the Commerce Clause. In *Morrison*, the conservative majority of five cited the *Cooper* principle of judicial supremacy to deny being bound by congressional findings grounding VAWA on the commerce power. Though Justice Anthony Kennedy joined the *Lopez* five-to-four majority, his concurring opinion specifically defended congressional reliance upon the commerce power as the basis for Title II. Five years later in *Morrison*, the same five-justice majority employed the *Cooper* judicial supremacy principle to deny legislative findings that gender rights claims were worthy of Commerce Clause protection, raising the question of whether the Court conservative majority might now consider overturning Title II protection against racial discrimination, which also depended on congressional findings.

In *Bush v. Gore*, the same conservative majority drew upon the judicial supremacy principle to strike down the Florida Supreme Court electoral vote decision. Following established Florida precedent, the state supreme court held that Florida laws governing disputed vote counts in any election should be construed to authorize as much lawful voter participation as possible. On appeal, lawyers representing Republican presidential candidate Bush argued, however, that such an interpretation of Florida law violated the Fourteenth Amendment Equal Protection Clause. Chief Justice William H. Rehnquist's opinion in support of the five-to-four majority per curiam order upheld this interpretation, overturning the Florida Supreme Court. As a result, the vote-counting did not proceed, giving the Florida electoral votes — and the national election as well — to Bush. Justice Ruth Bader Ginsburg's dissent pointed out that Rehnquist's opinion applied the judicial supremacy principle established in *Cooper v. Aaron* as followed in various other civil rights cases to strike down "a state court's portrayal of state law." Yet *Bush v. Gore* "involves nothing close to the kind of recalcitrance by a state high court that warrants extraordinary action by this Court," Ginsburg declared. "The Florida Supreme Court concluded that counting every legal vote was the overriding concern of the Florida Legislature when it enacted the State's Election Code. The court surely should not be bracketed with state high courts of the Jim Crow South."

The *Morrison* and *Bush* decisions, like the "memory and reality" the *OAH Newsletter* identified with the Little Rock confrontation, ignored the lessons of *Cooper v. Aaron.* The Little Rock NAACP began the *Cooper* litigation because Arkansas democratic politics opposed, and neither the Eisenhower administration nor Congress willingly supported, the equal justice principle established in *Brown* I. Enforced by the 101st Airborne, the litigation enabled the Little Rock Nine to overcome Faubus's and the segregationists' defiance on September 25, 1957; the Supreme Court *Cooper* decision during summer 1958, in turn, narrowed Faubus's political options, bringing about token desegregation of Central and Hall High Schools in 1959. Thus, without the *Brown* and *Cooper* decisions even the token racial desegregation of Little Rock public schools would have been delayed indefinitely had blacks had no other recourse than state and national democratic politics. Moreover, Martin Luther King, Jr. and the civil rights movement eventually defeated the Jim Crow racial apartheid system in the South by establishing "synergy" between nonviolent protest and federal court litigation, thereby mobilizing, in the name of liberal Christian consensus and cold war necessity, northern public support for passage of the Civil Rights Act of 1964 and the Voting Rights Act of 1965. Since the passage of these historic laws, state and national democratic politics sustained minority and gender rights claims within the limits federal litigation prescribed.

Measured against such ambivalence, the Little Rock Nine's courage and determination inspired continued faith in the ideal of equal justice. Each of the nine graduated from college and pursued successful careers. Thus, "the thing integration demonstrated is that, as you challenge the system," said Ernest Green, the oldest of the nine, in 1992, "it doesn't stop with schools. It extends to include all other arrangements and relationships. Once you open Pandora's box and let the genie out, you can't put the genie back in." In Little Rock, as a result of the *Cooper v. Aaron* litigation, a clash between the federal judiciary and elected officials ensured that more meaningful fulfillment of U.S. constitutional and democratic ideals would demand greater commitment and striving. "We're all a work in progress," Melba Pattillo Beals, also of the nine, was quoted as saying in 1997. "We just have to not lose faith and keep trying." Here was the enduring lesson of Little Rock, a lesson the nation has not yet fully grasped.

1953   President Dwight Eisenhower chooses California
            Republican governor Earl Warren as chief justice of
            the U.S. Supreme Court. Warren joins a Court
            divided over *Brown v. Board of Education*, in which
            NAACP Legal Defense Fund (LDF) lawyers argue
            for a construction of the Fourteenth Amendment
            Equal Protection Clause that would overturn *Plessy
            v. Ferguson* (1896). Its separate-but-equal doctrine
            underpins the state-imposed Jim Crow racial
            segregation system in primary and secondary public
            education. Division between the justices reflects
            contrary public and private images of race relations
            in the Jim Crow South and the rest of the nation, as
            well as the congressional stalemate over national
            civil rights legislation. This conflict creates, too,
            difficulties for the Eisenhower administration in
            establishing a consistent position toward civil rights
            in the United States and in cold war propaganda
            battles against communism. In Arkansas, the
            indigenous activism of the local NAACP within a
            context of white moderate racial politics has won
            some limitation of Jim Crow.

1954   Warren gains unanimous Court support for
            declaring that the "separate-but-equal" doctrine is
            inconsistent with the Equal Protection Clause.
            Commentators express surprise that the decision is
            unanimous. Symbolizing their unwavering
            commitment to the fundamental equal rights
            principle affirmed in *Brown*, the justices present a
            unified front. However, Warren achieves this
            unanimity by deferring to Justice Felix Frankfurter's
            position permitting federal courts to endorse
            gradual compliance in desegregation cases, which
            later causes confusion and controversy. Although
            Warren's opinion rests on recent precedent and
            established rules of evidence, critics claim that
            Brown is judicial activism, usurping congressional
            prerogative and states' rights. Meanwhile, though

some within the Eisenhower administration support the *Brown* decision, publicly and privately the president distances himself from it. The Little Rock School Board considers how to comply with *Brown;* local NAACP leaders accept this good faith effort because of the city tradition of racial moderation, as does newly elected Governor Orval E. Faubus.

1955

In *Brown* II, the Supreme Court unanimously authorizes local federal judges to accept school desegregation plans that proceed "with all deliberate speed." Shortly before the decision is announced, Little Rock school superintendent Virgil Blossom publicizes a plan that desegregates only Central High. The Little Rock NAACP decides to sue the school board. In Montgomery, Alabama, Martin Luther King, Jr., leads a boycott against segregated buses. Meanwhile, in rural east Arkansas, segregationist extremists resist desegregating the Hoxie school. Internationally reported incidents of violence there and elsewhere bring the limited involvement of the U.S. Department of Justice. Eisenhower enforces school desegregation in Washington, D.C., but expresses little regard for *Brown* and refuses to support a stronger civil rights bill advocated by Attorney General Herbert Brownell, Secretary of State John Foster Dulles (for cold war reasons), and congressional liberals on both sides of the aisle. Reflecting Arkansas racial moderation, Faubus maintains that desegregation is a local matter.

1956

Amidst disapproval from local white moderates and middle-class blacks, the Little Rock NAACP mobilizes poor black litigants in a federal lawsuit challenging the Blossom plan. School officials defend their phase program as a "good faith" start under *Brown* II. Prior to Judge John E. Miller's August decision in *Aaron v. Cooper* upholding the Blossom plan, segregationist Jim Johnson campaigns vigorously for a states' rights–interposition program reflecting the "massive resistance" the southern U.S. congressional delegation announces in the Southern Manifesto. In a successful summer gubernatorial primary reelection bid, Faubus proposes a more "moderate" interposition program than Johnson's. In Montgomery the boycott triumphs when the Supreme Court declares unconstitutional the segregated city buses. Despite Eisenhower's equivocation on civil rights issues, northern blacks support his reelection. Uprisings in Hungary and Poland, the Middle East Suez crisis, and African nationalist anticolonization movements aggravate, however, the cold war propaganda consequences of Eisenhower's inconsistency on civil rights.

January to July 1957   Early in the year the Arkansas legislature enacts Faubus's and Johnson's interposition measures, moderates triumph over segregationists in a Little Rock School Board election, and the U.S. Eighth Circuit Court of Appeals upholds Judge Miller's *Aaron v. Cooper* decision. The local NAACP does not appeal the decision. Instead it supports black students enrolling in Central High against Blossom's ultimately successful efforts to accept as few blacks as possible. By July, Little Rock segregationist publicity arouses expectations among many whites that interposition can defy the *Brown* decision and the court order desegregating Central High. Moreover, the segregationists expose the fundamental flaw of the Blossom plan: moderate-income and poorer white families living in the Central High district will experience racial desegregation, whereas Hall High, which serves more affluent whites in elite Pulaski Heights remains closed to blacks. Grasping the political benefits, Faubus secretly contacts segregationist leaders. Facing mounting tension, school officials quietly seek assistance from the justice department, but none is forthcoming.

August 1957   Secretly orchestrating phone calls to intimidate public officials and blacks, along with a rally on August 22 in Little Rock featuring the Georgia governor, segregationists sway public opinion in favor of interposition as the means to prevent racial desegregation. Meanwhile, Faubus and the segregationists secretly discuss using state police powers to block the federal desegregation order. Privately they consider, too, the possibility of Faubus running for a third term. Blossom and other school officials surreptitiously meet with Faubus, citing fear of public disorder and violence when school opens. Some school officials ponder Judge Miller's private suggestion that he will delay the implementation of the Little Rock desegregation plan if a state court case is brought to challenge the interposition laws. School officials do not pursue Miller's suggestion. But privately Faubus admits to U.S. justice department attorney Arthur B. Caldwell that he has participated in initiating a state court case seeking to delay desegregation because of impending violence. As a result of Faubus's public assertion that violence will result if blacks enter Central, the state judge on August 29 orders the desegregation plan halted. Responding to the request of school officials and the local NAACP, federal judge Ronald N. Davies orders desegregation to proceed.

September 1957   On September 2, Faubus reads a televised proclamation announcing that the Arkansas National Guard will prevent the desegregation of Central High scheduled to start the next morning. He justifies his action by employing state police powers to prevent disorder and violence on September 3. School officials ask the few black students admitted to Central to stay away pending federal court action. Under accepted constitutional law, Judge Davies declares, state police powers should be used to protect — not deny — rights if violence threatens or occurs. The judge, therefore, orders desegregation to proceed. Nevertheless, on September 4, the National Guard excludes nine black students from Central. Elizabeth Eckford's solitary attempt to enter the school amidst hostile whites is captured in a photograph circulated around the world. The ensuing confrontation between Arkansas and federal authorities receives global media attention. Davies orders Faubus to appear in court on September 20 to present evidence supporting his action. An FBI investigation reveals no evidence of Faubus's claims of impending violence.

Justice department lawyers privately attempt but fail to persuade Wiley Branton, the Arkansas LDF lawyer representing the black students, to agree to a delay in enforcing the desegregation order. In Newport, Rhode Island, on September 14, Eisenhower and Faubus meet but the governor remains defiant. Meanwhile, the justice department formally joins the case against Faubus, whose lawyers challenge the jurisdiction of both the federal government and the federal court. Although Faubus does not appear at the September 20 hearing, his lawyers, after denying court jurisdiction, leave the courtroom. Although, surprisingly, the justice department case does not include presentation of the FBI evidence, Davies, who previously had access to the report, orders desegregation to proceed. Faubus then withdraws the National Guard. On September 23, a mob forces the Little Rock Nine to withdraw after briefly attending classes at Central. Despite Eisenhower demanding the crowd to disperse, disorder persists. Finally, appealing to constitutional law and cold war necessity, Eisenhower dispatches to Little Rock the 101st Airborne units, which enforce the nine's admission to Central High on September 25.

1957–1958   The Little Rock Nine's admission to Central ends one confrontation and begins another. Throughout the school year the nine achieve academic success despite continuing harassment from a small but determined group of white students identified with the segregationists. In February 1958, Little Rock school officials seek from Judge Harry J. Lemley a two-and-one-half-year delay in the Little Rock desegregation plan. In May, a racially integrated audience including Martin Luther King, Jr., witnesses Ernest Green, the only senior among the nine, become the first black graduated from Central

High. The following month in *Cooper v. Aaron*, Judge Lemley grants school officials' requested delay. LDF lawyers pursue simultaneous appeals to both the U.S. Eighth Circuit Court and the Supreme Court, which declines review until the appeals court in special session reviews Lemley's order. By then, Faubus's primary campaign for third-term reelection as governor is well on the way to victory, espousing the segregationist platform of school closing and privatization to resist federal court-ordered desegregation.

1958–1959   In August 1958, the U.S. Eighth Circuit Court overturns Lemley's order, but grants a thirty-day delay enabling the Supreme Court to review *Cooper v. Aaron* in a historic special term from August 25 to September 29. U.S. and international media follow the proceedings in the most important racial desegregation case since *Brown*. Facing ongoing cold war propaganda battles in places such as Lebanon and Iraq, Eisenhower administration officials defend the Supreme Court and the *Brown* decision; Eisenhower himself is more supportive than ever. In Congress the conservative coalition is defeated in its attempt to weaken Supreme Court power. During the special term the justices reconsider the profound constitutional challenges Faubus's defiance epitomizes regarding the legitimacy of *Brown*. After protracted opinion making involving particularly Chief Justice Warren and Justices Brennan, Black, Harlan, and Frankfurter, the Court opinion resoundingly defends it own supremacy to interpret the U.S. Constitution. Ultimately, the Court opinion shapes the enforcement of school desegregation in Little Rock, influencing Martin Luther King, Jr., and future civil rights movement triumphs.

BIBLIOGRAPHIC ESSAY

Note from the series editors: The following bibliographic essay contains the primary and secondary sources that the author consulted for this volume. We have asked all authors in the series to omit formal citations in order to make our volumes more readable, inexpensive, and appealing for students and general readers. In adopting this format, Landmark Law Cases and American Society follows the precedent of a number of highly regarded and widely consulted series.

This book draws freely on other works I have published about the Little Rock confrontation and *Cooper v. Aaron* since 1981. I thank the publishers for permission to quote from the following: Tony A. Freyer, "Objectivity and Involvement: Georg G. Iggers and Writing the History of the Little Rock School Crisis," and "Crossing Borders in American Civil Rights Historiography," in Larry Eugene Jones, ed., *Crossing Boundaries: The Exclusion and Inclusion of Minorities in Germany and the United States* (New York: Berghahn Books, 2001), 172–191, 213–232; Tony A. Freyer, "The Past as Future: The Little Rock Crisis and the Constitution," in Elizabeth Jacoway and C. Fred Williams, eds., *Understanding the Little Rock Crisis: An Exercise in Remembrance and Reconciliation* (Fayetteville: University of Arkansas Press, 1999), 141–152; Tony A. Freyer, *The Constitution Resisted and School Desegregation*, Bicentennial of the U.S. Constitution Lecture Series (Bloomington: Indiana University Foundation, 1985); Tony A. Freyer, "Politics and Law in the Little Rock Crisis, 1954–1957," *Arkansas Historical Quarterly* 40 (Autumn 1981): 195–219; Tony A. Freyer, "The Little Rock Crisis Reconsidered," *Arkansas Historical Quarterly* 56 (Autumn 1997): 361–370; Tony A. Freyer, "*Cooper v. Aaron*: Incident and Consequence," *Arkansas Historical Quarterly* 65 (Spring 2006): 1–6; Tony A. Freyer, "Enforcing *Brown* in the Little Rock Crisis," *Journal of Appellate Practice and Process* 6, no. 1 (Spring 2004): 67–78. I hold the copyright for Tony A. Freyer, *The Little Rock Crisis: A Constitutional Interpretation* (Westport, Conn.: Greenwood, 1984).

All official published case citations in this book may be located by standard title search on Westlaw, Lexis-Nexis, or other U.S. Supreme Court databases. Note that although a court may issue an order on a given date, the opinion supporting the order usually is published the following day or later.

The photographs referred to in the introduction were taken by Larry Obsitnik (Little Rock Nine entering Central High under military escort) and Ira Wilmer Counts (Elizabeth Eckford and Hazel Bryant) courtesy of the *Arkansas Democrat Gazette* and Special Collections Division, University of Arkansas Libraries, Fayetteville.

The sources cited in the introduction are C. Vann Woodward, *The Strange Career of Jim Crow* (New York: Oxford University Press, 1957); S. F. Lawson, "Freedom Then, Freedom Now: The Historiography of the Civil Rights Movement," *American Historical Review* 96 (1991): 456–471; David J. Garrow, *Bearing the Cross: Martin Luther King, Jr., and the Southern Christian Leadership Conference* (New York: William Morrow, 1986); Taylor Branch, *Parting the Waters: America in the King Years, 1954–1963* (New York: Simon and Schuster, 1989); Taylor Branch, *Pillar of Fire: America in the King Years, 1963–1965* (New York: Simon and Schuster, 1998); Jack Bass, *Taming the Storm: The Life and Times of Judge Frank M. Johnson, Jr., and the South's Fight over Civil Rights* (New York: Doubleday, 1993); Mark V. Tushnet, *Making Civil Rights Law: Thurgood Marshall and the Supreme Court, 1936–1961* (New York: Oxford University Press, 1994); Michael J. Klarman, *From Jim Crow to Civil Rights: The Supreme Court and the Struggle for Racial Equality* (New York: Oxford University Press, 2004); Juan Williams, *Eyes on the Prize: America's Civil Rights Years, 1954–1965* (New York: Penguin, 1987); Michal R. Belknap, *Federal Law and Southern Order: Racial Violence and Constitutional Conflict in the Post-Brown South* (Athens: University of Georgia Press, 1987); D. R. Goldfield, *Black, White, and Southern: Race Relations and Southern Culture, 1940 to Present* (Baton Rouge: Louisiana State University Press, 1991); Gavin G. Wright, *Old South, New South: Revolutions in the Southern Economy since the Civil War* (New York: Oxford University Press, 1986); Mary L. Dudziak, "The Little Rock Crisis and Foreign Affairs: Race, Resistance, and the Image of American Democracy," *Southern California Law Review* 70, no. 6 (September 1997): 1641–1716; George M. Fredrickson, *The Comparative Imagination: On the History of Racism, Nationalism, and Social Movements* (Berkeley: University of California Press, 1997); Derrick Bell, Jr., "*Brown* and the Interest-Convergence Dilemma," *Harvard Law Review* 93 (1980): 518–533.

The introduction also cites Richard Kluger, *Simple Justice: The History of Brown v. Board of Education and Black America's Struggle for Equality* (New York: Alfred A. Knopf, 1976); from *Arkansas Historical Quarterly* 56 (Autumn 1997), Special Issue: 40th Anniversary of the Little Rock School Crisis, edited by David L. Chappell, the following articles: David L. Chappell, "Editor's Introduction," ix–xvi; Azza Salama Layton, "International Pressure and the U.S. Government's Response to Little Rock," 257–272; John A. Kirk, "The Little Rock Crisis and Postwar Black Activism in Arkansas," 273–293; Mark Newman, "The Arkansas Baptist State Convention and Desegregation, 1954–1968," 294–313; Richard H. King, "American Dilemmas, European Experiences," 314–333; Allison Graham, "Remapping Dogpatch: Northern Media on the Southern Circuit," 334–340; C. Fred Williams, "Class: The Central Issue in the 1957 Little Rock School Crisis," 341–344; Elizabeth Jacoway, "Down from the Pedestal: Gender and Regional Culture in a Ladylike Assault on the Southern Way of Life," 345–352; Tony Badger, "'The Forerunner of Our Opposition': Arkansas and the Southern Manifesto of 1956," 353–360; Tony A. Freyer, "The Little Rock Crisis Reconsidered," 361–370; and Adam Fairclough, "The Little Rock Crisis; Success or Failure for the NAACP?" 371–375; G. C. [*sic*] Iggers, "An Arkansas Professor: The NAACP and the Grass Roots," in W. and J. C. Record, eds., *Little Rock, U.S.A.: Materials for Analysis* (San Francisco: Chandler, 1960), 283–291; and Freyer, "Crossing Borders," 213–232.

The initial three chapters of this study outlining the events, context, and sources quoted preceding (1954–1957) and culminating in the Little Rock school desegregation crisis of August–September 1957 draw on the following secondary works: The leading work on the Little Rock NAACP is John A. Kirk, *Redefining the Color Line: Black Activism in Little Rock, Arkansas, 1940–1970* (Gainesville: University Press of Florida, 2002); the best study of Wiley Branton's role in the Little Rock litigation is Judith Kilpatrick, "Wiley Austin Branton and *Cooper v. Aaron:* America Fulfills Its Promise," *Arkansas Historical Quarterly* 65 (Spring 2006): 7–21; Judith Kilpatrick, "Wiley Austin Branton," paper presented at the New York University Legal History Colloquium, February 9, 2005 (quoted with permission); and Judith Kilpatrick, "Wiley Austin Branton and the Voting Rights Struggle," *University of Arkansas at Little Rock Law Review* 26 (Summer 2004): 642–701. See also Freyer, "Objectivity and Involvement," 172–192; and Brian James Daugherty, "'With All Deliberate Speed': The NAACP and the Implementation of *Brown v. Board of Education* at the Local Level, Little Rock, Arkansas," M.A. thesis, University of Montana, 1997. For the Little Rock School Board position, see Elizabeth Jacoway, "Richard C. Butler and the Little Rock School Board: The Quest to Maintain 'Educational Quality,'" *Arkansas Historical Quarterly* 65 (Spring 2006): 24–38; and, for a comparison of the Little Rock moderate elite to their counterparts in other southern cities, Elizabeth Jacoway and David R. Colburn, eds., *Southern Businessmen and Desegregation* (Baton Rouge: Louisiana State University Press, 1982). The best study of Faubus, which deals extensively with the years preceding, including, and immediately following the crisis, is Roy Reed, *Faubus: The Life and Times of an American Prodigal* (Fayetteville: University of Arkansas Press, 1997).

For Eisenhower administration positions on civil rights and foreign affairs in the first three chapters see Herbert Brownell with John P. Burke, *Advising Ike: The Memoirs of Attorney General Herbert Brownell* (Lawrence: University Press of Kansas, 1993); Mary L. Dudziak, *Cold War Civil Rights: Race and the Image of American Democracy* (Princeton, N.J.: Princeton University Press, 2000), 115–151; and Thomas Borstelmann, *The Cold War and the Color Line: American Race Relations in the Global Arena* (Cambridge, Mass.: Harvard University Press, 2001). A roughly contemporary account of cold war confrontations, including the chronology followed in this study, is Alexander DeConde, *A History of American Foreign Policy* (New York: Charles Scribner's Sons, 1963). On the segregationist extremists, see Frances Lisa Baer, "Race over Rights: The Resistance to Public School Desegregation in Little Rock, Arkansas, and Beyond, 1954–1960" (Ph.D. diss., University of Alabama, 2004); Graeme Cope, "'Honest White People of the Middle and Lower Classes'?: A Profile of the Capital Citizens' Council during the Little Rock Crisis of 1957," *Arkansas Historical Quarterly* 61 (Spring 2002): 37–58; Graeme Cope, "'A Thorn in the Side'? The Mothers' League of Central High School and the Little Rock Desegregation Crisis of 1957," *Arkansas Historical Quarterly* 57 (Summer 1998): 160–190; Graeme Cope, "'Marginal Youngsters' and 'Hoodlums of Both Sexes'? Student Segregationists during the Little Rock Crisis," *Arkansas Historical Quarterly* 63 (Winter 2004), 380–403; and Numan V. Bartley, "Looking Back at Little Rock," *Arkansas Historical Quarterly* 25 (Summer 1966): 101–116.

On the cultural politics of race, including the appeal of states' rights ideology and interposition in Little Rock and Arkansas (1954–1959), see David L. Chappell, *A Stone of Hope: Prophetic Religion and the Death of Jim Crow* (Chapel Hill: University of North Carolina Press, 2004) and Robert J. Norrell, *The House I Live In: Race in the American Century* (New York: Oxford University Press, 2005). For the racial politics and images defining interposition, see Corinne Silverman, *The Little Rock Crisis* (Tuscaloosa: University of Alabama Press, 1958); John Chambers, "Media Images of the Little Rock Crisis," unpublished research report in Tony A. Freyer's possession, April 28, 2000; Freyer, *The Little Rock Crisis*; David L. Chappell, "The Divided Mind of Southern Segregationists," *Georgia Historical Quarterly* 82 (1998): 45–72. Still useful is Numan V. Bartley, *The Rise of Massive Resistance and the Politics of the South during the 1950s* (Baton Rouge: Louisiana State University Press, 1969); but see Baer, "Race over Rights." On interest group politics prior to the crisis, see Boyce Alexander Drummond, Jr., "Arkansas Politics: A Study of a One-Party System" (Ph.D. diss., University of Chicago, 1957).

Manuscript collections and/or primary sources include, regarding Little Rock NAACP materials, the Georg Iggers Papers donated to the University of Arkansas at Little Rock Archives, including Georg Iggers to Tony Freyer, September 17, 1980; Franz Adler to Georg Iggers, February 9, 1954; and Iggers to Adler, May 10, 1954. See also Virginia Brady Perschbacher (Director of Library Services, Philander Smith College) to Tony Freyer, July 7, 1997, based on *President's Annual Report, 1955–1959* (in Freyer's possession). In addition to Daisy Bates, *The Long Shadow of Little Rock: A Memoir* (Fayetteville: University of Arkansas Press, 1987), essential manuscript materials for Daisy and L. C. Bates are the Daisy Bates Papers (State Historical Society of Wisconsin, Archives Division). At the Library of Congress Manuscript Division, see National Association for the Advancement of Colored People,

Group III, General Office Files, Arkansas; Mason File, NAACP Legal Defense and Education Fund, Inc.; Schools, General File, NAACP Legal Defense and Education Fund, Inc. See also, Melba Pattillo Beals, *Warriors Don't Cry: A Searing Memoir of the Battle to Integrate Little Rock's Central High* (New York: Simon and Schuster, 1994). In the Dwight D. Eisenhower Administration Oral History Project (Columbia University), see Wiley Branton (1973); William G. Cooper (1971); Harold Engstrom (1971); Amis Guthridge (1972); and A. F. House (1973).

On the Eisenhower administration, including the justice department, see the Arthur B. Caldwell Papers (University of Arkansas, Fayetteville); William F. Rogers Papers (Dwight D. Eisenhower Library, Abilene, Kansas); James C. Hagerty Papers (Dwight D. Eisenhower Library, Abilene, Kansas); Federal Bureau of Investigation Report — Little Rock, 44-12284-933 [n.d.] (FBI, Washington, D.C., and the University of Arkansas at Little Rock Archives); Federal Bureau of Investigation Report — Little Rock, 44-12284-937 [n.d.] (FBI, Washington, D.C.); Federal Bureau of Investigation Report — Little Rock, 44-12285-855 [n.d.] (Washington, D.C.); Osro Cobb, "*United States v. Governor Orval E. Faubus et al.*," manuscript located in University of Arkansas at Little Rock Archives; and especially, John Thomas Elliff, "The United States Department of Justice and Individual Rights, 1937–1962" (Ph.D. diss., Harvard University, 1968). Sources for the Little Rock school officials' position include, in addition to Elizabeth Jacoway, "Richard C. Butler" ; the Virgil T. Blossom Papers (Special Collections, University of Arkansas Libraries, Fayetteville); Richard C. Butler Case Files, *Cooper v. Aaron* (originals in Butler's and his legal heir's possession, copy of originals in Freyer's possession, used with permission); and Leon B. Catlett Case File, *Cooper v. Aaron* (in Freyer's possession, used with permission).

See also Virgil T. Blossom, *It Has Happened Here* (New York: Harper and Brothers, 1959); Elizabeth Huckaby, *Crisis at Central High: Little Rock, 1957–1958* (Baton Rouge: Louisiana State University Press, 1980); and Irving J. Spitzberg, Jr., *Racial Politics in Little Rock, 1954–1964* (New York: Garland, 1987). Also, throughout the three chapters dealing with the crisis and/or its antecedents I use as primary sources Orval Eugene Faubus, *Down from the Hills* (Little Rock: The Pioneer, 1980); "The Story of Little Rock — As Governor Faubus Tells It," *U.S. News & World Report*, June 20, 1958, pp. 101–106; and Brooks Hays, *A Southern Moderate Speaks* (Chapel Hill: University of North Carolina Press, 1959).

I also draw upon my own interviews with the following participants, all cited in Freyer, *The Little Rock Crisis*, except for the Lee Lorch interview: Harry Ashmore, Santa Barbara, June 2, 1981; Wiley Branton, Washington, D.C., December 11, 1979; William J. Brennan, Jr., Washington, D.C., March 3, 1980; Richard C. Butler, Little Rock, February 5, 1980; Leon B.

Catlett, Little Rock, July 1, 1980; Ronald N. Davies, Washington, D.C., April 16, 1980; Orval E. Faubus, Little Rock, July 15, 1980; A. F. House, Little Rock, June 16, 1980; James Johnson, Little Rock, September 4, 1980; Lee Lorch, Toronto, Canada, June 10, 2006; J. L. (Bex) Shaver, Wynne, Arkansas, August 15, 1980; W. J. Smith, Little Rock, September 3, 1980; and Ozell Sutton, Atlanta, Georgia, November 14, 1980.

Although most of the primary and secondary sources suggest the stages of the *Cooper v. Aaron* litigation (1956–1958), the following focus most directly on constitutional-legal materials, particularly those used in Chapters 4, 5, and 6 (first section). For a sense of the litigation as it unfolded at the time see Volumes 1–4 of *Race Relations Law Review*. The full record at the federal district court level is *Aaron v. Cooper*, Case 3113, Entry ERA20, Civil Case Files, U.S. District for the Western Division of the Eastern District of Arkansas, Record Group 21, National Archives and Record Administration, Fort Worth, Texas. Two contemporary accounts of the litigation emphasizing the Supreme Court August special term appear in J. W. Peltason, *Fifty-Eight Lonely Men: Southern Federal Judges and School Desegregation* (New York: Harcourt, Brace, 1961) and Anthony Lewis, *Portrait of a Decade: The Second American Revolution* (New York: Random House, 1964). Two recent accounts are Raymond T. Diamond, "Confrontation as Rejoinder to Compromise: Reflections on the Little Rock Desegregation Crisis," *National Black Law Journal* 11 (1989): 151–176; and Keith E. Whittington, "The Court as the Final Arbiter of the Constitution: *Cooper v. Aaron* (1958)," in Gregg Ivers and Kevin T. McGuire, eds., *Creating Constitutional Change: Clashes over Power and Liberty in the Supreme Court* (Charlottesville: University of Virginia Press, 2004), 9–20.

The leading study of *Brown* and the "unanimity" principle in relation to *Cooper v. Aaron* is Dennis J. Hutchinson, "Unanimity and Desegregation: Decisionmaking in the Supreme Court, 1948–1958," *Georgetown Law Journal* 68 (October 1979): 1–87. Two prominent accounts of the effect of the *Cooper* litigation on the Warren Court and national politics are Lucas A. Powe, Jr., *The Warren Court and American Politics* (Cambridge, Mass.: Harvard University Press, 2000) and Michal R. Belknap, *The Supreme Court under Earl Warren, 1953–1969* (Columbia: University of South Carolina Press, 2005). Earl Warren, *The Memoirs of Earl Warren* (New York: Doubleday, 1977) and William O. Douglas, *The Court Years, 1939–1975: The Autobiography of William O. Douglas* (New York: Vintage, 1981) include valuable insights on *Cooper v. Aaron*. The case is also discussed in Bernard Schwartz, *Super Chief Earl Warren and His Supreme Court: A Judicial Biography* (New York: New York University Press, 1983); G. Edward White, *Earl Warren: A Public Life* (New York: Oxford University Press, 1982); Roger K. Newman, *Hugo L. Black: A Biography* (New York: Pantheon, 1994); Tinsley E. Yarbrough, *John Marshall Harlan: Great Dissenter of the Warren Court* (New York: Oxford University

Press, 1992); and Craig Alan Smith, *Failing Justice: Charles Evans Whittaker on the Supreme Court* (Jefferson, N.C.: McFarland, 2005).

In this book I quote from and use principally the *Cooper v. Aaron* case files from the William J. Brennan Papers and the Harold H. Burton Papers, Library of Congress Manuscript Division; the Felix Frankfurter Papers, Harvard Law Library Special Collections and Library of Congress Manuscript Division; and the John Marshall Harlan Papers, Seeley G. Mudd Manuscript Library, Princeton University, Box No. 57. I also consulted the Hugo L. Black Papers, Library of Congress Manuscript Division and Tom C. Clark's draft dissent in *Cooper*, in the Tom C. Clark Papers, Tarleton Law Library, University of Texas at Austin. Harlan's and Frankfurter's case files include complete opinions, briefs, and court papers for the case from Lemley's decision and its appeals and resulting orders in the U.S. Eighth Circuit Court of Appeals to the U.S. Supreme Court August special term. Many of those same records are also available in Philip B. Kurland and Gerhard Casper, *Landmark Briefs of the Supreme Court of the United States: Constitutional Law* (Arlington, VA: University Publications of America, 1975). The Harry J. Lemley Papers (two boxes) in the University of Arkansas at Little Rock Archives include many of the affidavits and newspapers providing evidence for his opinion as well as correspondence, including the letter from R. B. McCulloch quoted in the text.

Other citations are from Fred N. Fishman to Justice Frankfurter, October 10, 1958, Fred N. Fishman Papers, Harvard Law Library Special Collections and Tony Freyer interview with John H. Mansfield, May 12, 2006, including handwritten passage quoted in text (with permission) from unpublished opinions of Felix Frankfurter, *Aaron v. Cooper* (June 30, 1958), original in Mansfield's possession. Also, the text quotes passages from a memorandum by Peter M. Fishbein, Justice Brennan's clerk, located in the William J. Brennan Papers, *Cooper v. Aaron* case files, Library of Congress Manuscript Division.

Accounts of the NAACP Legal Defense Fund arguments and preparation of the appellate briefs in *Cooper v. Aaron* appear in Jack Greenberg, *Crusaders in the Courts: How a Dedicated Band of Lawyers Fought for the Civil Rights Revolution* (New York: Basic Books, 1994); William L. Taylor, *The Passion of My Times: An Advocate's Fifty-Year Journey in the Civil Rights Movement* (New York: Carroll and Graf, 2006); and Tushnet, *Making Civil Rights Law*.

In the first section of Chapter 6 regarding the conflicted implementation of *Cooper v. Aaron* through the moderates' regained control of Little Rock schools, see Sara Murphy, *Breaking the Silence: Little Rock's Women's Emergency Committee to Open Our Schools, 1958–1963* (Fayetteville: University of Arkansas Press, 1997); Baer, "Race over Rights," chaps. 9 and 10; Spitzberg, *Racial Politics*, 82–141; Robert L. Brown, "The Third Little Rock Crisis,"

Arkansas Historical Quarterly 65 (Spring 2006): 39–44; Kirk, *Redefining the Color Line,* 133–138; Reed, *Faubus,* 244–259; Henry M. Alexander, *The Little Rock Recall Election,* Eagleton Institute Cases in Practical Politics no. 17 (New York: McGraw-Hill, 1960); and Elizabeth Jacoway, "Down from the Pedestal," 345–352, and her book *Turn Away Thy Son: Little Rock, the Crisis that Shocked the Nation* (New York: Free Press, 2007).

For the remaining three sections of Chapter 6, the sources include Martin Luther King, Jr., with Clayborne Carson, ed., *The Autobiography of Martin Luther King, Jr.* (New York: Warner, 1998), including quoted passages from "Letter from a Birmingham Jail," 188–204; Bass, *Taming the Storm;* Tony A. Freyer, ed., *Defending Constitutional Rights: Frank M. Johnson* (Athens: University of Georgia Press, 2001); Michael Meltsner, *The Making of a Civil Rights Lawyer* (Charlottesville: University of Virginia Press, 2006); Garrow, *Bearing the Cross;* Branch, *Parting the Waters;* Tushnet, *Making Civil Rights Law;* R. H. King, "American Dilemmas, European Experiences," 314–333; Mark Newman, "The Arkansas Baptist State Convention and Desegregation, 1954–1968," 294–313; Allison Graham, "Remapping Dogpatch," 334–340; Julian Bond, "Introduction," in Juan Williams, *Eyes on the Prize,* xiii–xiv; Daniel J. Boorstin, *The Image: A Guide to Pseudo-Events in America* (New York: Harper, 1964 [1961]); Raymond Arsenault, *Freedom Riders 1961 and the Struggle for Racial Justice* (New York: Oxford University Press, 2006); J. L. Chestnut, Jr., and Julia Cass, *Black in Selma: The Uncommon Life of J. L. Chestnut, Jr.* (New York: Farrar, Straus, and Giroux, 1990).

Of the many studies of federal court–enforced desegregation from the 1960s to the 1980s, including Title VI of the Civil Rights Act of 1964, see George R. Metcalf, *From Little Rock to Boston: The History of School Desegregation* (Westport, Conn.: Greenwood, 1983); David L. Kirp, *Just Schools: The Idea of Racial Equality in American Education* (Berkeley: University of California Press, 1982); Kluger, *Simple Justice,* 748–778; Howard I. Kalodnor and James J. Fishman, eds., *Limits of Justice: The Courts' Role in School Desegregation* (Cambridge, Mass.: Ballanger, 1978); Lino A. Graglia, *Disaster by Decree: The Supreme Court Decisions on Race and Schools* (Ithaca, N.Y.: Cornell University Press, 1976); Charles Vert Willie, *School Desegregation Plans That Work* (Westport, Conn.: Greenwood, 1984); Gary Orfield, *The Reconstruction of Southern Education: The Schools and the 1964 Civil Rights Act* (New York: John Wiley and Sons, 1969); Susan P. Stuart, "Indianapolis Desegregation: Segregative Intent and the Interdistrict Remedy," *Indiana Law Review* 14 (1981): 799–830; and Derrick A. Bell, Jr., "A School Desegregation Post-Mortem," *University of Texas Law Review* 62 (August 1983): 175–190.

In addition to the three Supreme Court cases, the sources for the epilogue are Damon Freeman, "Reexamining Central High: American Memory and Social Reality," *OAH Newsletter* (February 2000): 3, 6; Joel E. Anderson,

David L. Briscoe, Gary D. Chamberlain, Priscilla Nellum Davis, W. Dent Gitchell, Jim Lynch, Angela M. Sewall, Andy Terry, and Dianne D. Wood, *Plain Talk: The Future of Little Rock's Public Schools* (University of Arkansas at Little Rock Report, 1997); Brown, "The Third Little Rock Crisis," 39–44; Elizabeth Jacoway, "Introduction," in Jacoway and Williams, eds., *Understanding the Little Rock Crisis*, 1–22; Polly J. Price, "The Little Rock School Desegregation Cases in Richard Arnold's Court," *Arkansas Law Review* 58 (2005): 611–662; Christopher Coleman, Laurence D. Nee, and Leonard S. Rubinowitz, "Social Movements and Social Change Litigation: Synergy in the Montgomery Bus Protest," *Law and Social Inquiry* 30 (Fall 2005): 663–738; Jeffrey Rosen, "The End of Deference: *The Warren Court and American Politics* by Lucas A. Powe," *New Republic* (November 6, 2000): 39–45; Gary D. Rowe, "Constitutionalism in the Streets," *Southern California Law Review* 78 (January 2005): 401–456; Audrey Edwards and Craig K. Polite, "Don't Let Them See You Cry," *Parade Magazine* (February 16, 1992): 10, 13; and Associated Press, "Desegregation: A 'Work in Progress,'" *Tuscaloosa News*, August 10, 1997, p. 3B.

Aaron, John, 34
Aaron, Nadine, 96, 97, 138
Aaron v. Cooper
  appeal of, 68–76
  assigning, 53–54
  Brown II and, 87, 134
  decision in, 59–68
  filing of, 35, 36, 50, 52, 55, 56, 57
  political context of, 47
  pretrial misconceptions about,
    48–59
  racial tensions and, 48–59
ABA. *See* American Bar Association
Ableman v. Booth (1859), 173, 176
Adams, John, 186
Adams, Sherman, 121
Adler, Mrs. Franz, 25
Affirmative action, 166, 218, 221, 229
African independence movement,
    civil rights movement and, 215
Alabama Lawyer, 9
Alabama NAACP registration case,
    188
Alford, Dale, 205
Ali, Muhammad, 30
All deliberate speed standard, 164,
    177–178, 180, 182, 199, 227
  Brown I and, 162, 163, 177
  Brown II and, 148, 159–160, 166,
    182, 186, 190, 193, 196, 197, 225
  defining, 148, 162
  delay and, 163, 172, 181
  desegregation and, 61, 174–175,
    176, 186, 210, 214, 225
  federal supremacy and, 173
  questioning, 159–160, 171, 177,
    194, 200
  overturning, 218
  support of, 187, 188, 193

American Bar Association (ABA), 9,
    151, 152, 198
Andy Griffith Show, The (television
    show), 217
Angelou, Maya, 30
Antibusing amendment, 224
Anti-integration campaign, 39
Apartheid, 42, 159
Arendt, Hannah, 215–216
Arkansas Baptist, 216
Arkansas Commission of Education,
    23
Arkansas Conference of NAACP,
    51, 57
Arkansas Constitution, 208
Arkansas Democrat, 55, 62, 90, 150
  Blossom-House correspondence
    in, 71
  on Lemley, 144–145, 149
  Thomason and, 96
Arkansas Department of Education,
    144
Arkansas Gazette, 5, 19, 21, 55, 59,
    67, 83, 90, 129, 141, 146, 159
  Blossom-House correspondence
    in, 71
  on desegregation, 63
  Faubus in, 109
  on Little Rock School Board, 16
  Thomason and, 96
  on Williams, 18
Arkansas Industrial Development
    Commission, 71
Arkansas National Guard, vii, 110,
    115, 119, 125, 142, 144, 242,
    243
  at Central High, 2, 89, 111, 112,
    113, 114
  Eckford and, 233

Arkansas National Guard, *continued*
 Faubus and, 2, 112, 120, 128
 federalization of, 121, 122, 130,
  131, 136
 at Horace Mann High School,
  114
 mobilization of, 2
 potential violence and, 127
 white student harassment and, 138
Arkansas State Press, 28–29
 boycott of, 118, 137
Arkansas Supreme Court, 207, 209
Arsenault, Raymond, 221
Article 6 (U.S. Constitution), 80,
 108, 172–173
Ashmore, Harry, 5, 83, 129, 141,
 159
Atlanta Journal, 157, 159
Attendance zones, 24, 78, 97, 228

Badger, Anthony, 7, 8
Barrett, John, 140
Bates, Daisy, 20, 50, 91, 92, 171
 Blossom plan and, 25, 33
 Branton and, 52
 Faubus and, 89–90, 112, 114, 115
 federalization and, 136
 harassment of, 90, 95, 103, 118,
  129, 137
 interposition laws and, 84
 leadership by, 15, 204
 litigation and, 31, 81
 Little Rock Nine and, 117, 133,
  220
 phase program and, 33
 school board and, 18
 testimony of, 57, 58, 59
 Till murder and, 30
 white moderates and, 19
Bates, L. C., 20, 50, 137
 Blossom plan and, 25, 33
 Faubus and, 112
 harassment of, 90, 118

litigation and, 28, 31
 phase program and, 33
Belknap, Michal R., 7
Bell, Derrick, 1
Bell v. School City of Gary, Indiana
 (1963), 226
Bennett, Bruce, 82, 84, 103
 Faubus and, 86
 harassment by, 118
 membership lists and, 71
 state sovereignty and, 110
 suit and, 92, 95, 102
Bird, Marvin K., 64
Bird committee, 68
 interposition and, 65, 66
Birmingham, unrest in, 212, 236
Birth of a Nation, The (movie), 217
Black, Hugo L., 161, 180, 185, 193,
 194, 197, 244
 activism of, 158
 all deliberate speed and, 163, 164,
  177, 181, 199, 200
 delay and, 172
 desegregation and, 175
 on enforcement, 166
 Griffin and, 225
 opinion in *Cooper* and, 183, 184,
  185, 188, 189, 190, 214
 revision by, 176
 special term and, 151, 153, 155,
  156, 159
Black community, 2, 7, 12, 26–27,
 74
 civil rights activists and, 220
 intimidation of, 79
 legalism and, 94
 litigation and, 28–29, 32, 49, 50
 Little Rock NAACP and, 202
 maintaining order and, 95
 NAACP and, 77
 outsiders and, 51
 phase program and, 77
 states' rights and, 217

Bloody Sunday, 212
Blossom, Virgil, 110, 123, 129, 147, 211, 240, 242
    Branton and, 17, 21
    Brown I and, 20, 21
    criticism of, 28
    desegregation and, 19–20, 23, 24, 35, 47, 49, 60, 61, 70, 101, 105
    Faubus and, 48, 88, 95, 106, 113
    House correspondence with, 71
    interposition amendments and, 69
    interview of, 83, 143–144
    Little Rock NAACP and, 24–25, 78–79
    Miller and, 100
    phase program and, 49, 74, 75
    pressure on, 98–99
    publicity campaign by, 30
    pupil assignment law and, 77
    recruiting by, 57
    report by, 144
    resignation of, 203
    segregation and, 20, 48, 79
    Thomason case and, 106
    transfers and, 80, 91, 152
Blossom plan, 56, 58, 82, 83, 97, 112
    criticism of, 25, 28, 33, 35, 76
    described, 23
    enforcement of, 62, 94, 108, 109, 115
    revision of, 27, 51
    support for, 55
    See also Little Rock Phase Program
Bond, Julian, 4, 217
Bond, Mildred, 15
Booker, J. R., 25, 27, 28, 31
Boorstin, Daniel J., 219–220
Boycotts, 40
    Arkansas State Press, 118, 137
    Montgomery bus, 5, 30, 31, 93, 213, 218, 240, 241

Branch, Taylor, 5
Brandeis, Louis, 37, 186
Branscum, George P., 73, 74
Branton, Wiley, vii, 20, 48, 74, 87, 92, 114, 118, 206, 243
    Aaron and, 50, 52, 55, 56, 57
    Blossom and, 17, 21
    Blossom plan and, 12, 58
    civil rights work of, 51, 52
    Cooper and, 204–205
    Davies and, 107, 115
    desegregation and, 21, 121, 148
    hopefulness of, 33, 34
    House and, 77
    leadership by, 15, 16
    Lemley stay and, 150
    litigation and, 33–34, 47, 51, 55, 60, 61, 122, 123, 145, 151
    on Little Rock crisis, 131
    Maeguineas and, 117
    phase program and, 75
    Tate and, 52, 53
    Till murder and, 30
Brennan, William J., viii, 188, 244
    all deliberate speed and, 164, 176, 177, 181, 183, 197, 200
    appointment of, 159
    Brown I and, 163
    Brown II and, 163, 176, 198–199, 201
    Constitution and, 174, 193
    desegregation and, 162–163, 166–167
    Douglas and, 179
    enforcement authority and, 182
    federal supremacy and, 173, 177
    Fourteenth Amendment and, 175, 176
    Harlan and, 179, 180, 189
    Hoxie precedent and, 174
    JMH draft and, 180
    joining formula and, 182
    judicial supremacy and, 169–177

Brennan, William J., *continued*
  Keyes and, 228
  opinion in *Cooper* and, 167, 169,
    172, 173, 175–176, 181, 184,
    185, 189, 190, 192–193, 194,
    197, 199, 210, 214
  oral arguments in *Cooper* and, 161
  special term and, 151, 152, 153,
    154, 159, 160
  Supremacy Clause and, 180–181,
    182, 186
  Warren and, 172
Brewer, Herbert, 40, 82
Briggs v. Elliott (1955), 54, 80
Browder v. Gayle (1956), 30
Brown, Minnejean, 133, 211
  challenge for, 112
  harassment of, 139
  transfer of, 79
Brown, Robert Ewing, 73, 74, 81, 87
Brown, Robert L., 204
Brown v. Board of Education I (1954),
    viii, 14, 36, 42, 67, 93
  all deliberate speed and, 162, 163,
    177
  citing, 59–60
  civil rights struggle and, 3
  compliance with, 16, 22, 46, 49,
    51, 53, 63, 94, 117, 155, 170,
    203, 210
  Constitution and, 193, 211, 223
  Cooper and, 1, 3, 210, 234
  criticism of, 8, 9, 46, 155
  defense of, 152, 182, 183, 191,
    192, 199, 209
  desegregation and, 6, 56, 80, 169,
    187, 244
  disappointed hopes and, 15–22
  educational opportunity and, 230
  enforcement of, 11, 41, 43–44,
    65, 87, 224
  fiftieth anniversary of, 233

influence of, 7, 166, 233
  resistance to, 10, 37, 155, 158
  segregation and, 3, 228
  unanimity in, 178
Brown v. Board of Education II
    (1955), viii, 13, 14, 15, 23, 45,
    56, 69, 88
  Aaron and, 87, 134
  amicus brief for, 43, 65
  black activism and, 22
  community hostility and, 162
  compliance with, 40, 53, 170,
    185, 198
  constitutional rights and, 146
  decision to sue and, 22–34
  defense of, 169
  disagreements in, 150, 200
  enforcement of, 38, 44, 159, 164,
    213
  equity relief and, 54, 75
  interpretations of, 146
  remedial decree in, 24, 62, 78, 197
Brownell, Herbert, 38, 83, 116, 121,
    240
  Brown I and, 43–44
  Caldwell and, 82
  civil rights bill and, 41, 42, 44, 67
  desegregation and, 67
  discretion and, 53
  federalization and, 129–130
  Jim Crow and, 43
  opposition to, 39
  regular troops and, 130
  resignation of, 141
  Title III and, 45, 46, 77, 82
Bryant, Hazel, 232
Buchanan v. Warely (1917), 180
Bunch, Ralph, 125
Burger, Warren, 228
Burke, John M., 158
Burlingham, C. C., 188–189
Burrows, William, 158

Burton, Harold H., 179, 181, 193, 197, 199
  all deliberate speed and, 174–175
  Brown I and, 171
  desegregation and, 175
  Fourteenth Amendment and, 176
  opinion in *Cooper* and, 167, 171, 175, 184, 188
  retirement of, 170–171, 194
  special term and, 151, 152, 153, 155, 158
  Supremacy Clause and, 164
  unanimity and, 165
Bush, George W., 232
Bush v. Gore (2000), 232, 236–237
Busing, 218, 221, 223, 224, 227
  compliance with, 234
  concerns about, 219, 225
  desegregation and, 228
Butler, John Marshall, 190
Butler, Richard C., 163, 164, 196
  brief by, 74
  Brown II and, 198
  delay and, 153, 157
  desegregation and, 154
  Faubus's influence and, 155
  Frankfurter and, 167
  litigation and, 145, 152, 154–155, 156, 158, 159, 160, 166
  opinion and, 190
  Warren and, 165
Byrnes, James, 9, 10, 67

Caldwell, Arthur B., 67, 83, 84, 88, 114, 242
  Brownell and, 82
  delaying desegregation and, 105
  Faubus and, 103, 104, 109, 124
  Hoxie precedent and, 99
  litigation and, 85
  report by, 107
  Title III and, 77

Canons of Legal Ethics, 58
Capital Citizens' Council, 73, 78, 83, 84, 85, 206
  black transfers and, 80
  class tensions and, 88
  phase program and, 76
Carter, Jimmy, 224
Carter, John L., 52, 55
Carter, Robert L., 74
Catlett, Leon, 57, 58, 59
  House and, 73, 74
  interposition measures and, 69
Center for National Policy Review, 223
Central High School
  Arkansas National Guard at, 2, 89, 111, 112, 113, 114
  attendance zone for, 97
  black students at, 27–28, 31, 95, 202
  desegregation at, 24, 35, 47, 49, 73, 74, 79, 86, 87, 90, 103, 104, 105, 107, 112, 210, 211, 225, 233, 237, 240, 242, 243
  integration at, 19, 76, 77, 79, 91, 162
  101st Airborne at, 11, 130–131, 135–136, 143, 216–217
  potential violence at, 94, 105, 128–129
  segregation at, 35, 36
  transfer to, 78, 79
Charter of the United Nations, 133
Chestnut, J. L., Jr., 220
Citizens' councils, 30, 36, 39, 64, 87, 90, 91
  discourse of, 96–97
  Little Rock NAACP and, 81
  resistance by, vii, 29
  See also Capital Citizens' Council
Civil disobedience, 38, 93, 213
Civil obedience, 93, 213

Civil rights, 38, 202
  confrontation over, 2, 126
  enforcement of, 123, 124, 125,
    126, 218
  federal equivocation on, 41
Civil Rights Act (1957), 218
  Title III of, 44, 45, 46, 47, 48, 67,
    77, 82, 84, 88, 89, 93, 101, 104,
    124
Civil Rights Act (1960), 218
Civil Rights Act (1964), 4, 212, 225
  desegregation and, 222
  educational opportunity and, 230
  passage of, 214, 237
  Title II of, 44, 235, 236
  Title VI of, 218, 222, 226, 227, 230
Civil rights activists, 5, 141, 201,
    212, 226
  black community and, 220
  federal supremacy and, 217
  McCarthyism and, 214
Civil Rights Cases (1883), vii
Civil Rights Commission, 44, 222,
    225
Civil rights laws/legislation, 47, 67,
    82, 84, 86, 93, 99, 222, 225
  compliance with, 41
  enforcement of, 223
  nonenforcement of, 37
  support for, 45–46
Civil rights movement, 1, 7, 10, 11,
    201, 202, 204, 236, 237, 244
  African independence movement
    and, 215
  Brown I and, 3
  Cooper and, 12, 211, 214, 217
  federal court litigation and,
    211–218
  images/actualities of, 218–224
  LDF and, 213
  Little Rock crisis and, 216
  stereotypes and, 217
  violence of, 219–220

Clark, Jim, 212
Clark, Kenneth B., 139
Clark, Thomas, 167, 181, 185, 193
  on Brennan/Fourteenth
    Amendment, 175
  Brown I and, 163–164
  delay and, 154
  dissent and, 164, 197
  Frankfurter and, 188
  Frankfurter's concurring opinion
    and, 184
  JMH draft and, 177, 179
  opinion and, 171, 188, 190
  special term and, 151, 152, 153,
    158, 159
  Supremacy Clause and, 164
Clark litigation (1966), 219
Clement, Frank, 141
Clinton, Bill, 219
Cobb, Osro, 117, 118–119, 128,
    129, 140
  desegregation order and, 121
  harassment and, 139
Cohens v. Virginia (1821), 163
Cold war, vii, 41, 89, 135, 216, 221,
    237
  desegregation and, 192
  Eisenhower and, 190, 191–192
  Little Rock crisis and, 132
  patriotism and, 218
  propaganda of, 11, 12, 67, 192,
    193, 199, 214, 239, 241
Collins, Leroy, 141
Colonialism, segregation and,
    215
Commerce Clause, 232, 235, 236
Committee to Retain Our
    Segregated Schools (CROSS),
    209
Communism, 132
  nonviolence and, 215
  segregation and, 205
Conner, Bull, 212, 236

Constitution Party, 73
Constitutional rights
 enforcement of, 154, 173
 preservation of, 137, 173
Constitutional supremacy, 80, 199,
 216, 217
Constitutional symbolism, 217, 223,
 224
Cooper, William G., 15, 34–35, 60,
 105
Cooper v. Aaron (1958)
 arguments in, 135
 Brown I and, 1, 3, 210, 234
 Brown II and, 169
 challenging, 144–151
 criticism of, 9
 defiance of, 200, 230
 impact of, 157, 202, 210, 211
 implementing, 202–211
 legacy of, ix, 1, 230, 232, 235,
  238
 opinion in, 161, 168, 169,
  170–172, 182, 189–201, 214
 oral arguments in, 160, 161
 references to, 232, 235
Cope, Graeme, 109, 145–146
 on mothers' league, 96
 on white parents, 97–98
Counts, Ira Wilmer, 232
Crenchaw, J. C., 31, 50, 57, 137
 Blossom plan and, 26, 33, 58
 Branton and, 52
CROSS (Committee to Retain Our
 Segregated Schools), 209

Davies, Ronald N., 7, 114, 130, 145,
 170, 172, 196
 Aaron and, 108–109
 appointment of, 107, 119–120
 Branton and, 115
 Cooper and, 147
 criticism of, 120
 delay and, 115, 149

departure of, 144
Faubus and, 108, 109, 110, 119,
 121, 122, 123, 124, 125, 127,
 142, 242–243
FBI investigation and, 116,
 118–119
injunction by, 112, 126, 127–128,
 195
interposition laws and, 113
Miller and, 119, 120
Thomason case and, 109, 143
Defenders of State Sovereignty and
 Individual Liberty, 158
Defiance-compliance strategy, 120,
 128, 143
Denver School Board, 228
Department of Health Education
 and Welfare (HEW), 224
 community reviews by, 222, 223,
  227
Desegregation, 5, 8, 11, 12, 24, 26,
 39, 49, 59, 73, 85, 86
 Aaron and, 54, 67
 accommodationist approach
  toward, 33
 accomplishing, 64, 76, 212, 223
 affirmative duty for, 229
 all deliberate speed and, 61,
  174–175, 176, 186, 210, 214,
  225
 Brown I and, 6, 56, 80, 169, 187,
  244
 Brown II and, 22, 34, 70, 75, 76,
  78, 94, 163
 confronting, 14, 28, 34, 36, 39,
  40, 96, 212, 223
 Cooper and, 233
 delaying, 42, 78, 87, 100–101, 102,
  103, 105, 109, 110, 111, 115,
  146, 170, 172, 193, 214, 242
 enforcement of, 6, 41, 44, 46, 76,
  90, 107, 109, 111, 119, 136,
  142, 192, 197, 218, 243

Desegregation, *continued*
  Faubus and, 16, 41, 46, 48, 69,
    86, 94, 99, 101, 204, 212, 237
  federal government and,
    121–122, 140
  good faith efforts at, 127, 177
  limited, 18, 35, 78, 134
  phases of, 23–24, 52
  program for, 233, 234
  public stand on, 29, 206
  support for, 6, 113, 199, 216, 219,
    234
  token, 202, 225, 237
Desegregation order, 75, 76, 91
  delaying, 115, 116, 136, 142, 144,
    148, 161, 166
  enforcement of, 100, 123, 124,
    154, 161, 186, 192
Desegregation plan, 15, 21, 61, 69,
    173, 175, 243
  delaying, 135, 181, 229
  enforcement of, 174, 187
Diocese of Little Rock, 16
Dirksen, Everett, 152
Discrimination, 26, 36, 53, 173,
    236
  African Americans and, 235
  class, 85
  Faubus and, 103, 204
  institutional/societal, 216
  intentional, 229
  public school, 178
  reverse, 221
Dissent, Arendt in, 215
Douglas, William O., 57, 161, 193
  activism of, 158
  Brennan and, 179
  Cooper and, 160
  joining formula in *Cooper* and, 182
  opinion in *Cooper* and, 171, 175,
    180, 188, 198
  registration requirements and,
    154

special term and, 151, 153, 164,
    183
Du Bois, W. E. B., 14
Dudziak, Mary L., 11
Dulles, John Foster, 43, 45, 130, 240
Dunaway, Edwin F., 90
Dunbar Junior High School, 18, 26,
    78, 94
Dylan, Bob, 30

East African Standard, 125
Eastland, James, 36, 37
Eckford, Elizabeth, 210, 232–233,
    242
  Arkansas National Guard and, 233
  challenge for, 112
  harassment of, 115, 125, 211
  Lorch and, 118
  presentation by, 232
  transfer of, 79
Edmund Pettus Bridge, 212
Educational opportunity, 227, 229,
    230
Egyptian Gazette, 125
Eisenhower, Dwight D.
appointments by, 159
  Arkansas National Guard and, 2
  Brown I and, 43–44, 46, 64, 67,
    132, 134, 190, 191, 193, 214,
    220
  Brown II and, 14
  civil rights and, 38, 43, 44, 45–46,
    48, 67, 123, 124, 220
  cold war and, 190, 191–192
  Cooper and, 169, 191, 192, 193
  desegregation and, 67, 68, 191
  enforcement and, 126, 182
  equivocation by, 3, 10–11, 15,
    22–23, 41–46, 62, 88, 124, 158,
    220, 241
  Faubus and, 116, 120, 121, 124,
    133, 149, 191, 205, 243
  federalization and, 131

gradualism and, 192
integration and, 157
intervention by, 90, 121–122
leadership of, 192
Little Rock crisis and, 2,
   125–126, 131, 138, 140, 144
101st Airborne and, 89, 140,
   216–217
propaganda battle and, 11
separation of powers and, 67
southern strategy of, 11
support for, 136, 140
Title III and, 45, 46, 48
Warren and, 181, 239
Ellison, Ralph, 216
Engstrom, Harold J., 102
Equal justice, 164, 179, 216, 224,
   230, 231
   Brown I and, 77, 226, 237
   Cooper and, 202
Equal protection, 129, 172
Equal Protection Clause, 159, 236,
   239
Executive Order 10730, 130–131
Eyes on the Prize (documentary), 6

Fairclough, Adam, 6
Faubus, Orval E.
Brown I and, 15, 81
   Brown II and, 14, 47
   compliance by, 116, 119, 121,
      128, 142
   constitutional obligations and, 134
   Cooper and, 182, 184, 203
   criticism of, 125, 141, 149
   defiance by, 90, 99–112, 115, 116,
      125, 127, 128, 143, 153, 159,
      180, 181, 182, 184, 190, 194,
      199, 200, 209, 210, 214, 218,
      244
   delay and, 101, 104, 105, 115, 142
   demagoguery of, 120, 141, 166
   economic program by, 64, 72, 73

Eisenhower and, 116, 120, 121,
   124, 133, 149, 191, 205, 243
electoral strategy of, 142–143
on federal authorities, 109
influence of, 155, 205
injunction against, 126, 127–128,
   195
moderates and, 62, 96, 149
political calculations of, 70,
   89–90, 120, 141
potential violence and, 107,
   110–111, 113, 123, 125, 127
pressure on, 68, 98–99
proclamation by, 115, 116
reelection of, 47, 57, 72, 73
special elections and, 168, 170
tax increase and, 72, 73
Faubus v. United States (1958), 122,
   142, 147, 195
Faulkner, William, 67
Federal Bureau of Investigation
   (FBI) 40
   civil rights cases and, 140
   evidence from, 104
   investigation by, 115–116,
      118–119, 125
   report by, 123, 141
Federal intervention, 81, 124, 132,
   140
Federal litigation
   civil rights movement and,
      211–218
   images of, 220–221
Federal supremacy, 89, 140,
   172–173, 174, 177, 183, 187
   all deliberate speed and, 173
   civil rights activists and, 217
   Cooper and, 217–218
   media and, 217
   principle of, 137
Federalism, 192, 193, 217
   desegregation and, 68
   states' rights versus, 9

Fifteenth Amendment, 37, 221
Fishman, Fred N., 200
Flaherty, Donald, 192
Fletcher, Albert L., 16
Florida Election Code, 237
Florida Legislature, 237
Florida Supreme Court, 232, 236, 237
Fourteenth Amendment, 40, 159,
    174, 175, 221
  Brown I and, 183
  Burton revision of, 176
  discrimination and, 178
  equal protection and, 172
  Equal Protection Clause of, 236,
    239
  nonenforcement of, 37
  segregation and, 183
Frankfurter, Felix, viii, 53, 181, 239,
    244
  all deliberate speed and, 164, 176,
    187, 188, 193
  briefs for, 157
  Brown II and, 201
  Butler and, 167
  Clark and, 188
  concurring opinion in *Cooper* by,
    169, 170, 176, 184–189, 190,
    194, 195, 197, 198, 199, 200
  criticism of, 195
  decision making and, 194–195
  delay and, 172
  desegregation and, 154, 175, 180,
    198, 210
  Faubus and, 198
  gradualism and, 160
  Harlan and, 159, 165
  JMH draft and, 177, 179
  joining formula and, 182
  judicial restraint and, 158
  on lawlessness, 186
  memorandum by, 195–196, 197,
    198
  opinion and, 167, 172

southern moderates and, 161
special term and, 151, 153, 156
Supremacy Clause and, 186
unanimity and, 178, 194
Warren and, 165, 185, 189
Frederickson, George M., 3
Freedom Riders, 5, 221
*Freedom Riders 1961 and the Struggle
    for Racial Justice* (Arsenault), 221
Freund, Paul, 9
Fulbright, J. William, 8, 158, 165

Gardner, Archibald K. in *Cooper*,
    119, 145, 151
Garrow, David J., 5, 92
Ginsburg, Ruth Bader, 236, 237
Goldfield, David, 7
Gone with the Wind (movie), 217
Gore, Albert, 232
Gradualism, 5, 6, 34, 94, 126, 192,
    209
  Brown I and, 132
  Brown II and, 160, 210
  Faubus and, 160
Green, Ernest, 133, 211, 237, 243
  challenge for, 112
  graduation of, 144, 204
  harassment of, 139
  King and, 204
  transfer of, 79
Green v. County School Board (1968),
    227
Griffin, Marvin, 95, 102, 104, 109,
    113
  phase program and, 105
  rally and, 90, 96, 103
Griffin v. County School Board (1964),
    225
Gulley, Tom, 94
Guthridge, Amis, 30, 31, 39, 81, 87,
    101, 102, 103, 207
  on Faubus, 40
  interposition and, 71

open letter by, 80
race/class antagonisms and, 36
state sovereignty and, 110
suit by, 95
violence threat and, 96

Hall High School, 24, 84, 88, 241
 attendance zone for, 97
 black students at, 202, 209
 desegregation at, 35, 80, 204,
  210, 225, 237
 segregation at, 143
 transfer requests to, 152
Harlan, John Marshall, 167, 174,
  185, 244
 all deliberate speed and, 177–178
 Brennan and, 179, 180, 189
 briefs for, 157
 Buchanan and, 180
 Cooper and, 160
 delay and, 166
 on desegregation, 160
 on Fourteenth Amendment, 178
 Frankfurter and, 159, 165
 joining formula in *Cooper* and,
  182, 194
 judicial restraint and, 158
 opinion in *Cooper* and, 167, 170,
  172, 177, 181, 184, 188, 189,
  197
 oral arguments and, 161
 special term and, 151, 163
 Supremacy Clause and, 164
 unanimity and, 177–184, 193
Harper, Thomas, 122
Harris, M. Lafayette, 50, 51, 55
Harris, Roy V., 95, 102
 rally and, 90, 96, 103
Hays, Brooks, 8, 120, 205
HEW. *See* Department of Health
  Education and Welfare
Hodges, Luther H., 141
Holmes, Oliver Wendell, 186

Hoover, J. Edgar, 140
Horace Mann High School, 30, 77,
  79, 94, 112, 113, 148, 149
 Arkansas National Guard at,
  114
 auto mechanics at, 56
 black students at, 28, 31
 opening of, 32
 registration strategy at, 49
 transfer from, 78
House, Archie F., 57, 58, 70, 82, 88,
  107, 109
 Blossom correspondence with, 71
 Branton and, 77
 Catlett and, 73, 74
 Hoxie precedent and, 99
 interposition measures and, 69
 interviewing, 83
 litigation and, 122
 New York NAACP and, 75
 petition by, 108
 phase program and, 54–55,
  59–60, 62
Howell, Max, 71
Hoxie, 45, 88, 156
 desegregation in, 64, 66, 84, 121
 disorder in, 63, 71, 95
 precedent, 99, 104, 174
Hoxie School Board, intimidation
  campaign and, 40–41, 44
Huckaby, Elizabeth, 147
Hughes, Charles Evans, 159, 176
Human rights, 132, 133
Humphrey, Hubert, 226

Identity politics, 9, 41, 47, 86
Iggers, Georg, 6, 7, 18, 19, 24, 48
 Blossom plan and, 25, 26
 Harris and, 50, 51
 litigation and, 31, 32, 33, 51
 report by, 17
 soliciting by, 50, 51
 on suit, 28

Hoxie, AR (handwritten annotation)

Iggers, Wilma, 18, 19, 31, 48
  litigation by, 32
  report by, 17
Image: A Guide to Pseudo-Events in America, The (Boorstin), 219
Integration, 17, 91, 116, 144, 157, 162, 219, 235
  Brown II and, 29
  complete, 76
  court-sanctioned, 229
  delaying, 77, 92, 147, 162, 167
  desegregation and, 230
  enforcing, 113, 191, 203
  meaningful, 229
  mongrelization and, 40
  opposition to, 68, 92, 97
  plan for, 18, 205–206
  privatization and, 190
  segregation and, 79, 224, 226
  support for, 234
  token, 219
  violence surrounding, 125
International media
  Little Rock crisis and, 125–126, 149–150
  special term and, 192
Interposition, 47, 48, 57, 62, 68–69, 71, 74, 75, 85, 90, 96, 143, 186
  economic program and, 72–73
  clash over, 67
  Faubus and, 63, 64, 65, 67, 70, 77
  symbolism aroused by, 73
Interposition laws, 65, 68, 70, 77, 82, 83, 86, 98, 101, 113, 147, 155
  enforcement of, 86
  litigating, 84, 100, 102, 105, 114
  passage of, 69, 72
Ivey, W. P., 147

Jackson, Andrew, 186
Jackson, Margaret, 97
Jenner, William, 190
Jenner-Butler bill, 194, 196

Jet magazine, Till murder and, 29
Jim Crow, 3, 8, 12, 19, 22, 26, 33, 37, 42, 75, 186, 230, 233
  defending, 4
  dilemma of, 5–6, 14
  overturning, vii, 4–5, 59, 201, 237, 239
  propaganda battle and, 43
Johnson, Frank, 5, 214
  Freedom Riders and, 221
  Selma march and, 213
Johnson, James, 39, 47, 98, 103, 143, 207, 240, 241
  Faubus and, 63–64, 66, 70, 86, 104, 110, 112
  interposition and, 63, 64, 66–67
  opposition strategy of, 38
  political discourse of, 36–37
  state sovereignty and, 110
  states' rights party and, 66
Johnson, Lyndon
  HEW community reviews and, 223, 227
  Jenner-Butler bill and, 194
  Smith bill and, 152
Johnson Amendment, 37, 41, 63, 68, 69, 70
Joining formula in *Cooper*, 182, 184, 189, 194, 198
Jones, Effie, 210
Jones, Scipio Africanus, 25, 26, 51, 59
Judicial activism, 10, 158, 159, 164, 171, 221
  criticism of, 152
  divergent outcomes of, 224–231
  judicial restraint and, 172
  opposition to, 182
Judicial restraint, 152, 158, 159, 164, 223, 225
  judicial activism and, 172
Judicial supremacy, 12, 169–177, 182, 200, 211
  Cooper and, 156, 158, 216, 236

Karam, James (Jimmy) T., 87
KARK radio, Griffin speech on, 103
Kennedy, Anthony, 236
Kennedy, John F., 221
Keyes v. Denver School District No. 1
  (1973), 227–228
Kilpatrick, James J., 37
King, Martin Luther, Jr., vii, 5, 92,
  139, 192, 212, 240
  civil rights movement and, 237,
  244
  Faubus and, 3
  federal litigation and, 213
  Green graduation and, 204
  Jim Crow and, 4
  LDF and, 213, 214
  leadership of, 220
  legalism and, 93, 213
  litigation and, 214
  Little Rock crisis and, 1, 220
  mass action and, 94
  Meltsner and, 214
  nonviolence and, 213, 215
  threats against, 30
Kirk, John A., 6, 7
Kirp, David L., 224
Klarman, Michael J., 4
Kluger, Richard, 223
Ku Klux Klan, 29, 212, 221, 230

Laws, Clarence, 137, 138, 139–140
LDF. *See* Legal Defense Fund
Leflar, Robert, 198
Legal Defense Fund (LDF), viii, 4,
  17, 20, 24, 33, 74, 90, 92, 117,
  118, 126, 206, 220, 243, 244
  Blossom plan and, 76
  Branton and, 52
  Browder and, 30
  Brown I and, 19, 21, 181, 239
  Brown II and, 146, 148
  civil rights movement and, 213
  Cooper and, 78, 202, 204–205

delay and, 135
enforcement and, 205
King and, 213, 214
litigation by, 49, 56, 57, 84, 113,
  151, 199, 203, 212, 213
Marshall and, 52, 108, 165,
  204–205
Miller and, 190
Morris and, 26
NAACP split with, 204
privatization and, 203
review by, 32
school board petition and, 145
student rights and, 116
Legal Redress Committee
  (Arkansas NAACP), 33, 51
Legalism, 93, 94, 213
Lemley, Harry J., 119, 161, 172,
  195, 196, 200, 243
  Brown II and, 146, 147–148
  Cooper and, 244
  criticism of, 149–150, 151
  delay and, 135, 144–145, 148,
  153, 156, 198
  Eisenhower and, 149
  Faubus and, 146
  reversing, 157, 165, 167, 170, 190
  southern customs/mores and,
  145
Lenin, Vladimir, 215
"Letter from a Birmingham Jail"
  (King), 213
Lewis, Anthony, 210
Life magazine, 40
Lincoln, Abraham, 185, 188
Little Rock Chamber of
  Commerce, 205
Little Rock Citizens' Council, 30,
  36, 87, 90
  Blossom plan and, 35
  Faubus and, 95
  Hoxie and, 63
  strategy of, 37

Little Rock crisis, 2, 6, 10
   civil rights movement and, 216
   cold war and, 132
   described, 112–127
   legacy of, 211–218
   propaganda consequences of,
     130, 136
Little Rock Mothers' League, 138
Little Rock NAACP, 6, 41, 81, 84,
   126
   Aaron appeal by, 78
   black community and, 93, 202
   Blossom and, 24–25, 78–79
   Blossom plan and, 25, 27, 82
   Branton and, 55
   Brown I and, 15, 19, 240
   challenge by, 7
   citizens' councils and, 81
   Cooper and, 5, 83, 117, 237
   cooperation with, 19
   court defeat and, 76, 77
   credibility for, 94
   desegregation and, 15, 233
   interposition politics and, 68–69
   litigation and, 12, 15, 22, 30, 33,
     34, 35, 47, 48–49, 55, 56–57,
     203, 217, 220
   Little Rock School Board and,
     16–18
   Lorch and, 118, 137, 138
   minimalist plan and, 14
   phase program of, 78, 211
   split in, 26
   Title III and, 46
   white violence and, 29
   See also Bates, Daisy
Little Rock Nine, 116, 123, 126,
   129, 185
   academic success for, 135, 211
   Bates and, 220
   constitutional rights of, 117, 135
   desegregation and, 138–139
   harassment of, 128, 135, 136, 204

   heroism of, 233, 237
   motivations of, 79
   Springarn Medal for, 204
   support for, 216
   teachers and, 118
   triumph of, 135–144
   See also individual names
Little Rock Phase Program, 47, 49,
   59–60, 74
   Aaron and, 85
   affirmation of, 67
   black community and, 77
   Brown I and, 85
   Brown II and, 28, 54, 60, 61
   class discrimination and, 85
   criticism of, 33, 76, 105
   delaying, 107
   NAACP and, 51
   problems with, 48, 61, 70
   publication of, 27
   segregationists and, 81
   support for, 30, 54–55, 77, 81
   testing, 75
   See also Blossom plan
Little Rock Public Library, 23–24
Little Rock Public Schools, 31
Little Rock School Board, 26, 41,
   60, 82, 83, 94, 141, 149, 152,
   158, 183, 205, 241
   Aaron and, 14, 47–48
   Brown I and, 6, 14, 15, 240
   constitutional requirements and,
     16
   Cooper and, 65
   desegregation and, 15, 21, 126
   disabling, 185
   integration and, 203
   interposition campaign and, 63
   Little Rock NAACP and, 17–18
   NAACP and, 12, 16–17
   pressure on, 68
   privatization and, 203
   teachers' contracts and, 207

Little Rock School District (LRSD),
19, 35, 148, 234, 235
London Times, 125–126
Look magazine, Till murder and, 30
Lorch, Grace, 82, 83
  Eckford and, 115, 118
  harassment of, 137, 138
Lorch, Lee, 56, 82, 83, 92
  Blossom plan and, 26
  harassment of, 137, 138
  litigation and, 31, 33
  NAACP and, 118, 137, 138
  soliciting by, 50, 51
Los Angeles Mirror-News, 157
Los Angeles Watts race riots, 218
Lovell, J. A., 81
LRSD. *See* Little Rock School
  District
Lucy, Autherine, 42

Maeguineas, Donald B., 117, 121
Mann, Woodrow Wilson, 94, 114,
  129, 130
Marbury v. Madison (1803), viii, 172,
  178, 179
Marshall, John, 172, 174, 176
Marshall, Thurgood, viii, 4, 55, 74,
  118, 145, 152, 206
  civil rights work of, 52
  delay and, 148
  on democracy, 215
  discretion and, 53
  intervention and, 117
  Lemley stay and, 150
  litigation and, 108, 122, 123, 151,
    153, 155, 165, 167, 204–205,
    214
  Morris and, 26
  See also *Cooper v. Aaron*,
    arguments
Massery, Hazel, 232–233
Matthes, Marion C., 150–151
Matthews, Jess W., 144, 147

Matthews, Kay, 122
Mboya, Tom, 215
McCarthyism, 214
McCulloch, R. B., 71, 110
  all deliberate speed and, 200
  Brown II and, 65, 66
  interposition and, 143
  litigation and, 93
McFaddin, E. F., 208
McKeldin, Theodore R., 141
McMath, Sidney, 129
M'Culloch v. Maryland (1819),
  viii
Meador, Daniel J., 225, 229
Media
  black community and, 217
  federal supremacy and, 217
  international, 125–126, 149–150,
    192
  Little Rock crisis and, vii,
    125–126, 149
  propaganda consequences and, 130
  special term and, 151
Meltsner, Michael: on King, 214
Miller, John E., 48, 57, 63, 70, 79,
  83, 106, 199, 242
  Aaron and, 240
  Blossom and, 100
  Blossom plan and, 75
  Briggs and, 61, 80
  Brown II and, 60, 62
  constitutional obligations and, 134
  Cooper and, 47, 49, 53–54, 59,
    61–62, 94, 108, 147, 170
  court order by, 77, 88
  crisis and, 89
  Davies and, 119, 120
  desegregation and, 73, 76, 101,
    109, 190, 206
  enforcement and, 205
  equity powers and, 54, 61
  equivocation by, 210
  ethics problems for, 123

Miller, John E., *continued*
  Faubus and, 99, 101, 111
  interposition laws and, 100, 102,
    105
  phase program and, 54, 62, 67, 74
  privatization and, 203
  reasonableness standard and, 99
  Thomason case and, 107
  Upton and, 100
Milliken v. Bradley (1974), 228, 229
Minnick, John Bradley, 158
Minority rights, 214, 215, 223
Montgomery bus boycott, 5, 30, 31,
  93, 213, 218, 240, 241
Moore v. Dempsey (1923), 59
Morris, Sue, 26
Morrison, de Lesseps S., 219
Morsell, John H., 125
Mothers' League of Central High,
  95, 105, 107
  discourse of, 96–97, 98
  opposition by, 90–91, 96
Mothershed, A. L., 138
Mothershed, Thelma, 79, 138, 211
  challenge for, 112
Muller v. Oregon (1908), 37
Murray, Pauli, 220
Myrdal, Gunnar, 14

National Association for the
  Advancement of Colored
  People (NAACP), 39, 40, 81,
  99, 108, 140, 157, 242
  Aaron and, 241
  activism of, 12, 26
  black community and, 77
  Brown and, 17, 32
  Cooper and, 7
  cooperation with, 19
  Delta black voters and, 64
  Faubus and, 86
  identification with, 26
  LDF split with, 204

  legal aid from, 50
  litigation and, 27, 29, 47, 49, 55,
    56, 61, 214
  Little Rock crisis and, 2, 89
  LRSB and, 12
  marginalization of, 32, 82
  phase program and, 51
  resolution by, 22
  segregationist bills against, 207
  Till murder and, 30
  See also Arkansas Conference of
    NAACP; Little Rock NAACP;
    New York NAACP
National Association for the
  Advancement of Colored
  People (NAACP) Education
  Committee, 17
National Association for the
  Advancement of Colored
  People (NAACP) State
  Conference of Branches, 15
National Guard. *See* Arkansas
  National Guard
New Deal, 8, 39
New Jersey Supreme Court, 163
New Lincoln High School, 139
New York NAACP, 83
  House and, 75
  influence of, 118, 137
  King and, 213
  racial status quo and, 92
New York Post
  Blossom interview in, 143–144
  on Faubus, 149
Newsweek, 149
Nixon, Richard M.
  desegregation and, 224
  HEW community reviews and,
    227
  judicial restraint and, 223
Nonviolence, 1, 213, 216
  communism and, 215
Norfolk *Virginian-Pilot*, 151, 152

"Obstruction of Justice in the State
of Arkansas" (Eisenhower), 129
Office of Education, 222, 226
101st Airborne "Screaming Eagle"
Division, 2, 211, 237, 243
at Central High, 11, 130–131,
135–136, 143, 216–217
dispatching, 89
*Organization of American Historians
(OAH) Newsletter,* 232, 237

Parent teacher associations (PTAs),
94
Parks, Rosa, 4
Parochial schools, desegregation of,
16
Pattillo, Melba, 91, 211, 238
challenge for, 112
harassment of, 139
transfer of, 79
Peltason, J. W., 210
Phase program. *See* Little Rock
Phase Program
Philander Smith College, 26,
50, 55
Iggers and, 17
Lorch and, 137
"Plan for School Integration—Little
Rock School District," 23
Plessy v. Ferguson (1896), viii, 37,
159, 239
Police powers, 10, 93, 116, 122,
208, 211, 217
Faubus and, 123, 142, 213–214
Pope, Walter, 122
Potts, Marvin H., 83, 94, 105
Pound, Roscoe, 186
Powell, Jay, 147
Powell, Terrell, 208
Privatization, 136, 152, 175, 184,
199, 227
Faubus and, 135, 142, 169, 190,
210

integration and, 190
law, 165, 190, 210
LDF and, 203
movement, 231
segregation/segregationists and,
96, 135, 169, 204
Propaganda, 43, 130, 136, 140
cold war, 11, 12, 67, 192, 193,
199, 214, 239, 241
segregation and, 215
Pruden, Wesley, 87, 95, 101, 103
Christian racism of, 143
violence threat and, 96
PTAs (Parent teacher associations),
94
Public accommodations, 212, 219
Public opinion, 212, 220
Faubus and, 96, 164
split in, 216–217
Pulaski County Chancery Court,
95, 102
Pulaski County Special School
District, 28
Pulaski Heights, 25, 74, 76, 80, 84,
90, 97, 143, 204
desegregation and, 35
Pupil assignment laws, 69–70, 77,
211, 225, 226

Rabb, Maxwell, 129, 130
Race mixing, 19, 73, 81, 97, 227
opposition to, 96
Race relations, 16, 19, 20, 46, 59,
86, 87, 112, 149, 216, 229
desegregation and, 60
improving, 57
in Little Rock, 25, 219
Racial equality, 26, 34, 60, 232–233
Racial justice, vii, 14, 211–212
Racial struggle, images/actualities
of, 218–224
Racial tensions, 14, 47, 48–49, 64,
70, 218

Racial violence, 8, 12, 22, 24, 41,
    45, 221
Racism, 10, 112
    Christian, 143
    public, 111
    romantic, 217
Rankin, J. Lee, 196
    argument in *Cooper* by, 155, 165,
        167, 182
    Brown I and, 152, 158, 191
    compliance and, 155
    constitutional obligation and,
        193
    delay and, 157
    federalization and, 129–130
    on law and order, 167
    on Supreme Court, 156
Rath, Henry V., 74
Ray, Gloria
    challenge for, 112, 211
    harassment of, 139
    transfer of, 79
Reagan, Ronald, 224
Reasonableness doctrine, 99, 114,
    146
Rector, William F. "Billy," 102
Reed, Murry O.: *Thomason* case
    and, 105, 106, 107
Reed, Roy, 90, 98, 100, 101
    on Faubus, 89
"Reexamining Central High:
    American Memory and Social
    Reality" (Eckford and
    Massery), 232–233
"Reflections on Little Rock"
    (Arendt), 215
Rehnquist, William H., 236
Richmond *News Leader*, 37
Roberts, Terrance, 211
    challenge for, 112
    harassment of, 138–139
    transfer of, 79
Robinson, Elsie, 210

Rockefeller, Winthrop, 71, 110
Rockwell, Lincoln, 221
Rogers, William, 141, 144, 158
    Brown I and, 152, 182, 191, 193
Romaine, O. W., 147
Roosevelt, Franklin D., 11, 36
    Court confrontation and, 159, 194
    Lemley and, 145
    Miller and, 59
Rose, U. M., 198

San Diego, desegregation, 91
Save Our Schools Committee, 73
School closing crisis, 190, 191, 203,
    204, 205
School closing laws, 165, 172, 208,
    209, 210
    Faubus and, 167, 203
School officials
    Faubus and, 103, 143, 144
    Lemley and, 147–148
SCLC. *See* Southern Christian
    Leadership Conference
Segregation, 5, 14, 17, 25, 30, 46,
    72, 116
    abolition of, vii, 4, 18, 21, 178,
        183
    boycott against, 240
    colonialism and, 215
    communism and, 205
    compulsory, 187
    continuing, 114
    de jure, 228
    equal protection and, 172
    federal equivocation on, 41
    integration and, 79, 224, 226
    maintaining, 20, 101, 113, 228
    privatization and, 96, 204
    prohibiting, 226
    propaganda and, 215
    sanctioning, 229
    termination of, 189
Segregation laws, 132, 213

Segregationists, 2, 8, 42, 205, 209, 210, 240
  Aaron and, 47
  bills by, 207
  Blossom plan and, 35
  constitutional claims of, 193
  contempt proceedings against, 104
  Cooper and, 48, 68–76
  defiance by, vii–viii, 10, 15, 28, 34–41, 88, 89, 97, 184, 218
  desegregation and, 68, 101, 109
  discrimination and, 204
  election of, 206
  enforcement and, 202
  Faubus and, vii, 65, 85–86, 87, 96, 98, 99, 112, 136, 139, 241–242
  influence of, 166
  injunction against, 106, 124
  interposition and, 48, 67, 77
  phase program and, 81
  pressure from, 68
  privatization and, 135, 169, 204
  teacher removal and, 207, 208
  threat by, 47, 83
  violence by, 134
  white students and, 136
Selma march, 4, 5, 212, 213, 220
Senate Judiciary Committee, 141
Separate but equal, 17, 19, 23
  Brown I and, 13–14, 60, 159
  Equal Protection Clause and, 239
  inherent inequality of, 60, 159
  overturning, 13–14
Separation of powers, 42, 44, 46, 124
  Cooper and, 11
Shaver, J. L. (Bex), 64, 65, 66, 71, 86
Shivers, Allan, 101, 110
  desegregation and, 42
  federal intervention and, 81
  privatization and, 96

Shropshire, Jackie L., 20, 25, 26
Shuttlesworth v. Birmingham Board of Education (1958), 225
Simple Justice (Kluger), 223
Slaughter House Cases (1873), vii
Smith, Roland S., 93
Smith, William J., 87, 101, 106, 120
  Faubus and, 72, 110–111
  interposition laws and, 102
  proclamation by, 113, 116
Smith bill, 182, 196
Smith v. Texas, 173, 178, 179, 180
SNCC. *See* Student Non-violent Coordinating Committee
South China Morning Post, 191, 192
Southern Christian Leadership Conference (SCLC), 92, 220
Southern Manifesto, 8, 38, 240
  desegregation and, 39
  Eisenhower vacillation and, 46
  interposition and, 66
  resistance and, 63
Southern Mediator, 29, 33, 49, 51, 55, 58, 78
Southern Regional Council, 25
Southern School News, 65, 105
  racial issues and, 67
  on Rector suit, 102
  on school board votes, 74
Southwest American, 149
Special term, 151–160, 161, 163, 164, 171, 183, 191, 192, 193, 195, 196, 225
  calling, 150
  media coverage for, 192
States' rights, 12, 47, 48, 62, 82, 85, 91, 96, 107, 120, 122
  Brown I and, 30
  Faubus and, 8, 10, 136
  federalism versus, 9
  ideology, 3, 34, 36, 37, 66, 111
  loss of, 97, 152
  preserving, 65

States' rights, *continued*
  segregation and, 15
  struggle against, 217
  symbolism, 68, 70
  testing, 81
  See also Interposition
Stennis, John, 149
Sterling v. Constantin (1932), 173
Stop This Outrageous Purge
    (STOP), 208, 210
Student Non-violent Coordinating
    Committee (SNCC), 214
Supremacy Clause, 69, 164, 179,
    180–181, 182, 186
  Brown I and, 178
Sutton, Ozell, 26, 33, 50
*Swann v. Charlotte-Mecklenburg
    Board of Education* (1971), 218,
    227, 228

Taney, Roger, 176, 180
Tate, U. Simpson, 55, 57, 74
  Blossom plan and, 76
  Branton and, 52, 53
  LDF and, 31
  oral argument by, 60, 61
Taylor, Maxwell, 130
Teachers
  integration/segregation views of,
    207
  removal of, 208
Teachers' contracts, 207, 208
Tenth Amendment, 122
Terry, Adolphine Fletcher, 208
Texas Rangers, 42, 81
Thirteenth Amendment, 37, 221
Thomas, Jefferson, 91, 210
  challenge for, 112
  harassment of, 139
  transfer of, 79
Thomason, Mary, 96, 97
  statements by, 110
  suit and, 105, 107, 109

Thomason case, 111, 112, 113, 114,
    119, 147
  appealing, 108
  Blossom and, 106
  Davies and, 109, 143
  Faubus and, 106, 107, 110, 142
  interpretation of, 142
  Miller and, 107
  Reed and, 105, 106, 107
  states' rights and, 107
Thompson, Estella, 210
Till, Emmett, 31, 41, 44, 67
  murder of, 29–30, 38, 43
Time, 149
Times of India, 125
Title III (Civil Rights Act [1957]),
    44, 46, 47, 67, 82, 93, 101
  defeat of, 48, 77, 84, 88, 99, 104,
    124
  opposition to, 45
Title VI (Civil Rights Act [1964]),
    218, 226
  desegregation and, 226
  enforcement of, 222, 227, 230
Tobacco Road (movie), 67, 217
Transportation, desegregation of,
    30, 67
Troublemakers, 141, 149
  prosecuting, 146–147, 155, 156,
    157, 166
Tushnet, Mark, 4

Unanimity, 193, 200
  Cooper and, 170–171, 178
  limits of, 177–184
  testing, 160–168
U.S. Army, 122
U.S. Chamber of Commerce,
    149
U.S. Code, 83, 130
  Section 241, 104
  Section 242, 104
  Section 331, 122, 131

Section 332, 122, 129, 131
Section 333, 122, 129, 131
Section 334, 129, 131
U.S. Constitution, viii, 7, 232
  Article 6 of, 80, 108, 172–173
  Brown I and, 193, 211, 223
  supremacy of, 129, 186, 187, 189
U.S. Department of Justice, 89, 240
  desegregation and, 42
  enforcement and, 224
  LDF lawsuit and, 203
U.S. Department of State, 68, 140
U.S. District Court for the Eastern
    District of Arkansas, 34
U.S. Eighth Circuit Court of
    Appeals, 7, 62, 74, 119, 147,
    148, 150, 151, 195, 244
  Aaron and, 153–154, 201
  appeal to, 108
  Brown II and, 75
  Cooper and, 173
  delay and, 135
  Faubus and, 142
  Lemley and, 145, 156
  Morris and, 26
  upholding, 167, 170, 190
U.S. Fifth Circuit Court, 227
U.S. House Un-American
    Committee, 118
United States Marshals, 128
U.S. Nazi Party, 221
U.S. News & World Report, 191
  Faubus and, 141–142, 145
  federal supremacy and, 183
  on oral arguments/per curium
    opinion, 171–172
U.S. Supreme Court, 10, 138
  attack on, 194
  censuring of, 152
  desegregation and, 224
  politicization of, 223
  special term of, 150, 151–160,
    192

*United States v. Jefferson County
    Board of Education* (1966), 227
United States v. Lopez (1995), 235,
    236
United States v. Morrison (2000),
    232, 235, 236, 237
United States v. Peters (1809), 173,
    176
University of Alabama, Wallace at,
    222
University of Arkansas,
    desegregation and, 23
University of Arkansas Law School,
    33
University of Mississippi,
    desegregation and, 222
Upton, Wayne, 73, 145, 147, 150,
    159, 160, 165
  delay and, 101
  interposition laws and, 100, 102
  Miller and, 100
  votes for, 74
Urban League, 25, 81

Vanderbilt University, racial issues
    and, 67
Violence Against Women Act
    (VAWA), 232, 235, 236
Virginia Law Review, 225
Voting rights, 45, 212, 213
Voting Rights Act (1965), 4, 212,
    214, 218, 237

Walker, Edwin A., 133, 138
Wallace, George, 220, 222
  defiance by, 214, 217
  desegregation and, 212, 223
Walls, Carlotta, 79, 112, 139, 211
Walls, Cartelyou, 79
Warren, Earl, viii, 41, 53, 57, 161,
    167, 174, 185, 198, 244
  activism of, 158
  all deliberate speed and, 164

Warren, Earl, *continued*
American people against, 158
Brennan and, 172
Brown I and, 170, 183, 239
Butler and, 165
civil rights bill and, 45–46
criticism by, 158
delay and, 166, 172
desegregation plan and, 154
Eisenhower and, 181
Frankfurter and, 165, 185, 189
JMH draft and, 180
joint opinion in *Cooper* and,
179
opinion in *Cooper* and, 170, 171,
172, 175–176, 181, 182, 183,
184, 188, 189, 210
separate-but-equal and, 159
special term and, 151–160, 183,
191, 195, 196
unanimity and, 178
Washington, Booker T., 26
Washington Post, 165, 199
White flight, 218, 225, 227, 235

White students, harassment by,
138–139
White supremacy, 6, 10, 11, 34, 35,
39–40, 215
preserving, 9, 38
Whittaker, Charles Evans, 152, 153,
154, 156, 161
appointment of, 159
LDF motion and, 151
opinion in *Cooper* and, 171, 175,
188
Supremacy Clause and, 164
Wilbern, Kay, 95, 102
Wilkins, Roy, 93, 125, 139–140
Williams, Thaddeus D., 19, 20, 25,
26, 31
Blossom plan and, 28
desegregation and, 21
litigation and, 33
on segregation, 18
suit and, 28
Women's Emergency Committee,
205, 208
Woodward, C. Vann, 4, 5–6

lawlessness of "massive resistance" / some injunctive
part of MLK's Birmingham situation   effort against

Cooper v. Aaron — how will this function?

1) "delay"

2) immediation

3) Frankfurter — middle — "constructive use of time" (187